COACHING IN PROFESSIONAL CONTEXTS

PRAISE FOR THE BOOK

'For years, I have turned to Christian van Nieuwerburgh to help me grow as a coach. This volume is yet another feather in his cap. Included within is a conceptual jump forward in the conversation about coaching: now that coaching is an established discipline it is time that we shift our focus to nuanced and contextual factors. Once again, van Nieuwerburgh proves that he is a pioneering thought leader in coaching. He has assembled a strong line-up of contributing authors.'
Dr Robert Biswas-Diener, Coach and Wellbeing Researcher

'Christian van Nieuwerburgh has brought an expert team of authors to reflect on the current state of best practice for coaching managers and senior employees across the breadth of professional services, with compelling insights and practical wisdom for all.'
Professor Andrew Godley, Director of Henley Centre of Entrepreneurship, Henley Business School

'This is a wonderfully accessible and practical book bringing together insights into specific professional contexts and implications for coaching. It provides some excellent evidence-based coaching tips as well as tips around operating within these various professional contexts. A must-have book for the coach's bookshelf.'
Ruth Hayes, Director, Felix Consulting and President, University of Sydney Coaching and Mentoring Alumni Chapter

'This insightful book raises and addresses the important issues associated with coaching in professional contexts. It will stimulate reflective practice for both trainee and experienced coaches. I congratulate Christian van Nieuwerburgh on editing this excellent book.'
Professor Stephen Palmer, President, International Society for Coaching Psychology

'This book provides an opportunity to explore and understand coaching in different environments and will develop confidence in coaches looking to broaden their remit, educate new coaches and allow us all to consider the opportunities that exist in our professional industry. It is written by smart, trusted experts and curated by one of our profession's innovative thinkers.'
Helen Tiffany, Managing Director, The Coach House and Past Vice Chair, Association for Coaching

'In describing clearly and in detail how coaching is used in a variety of professional contexts, this book prompts the reader to reflect upon their own experiences of coaching and to consider how to assimilate ideas from other settings. A valuable, thought-provoking and practical contribution to the coaching literature and profession.'
Professor Bob Thomson, Warwick Business School, University of Warwick

COACHING IN PROFESSIONAL CONTEXTS

EDITED BY **CHRISTIAN VAN NIEUWERBURGH**

Los Angeles | London | New Delhi
Singapore | Washington DC

Los Angeles | London | New Delhi
Singapore | Washington DC

SAGE Publications Ltd
1 Oliver's Yard
55 City Road
London EC1Y 1SP

SAGE Publications Inc.
2455 Teller Road
Thousand Oaks, California 91320

SAGE Publications India Pvt Ltd
B 1/I 1 Mohan Cooperative Industrial Area
Mathura Road
New Delhi 110 044

SAGE Publications Asia-Pacific Pte Ltd
3 Church Street
#10-04 Samsung Hub
Singapore 049483

Editor: Susannah Trefgarne
Assistant editor: Laura Walmsley
Production editor: Rachel Burrows
Marketing manager: Camille Richmond
Cover design: Lisa Harper-Wells
Typeset by: C&M Digitals (P) Ltd, Chennai, India
Printed and bound by Hobbs the Printers Ltd,
Totton, SO40 3WX

First published 2016

Library of Congress Control Number: 2015938327

British Library Cataloguing in Publication data

A catalogue record for this book is available from
the British Library

ISBN 978-1-4739-0670-9
ISBN 978-1-4739-0671-6 (pbk)

At SAGE we take sustainability seriously. Most of our products are printed in the UK using FSC papers and boards.
When we print overseas we ensure sustainable papers are used as measured by the Egmont grading system.
We undertake an annual audit to monitor our sustainability.

CONTENTS

About the Editor and Chapter Authors   vii
Acknowledgements   xiii
Companion Website   xv

1 The Importance of Understanding Professional Contexts   1
   Christian van Nieuwerburgh

2 Coaching for Optimal Functioning   11
   Gordon Spence

3 Manager as Coach: The Challenge   29
   Julia Milner and Alex Couley

4 Coaching for Career and Professional Development   41
   Julia Yates

5 Coaching in the Financial Services Industry   55
   Emma Fowler and John Ainley

6 Coaching within Professional Services Firms   75
   Caroline Flin and Ian McIntosh

7 Coaching in Local Government   91
   Colin Williams and Samantha Darby

8 Coaching in Healthcare Settings   101
   Vivien Walton and Julia Sinclair

9 Coaching Patients   115
   Rachel Hawley

10   Coaching in Schools   131
     John Campbell

11   Coaching in Higher Education   145
     Ioanna Iordanou, Agnieszka M. Lech and Veronica Barnes

     Framework for Practitioners 1: Coaching for Research Supervision 159
     Cathia Jenainati

12   Integrating Coaching and Positive Psychology in Education   169
     Clive Leach and Suzy Green

13   The Current State of Research   187
     Tim Theeboom

14   Coaching for Wellbeing at Work   199
     Lindsay G. Oades

15   Supervision for Learning   213
     Mary Watts, Esther Cavett and Sarah Dudney

16   Towards a Coaching Culture   227
     Christian van Nieuwerburgh

     Framework for Practitioners 2: The GROWTH Model   235
     John Campbell

     Framework for Practitioners 3: Supporting the Development
     of Coaching Cultures   241
     Tim Hawkes

     Perspective from Practice 1: What We Know From Elite Sports   245
     Pat McCarry

17   Towards a Philosophy of Coaching?   249
     Christian van Nieuwerburgh

Index   257

ABOUT THE EDITOR AND CHAPTER AUTHORS

Christian van Nieuwerburgh is Associate Professor of Coaching at Henley Business School. Seen as an international authority in the field of coaching, he regularly speaks at conferences in the USA, Europe, Australia and the Middle East. He is well published in the field of coaching and is the author of *An Introduction to Coaching Skills: A Practical Guide* (Sage, 2014). As Managing Director of Growth Coaching (UK) and Growth Coaching Online, Christian is committed to supporting the development of coaching in educational settings. Students, delegates, clients and peers describe him as an inspirational educator and empowering coach.

John Ainley is CEO of Alexander, the UK's most experienced provider of senior leadership coaching. He is a sought-after advisor and leader in business, culture and leadership, and over the past ten years he has built long-term deep trust partnerships with the world's top leaders, executive coaches and thought leaders. His work is characterised by a genuinely authentic approach to helping leaders simultaneously grow and lead exceptional lives and careers. He supports leadership teams to craft strategies that engage leaders and their followers to deliver change and outstanding business results.

Veronica Barnes is an experienced and highly motivated people development professional, with a passion for coaching. She worked for the Open University for 24 years, latterly as Head of Learning and Organisational Development. During this time she initiated a coaching programme, which led to the development of over 50 internal coaches and the foundations for a coaching culture at the university. She is a qualified coach and coach supervisor. She has spoken and written widely on developing and nurturing internal coaches. She now works as an independent coach and coaching supervisor.

John Campbell is the Executive Director of Growth Coaching International where he leads a team of coaches and facilitators that provides coaching and coach training services to educators across Australia, the Asia Pacific region and the UK. He is an experienced and inspirational executive coach and facilitator. In addition to his teaching qualifications he holds Master's degrees in Organisational Communication (University of Technology, Sydney) and in the Psychology of Coaching (University of Sydney).

Esther Cavett is an executive and career coach. Trained in psychological coaching, she was previously a senior partner in a large City law firm and a professional musician. She has coached in private practice and with various coaching and counselling organisations, working with people in occupations ranging from business and law to education, charity and the arts. She runs two mentoring programmes, one for maternity returners in the City and one for the business mentoring of early career professional musicians. She writes regularly on coaching-related topics and has an interest in the transfer of skills from one area of expertise to another.

Alex Couley is a director and principal trainer at the International Centre for Leadership Coaching. A leading expert in coaching, Alex is one of the Founding Fellows of the Institute of Coaching. He provides coaching to leaders across the globe and has trained more than one thousand workers in coaching methodologies, positive psychology and mental health interventions throughout Australia. He assisted numerous organisations to develop wellbeing programmes for their employees and has consulted on the implementation of coaching cultures. Alex has gained a significant reputation as a coach trainer and specifically in training managers to utilise coaching in the workplace.

Samantha Darby is People and Leadership Consultant at West Midlands Employers, responsible for the day-to-day management of the West Midlands Coaching and Mentoring Pool. Samantha has been involved in developing the pool since it began in 2007. She has led on the evaluation of all aspects of the project and worked with experts to create appropriate training and supervision support. Samantha has also been involved in supporting a number of leadership and development programmes from first line to manager to aspiring CEOs, and is a qualified executive coach.

Sarah Dudney is a business coach and founder of Ignite, an organisation that provides career coaching, outplacement and development services. She has over ten years' experience of search and recruitment in the City of London, working with asset management houses, banks and family offices in Europe, the Middle East, Africa and North America. Sarah has been writing on career management, recruitment and related issues in financial services for the *Financial Times*, Investment Pensions Europe, Professional Investor and Global Investor since 2005. Her earlier career was spent in Edinburgh working for AEGON in a corporate planning role.

Caroline Flin is an executive coach and leadership specialist working across a range of industries, including Professional Services. She is also a researcher in Psychology with a special interest in coaching, working on a number of projects through the University of East London. Previously, Caroline spent more than 15 years in corporate learning and development and was Head of Coaching at a 'Big Four' Professional Services Firm. She has a strong track record in developing internal coaching programmes and has designed and delivered learning solutions to UK and international audiences.

Emma Fowler is Director of Free Your Career Ltd. She is also an international executive coach and business consultant. Emma spent many years living in Asia and has experience of working with clients internationally. She has a BSc in Experimental Psychology and is currently studying for a Master's degree in Coaching Psychology. In her spare time, Emma is Trustee of the UK charity Shark Guardian. She is a committee member in her local tennis club and enjoys a wide range of hobbies including triathlon.

Suzy Green is a clinical and coaching psychologist and founder of The Positivity Institute. She is a leader in the complementary fields of Coaching Psychology and Positive Psychology. She lectured on Applied Positive Psychology for the Coaching Psychology Unit at the University of Sydney for ten years, and is an Honorary Vice President of the International Society for Coaching Psychology. Suzy is currently Adjunct Professor in the School of Business, University of Western Sydney, and holds honorary academic positions at the University of Wollongong, University of Melbourne Graduate School of Education, and the Institute for Positive Psychology and Education, Australian Catholic University.

Rachel Hawley is a senior lecturer at the Centre for Leadership in Health and Social Care, Sheffield Hallam University, and founder of Change Comes From Within Consulting. Holding a Master's degree in Coaching and Mentoring from Sheffield Business School, she is currently working towards her doctorate in Professional Studies. Rachel has over 25 years' experience of working with a wide range of public sector organisations at local, regional, national and European levels, where patient, public, learner and staff engagement has extensively underpinned her experience. She is experienced in managing high profile national projects and skilled in providing expert consultancy.

Ioanna Iordanou is a senior lecturer in Human Resource Management (Coaching and Mentoring) at Oxford Brookes University. Her research centres on the benefits of embedding coaching training and creative experiential learning in management education. As a coaching researcher and practitioner, she has a keen interest in the grounding of coaching as a standalone profession through empirical research. She is currently co-authoring a book on values and ethics in coaching with Rachel Hawley. She holds a PhD, an MA, and two professional qualifications in coaching from the University of Warwick.

Clive Leach works as an evidence-based organisational coach and facilitator providing executive, leadership and career development coaching, workshops and presentations within the government, education and corporate sectors. He is currently based in London but his practice extends to Asia and Australia. His recent experience includes designing and facilitating 'Positive Education' programmes supporting university and school leadership teams, faculty, students and parents. Clive is a graduate of the Master of Organisational Coaching programme at the University of Sydney. He is also the lead author of 'Flourishing Young People' featured in the peer-reviewed *Journal of Evidenced-based Coaching & Mentoring*.

Agnieszka M. Lech is a chartered psychologist and a Senior Fellow of the Higher Education Academy. Throughout her education and work experience, she has gained a broad understanding of the various aspects of training, coaching and teaching. She studied psychology in Poland and Canada and completed her MSc in Psychology at the University of Silesia in 2006. In 2012 she completed her PhD in Psychology (University of Kent). In addition, she has postgraduate qualifications in Coaching Psychology (University of East London) and in Journalism (University of Silesia), as well as an Award in Leadership Coaching and Mentoring (Chartered Management Institute).

Ian McIntosh is a career coach, studying for an MSc in Career Coaching at the University of East London. Ian previously qualified as a lawyer, spending over 20 years as a corporate partner with law firm Addleshaw Goddard LLP, where he chaired the firm's partner development programme. His current career coaching practice includes a coaching role within the University of York's careers team, and his individual coaching practice has a particular focus on clients within the professional services sector.

Julia Milner is an award-winning practitioner and academic in the area of leadership development, coaching and high performing organisational cultures. She is an Associate Professor in Organisational Psychology at Xi'an Jiaotong-Liverpool University in China, Honorary Associate Professor at the Sydney Business School (University of Wollongong) Visiting Professor at a Business School in Finland, and has worked at several universities in Australia and Europe. Julia is a director at the International Centre for Leadership Coaching (ICLC) and has received a German Coaching Award for her industry work. As a business coach and management consultant, she has worked with several large consultancies and international companies.

Lindsay G. Oades is an Associate Professor of Positive Psychology at the Centre for Positive Psychology, University of Melbourne. Lindsay's expertise in clinical, coaching and positive psychology is applied in business, health and education sectors. Lindsay has over 100 refereed journal articles, book chapters or books published or in press. As co-editor of the *International Journal of Wellbeing*, and on the Scientific Advisory Committee at the Institute of Coaching, McLean Hospital/Harvard, combined with being an associate of Maudsley International, Lindsay seeks to make a contribution to wellbeing in an international context.

Julia Sinclair is a qualified and experienced career and personal development coach with an extensive background in HR, recruitment and learning and development within the private and public sector. Her particular area of expertise over recent years has been within the medical field, providing career support ranging from medical school applicants to senior qualified doctors. She is dedicated to developing and supporting others to achieve their full potential and gain the confidence and skills required to fulfil their career journeys. She possesses a Postgraduate Diploma in Career Coaching and is a qualified trainer (CIPD), stress management practitioner and counsellor.

Gordon Spence is a course director of the Master of Business Coaching at Sydney Business School, University of Wollongong. He holds a PhD in coaching psychology from the University of Sydney and has over 12 years' postgraduate teaching experience in business coaching and employee wellbeing. He has maintained a private practice throughout. Gordon researches employee engagement, peak performance, mindfulness and the relational aspects of coaching. He has published several book chapters and peer-reviewed journal articles on these topics. He is past co-chair of the Science Advisory Council, Institute of Coaching, McLean Hospital/Harvard, and is currently co-editing *The SAGE Handbook of Coaching*.

Tim Theeboom is a researcher and lecturer at the University of Amsterdam (Work and Organisational Psychology Department). In his research, he focuses on the effectiveness of coaching in organisational settings and is especially interested in how coaches can facilitate the self-regulatory and problem-solving capacities of coachees. Tim also lectures on coaching psychology and career management (Master's level courses), and besides his work as an academic he also works as an organisational consultant (and coach) for the Positive Psychology Institute, and is a member of the Special Group in Coaching Psychology for the Dutch National Institute of Psychology (NIP).

Vivien Walton is a partner in The Dearden Partnership, and a coaching psychologist and personal and organisation development consultant who has been coaching in healthcare settings for 15 years. Viv also provides leadership and behavioural assessment to support the appointment of senior clinicians and executives, mainly in the NHS, through the company that she founded, Dearden Search and Selection. She has degrees in Economics and Psychology and a Master's in Coaching Psychology.

Mary Watts is an independent consultant, coaching psychologist and educator specialising in personal and professional learning and change. She is Emeritus Professor of Psychology at City University, London, where she was formerly Pro-Vice-Chancellor for Teaching and Learning. She is currently Director of Meyler Campbell Business Coach Programme. She is a Chartered Psychologist specialising in counselling, health and coaching psychology and a BPS Registered Supervisor. She is former chair of the British Psychological Society's Division of Counselling Psychology, the Psychotherapy Implementation Group and the Special Group in Coaching Psychology. Mary has considerable experience working with senior leaders in the context of organisational change.

Colin Williams is the Director of West Midlands Employers (WME) and leads the ongoing development and delivery of the support and services provided to Local Authorities and other public sector employers across and beyond the region. Covering a wide array of human resource and organisational development issues at a local, regional and national level, Colin has developed a strong reputation for adding value and innovating. He trained as a coach as part of the West Midlands Coaching and Mentoring Pool, and with the support of an excellent team at WME has successfully developed a range of effective and highly valued collaborative arrangements.

Julia Yates is Senior Lecturer in Psychology at the University of East London. She is also the programme leader for the MSc in Career Coaching. She has worked as a practitioner, director, trainer and writer in the field of career coaching for 15 years. Her research interests include the application of coaching tools to career work, career image, career decision making and pedagogical approaches. As a practitioner turned academic, Julia is passionate about strengthening links between the research community and career practitioners. Her recently published work, *The Career Coaching Handbook* (Routledge, 2013), provides an analysis of how career development theory can be applied in practice.

ACKNOWLEDGEMENTS

This book has been a pleasure to edit because of the wonderful people who have provided the chapters, case studies and frameworks and so my heartfelt thanks go firstly to them. I am particularly grateful for their thoughtful and thought-provoking contributions. It has been a great honour to collaborate with each of the 40 contributors. Their commitment, insights and good humour have made this a very enjoyable project.

Editing this book has allowed me to reflect on the professional contexts in which I work. Making a living in the field of coaching allows me to work with some amazing people.

I'd like to start by thanking everyone involved with the West Midlands Coaching Pool, particularly Samantha Darby and Rebecca Davies. This is where I developed my passion for coaching and the impact it can have within professional contexts.

I am also grateful to colleagues at the various higher education institutions for whom I have worked. My first academic role in the field of coaching was at the School of Psychology at the University of East London (UEL). I would like to thank Prof. Mark Davies, Dr Aneta Tunariu and Prof. Irvine Gersch for their professional and personal support. I'd also like to particularly thank Julia Yates, Dr Ashok Jansari, Dr Nash Popovic, Dr Tim Lomas, Dr Itai Ivtzan and Dr Kate Hefferon for their friendship and collegiality during my time at UEL. I have also appreciated the opportunity to work with Dr Ilona Boniwell on the International MSc in Applied Positive Psychology at Anglia Ruskin University. Working at Henley Business School is both a joy and a privilege and I am thankful for the warm welcome of colleagues. I am particularly grateful to Prof. Abby Ghobadian and Dr Patricia Bossons who have been very supportive to me during my early days at Henley. Working with passionate, motivated and ambitious postgraduate students at all of these institutions has been incredibly rewarding and inspiring.

I am thankful too for the opportunity to work on consultancy and training projects through a number of organisations. Through Growth Coaching United Kingdom and Growth Coaching Online I have been able to do some of the work that is closest to my heart: coaching in education. I am glad of the opportunity to work with and learn from my good friend and colleague, John Campbell. It's a great privilege to be able to work both with him and the Growth Coaching International team in Australia. I'd like to thank Andrea Giraldez, Margaret Barr and Andrea Berkeley for their enthusiasm and commitment to Growth Coaching work in the United Kingdom. AQR in the UK and Al-Rowad in the United Arab Emirates have allowed me to undertake consultancy and training in different parts of the world. I am grateful to them for allowing me to do this valuable and enjoyable work. Special thanks are also due to Doug Strycharczyk, Prof. Peter Clough and Helen Murray at AQR, and my friend Alaa Omar at Al-Rowad.

The opportunity to speak at conferences on coaching and positive psychology has allowed me to collaborate with some wonderful people. I am particularly grateful for any chance to meet and work with Dr Jim Knight of the Impact Research Lab in the USA, Helen Tiffany from The Coach House in the UK, Dr Suzy Green, Clive Leach and Claudia Owad of the Positivity Institute in Australia, and Andrew Stainer from the Helmsman Project.

This is my second book for Sage. Hopefully, there will be more to come! The professional support of the team is without equal. They are masters of dissemination. They are able to take thoughts and help transmit them to a global audience. Particular thanks are due to my editor Laura Walmsley who has supported me throughout the project, and Kate Wharton who initially commissioned this book.

As always, I greatly appreciate the wonderful support and warmth that I receive from my family as I consistently blur the lines between 'work' and 'life'! Special thanks are due to Cathia Jenainati, Christian Arthur van Nieuwerburgh and Tsuyu Tsuchida for their unconditional love. The Jenainati family are a consistent source of encouragement, kindness and support.

But the most important acknowledgement should go to you, the reader. Without you and your interest in the application of coaching within organisational settings, this book would not have been published. All of us who have contributed to its creation hope you will find it to be of value. I also hope that it will play some part in supporting you to achieve what you aspire to.

COMPANION WEBSITE

This book is accompanied by a companion website hosting 24 specially commissioned case studies, written by specialist practitioners. These case studies illustrate in practice some of the key theory and ideas around working in different coaching contexts that you have read in the book. Below is the complete list of case studies you can find on the website, **https://study.sagepub.com/coachingcontexts**

COACHING FOR CAREERS AND PROFESSIONAL DEVELOPMENT

- Case Study 1: Coaching using career theories
  Michelle Pritchard

- Case Study 2: Coaching mid-life career change
  Julia Yates

- Case Study 3: Coaching to 'get back on track'
  Julia Heynat

COACHING IN THE FINANCIAL SERVICES INDUSTRY

- Case Study 4: Executive coaching for top team members
  Andrew Sheridan

- Case Study 5: Using a coaching approach with the executive team
  John Ainley

- Case Study 6: Leadership development in a multinational bank
  Emma Fowler

COACHING WITHIN PROFESSIONAL SERVICES FIRMS

- Case Study 7: Preferred supplier list assessment and selection process
  Caroline Flin

- Case Study 8: Transition to partner programme
  Lucy Mair

COACHING IN LOCAL GOVERNMENT

- Case Study 9: West Midlands Coaching and Mentoring Pool
  Samantha Darby and Colin Williams

COACHING IN HEALTHCARE SETTINGS

- Case Study 10: Career coaching for a doctor
  Julia Sinclair

- Case Study 11: Coaching assistant directors within the NHS
  Vivien Walton

- Case Study 12: Coaching general practitioners
  Jane Cryer

COACHING PATIENTS

- Case Study 13: Coaching conversations, care and confidence
  Anya de Iongh

- Case Study 14: Better conversations, better care
  Penny Newman

COACHING IN SCHOOLS

- Case Study 15: Opening the coaching portals
  James Hayres and Nancy McNally

- Case Study 16: Empowering our greatest resource
  Peter Webster and Nicole Morton

COACHING IN HIGHER EDUCATION

- Case Study 17: Developing coaches and coaching staff
  Veronica Barnes

- Case Study 18: Coaching PhD students
  Agnieszka M. Lech

- Case Study 19: A student's perspective
  Olliver R. Lloyd

INTEGRATING COACHING AND POSITIVE PSYCHOLOGY IN EDUCATION

- Case Study 20: A strategic approach to enhance wellbeing
  Claire Dale and Clive Leach

- Case Study 21: A strength-based coaching programme
  Wendy Madden and Suzy Green

COACHING FOR WELLBEING AT WORK

- Case Study 22: Coaching for wellbeing
  Lindsay G. Oades

SUPERVISION FOR LEARNING

- Case Study 23: Experiences of coaching supervision
  Sarah Dudney

- Case Study 24: Finding time to think
  Esther Cavett

1

THE IMPORTANCE OF UNDERSTANDING PROFESSIONAL CONTEXTS

CHRISTIAN VAN NIEUWERBURGH

WHAT IS UNIQUE ABOUT COACHING IN PROFESSIONAL CONTEXTS?

The premise of this book is that it is helpful to consider the various ways in which professional contexts can impact on the experience of coaching. Right from the outset, it is important to reflect on this premise. Is it true that a coaching programme in a hospital is unlike a coaching programme within a university? Is coaching a senior executive within a multinational bank essentially different from coaching a senior executive working for a professional services firm? The process of drawing together the experiences and thoughts of a wide range of practitioners and academics to create this book has helped to start to formulate a considered response to these questions. Firstly, as you read this book, it will become apparent that particular contexts have nuances and perspectives that seem to be more pertinent than in others. This may be due to the nature of the business or the predisposition of the people who choose to work within a sector. Secondly, you will note that the ethos of coaching and some of its principles feature across all the professional contexts covered in this book. So we start our exploration of coaching in professional contexts with a challenging paradox: coaching is at once different and the same across professional contexts.

As you read through the book, please keep an open mind, noticing what is consistent and what varies. Although purists might argue that a coach does not need to know anything about the coachee's profession, executive coaching does not take place in a vacuum. It usually involves conversations about the challenges and opportunities of working and leading in fast-paced complex systems. While knowledge of these systems may not be a prerequisite for effective coaching within such contexts, the commercial reality is that a coach without professional credibility is unlikely to get business.

We will be approaching these questions from a number of angles, explicitly and implicitly. These discussions are informed by the real-life professional experiences of many of the contributing authors. Your own thoughts and experiences should be brought to bear in this process.

This book is rooted in professional practice. It is written by practitioners and for practitioners. By the word 'practitioner', we mean all professionals who share an interest in the use of coaching within organisational settings. This includes executive coaches, executives, managers, leaders and human resources (HR) and organisational development (OD) professionals. The contributors have experienced coaching within professional contexts from these various angles. The passion of the chapter authors is inspirational. It is clear that each is driven by a commitment to create flourishing workplaces through the use of coaching interventions – professional contexts that encourage engagement and motivation.

HOW SHOULD I READ THIS BOOK?

This first chapter will provide a broad introduction to the book, raising interesting questions for consideration and proposing some key definitions. Every chapter is summarised below in order to support you to focus your attention on those most immediately relevant. One of the purposes of this book is to provide practitioners and students of coaching with insights into the context of most interest to them. At the same time, it is hoped that reading about coaching within alternative contexts will spark new thoughts and possibilities. *Coaching in Professional Contexts* is structured so that some 'generic' chapters provide a theoretical frame for context-specific chapters. By generic, we mean that the chapters relate to coaching in organisations, regardless of the professional context. Chapters 2 to 4 relate to all professional contexts. Chapters 5 to 12 consider the use of coaching within specific fields. Chapters 13 to 17 will be of interest to anyone introducing coaching within an organisational setting. Many chapters are supported by case studies written by practitioners with direct, recent and relevant experience of the coaching under discussion.

So you, the reader, may wish to approach this book in a traditional manner, working your way through it from start to finish. Alternatively, you could start with an area of particular interest and then dip into other professional contexts out of interest. It is also possible to read the 'generic' chapters before reading context-specific chapters. As a team of authors, our intention has been to support the most effective use of coaching within organisational contexts. While we are all committed to finding ways that coaching can engage and motivate people within professional contexts, we are also keen to ensure that you will find this text interesting and relevant. So, any way that works for you is the best way of approaching this text.

WHAT IS COACHING?

It is not possible to avoid this question. And yet often it is not sufficiently discussed in professional contexts. The reality is that the term 'coaching' is used liberally to mean a broad range of interventions and approaches. This is the unspoken reality that many prefer to ignore. Due to its confidential nature and disparities about the way in which coaches are trained (if they are trained at all), there is sometimes little clarity about what is actually taking place under the banner of 'coaching'. On the one hand, this is welcome news for those who wish to see coaching taking place in as many contexts and within as many situations as possible. On the other hand, professional associations may be concerned about the quality assurance of interventions labelled 'coaching'. While we hope to see the continued growth of coaching within professional contexts, we believe that the lack of agreement about terminology can get in the way of successful implementation of coaching initiatives and programmes.

There are many excellent definitions of coaching being used. Perhaps best known within professional contexts is the phrase coined by Sir John Whitmore: 'Unlocking people's potential to maximize their own performance' (2009: 11). His book, *Coaching for Performance*, may have been the catalyst for the surge in the use of coaching in professional contexts in the UK soon after the first edition was published in 1992. In fact, the GROW model presented within this book is probably the most-used coaching process within organisations worldwide. With this in mind, it is essential to note that Whitmore's notion of coaching for performance was underpinned by a belief that this should be brought about simply by raising coachees' awareness and increasing their sense of personal responsibility. Whitmore follows up the well-known quote above by being very clear that coaching is about 'helping them to learn rather than teaching them' (2009: 11). In other words, coaching is a largely non-directive conversational intervention.

I have noted elsewhere that there is broad agreement in the literature that coaching:

1. 'Is a managed conversation that takes place between two people.

2. Aims to support sustainable change to behaviours or ways of thinking.

3. Focuses on learning and development'. (van Nieuwerburgh, 2014: 5)

While coaching and mentoring are similar conversational approaches that share many of the same skills (Willis, 2005), we propose that one (coaching) takes a primarily non-directive stance while the other (mentoring) is generally more directive. It is recognised that there is some overlap in the interventions and that both coaching and mentoring are effective and necessary ways of supporting the development of professionals. However, this text will focus on the use of *coaching* within professional contexts.

Executive coaching is a conversational process that leads to a change of thinking or behaviour with the aim of improving outcomes in professional contexts. It is the role of the executive coach to create an environment in which the coachee can reflect deeply and generate new ideas and personalised solutions. As opposed to life coaching, the concept of three-way contracting (between coachee, organisational client and coach) is central to executive coaching. This ensures that the coaching supports both the coachee (the client who receives the coaching) and the organisational client (the person who represents the entity that pays for the coaching). So the primary purpose of executive coaching is to support the client to achieve more of their potential and maintain or enhance their wellbeing *within* their organisational context.

HOW WERE THE PROFESSIONAL CONTEXTS CHOSEN?

It is acknowledged that not all professional contexts are covered in this book. The military, charitable and hospitality sectors, for example, do not appear. The various professional contexts included were chosen for two reasons. Firstly, it was important to include contexts in which coaching was being used extensively. Secondly, the choice was driven by the availability and expertise of the chapter and case study authors. A later edition of this book will no doubt include a greater number of professional contexts.

CONTROVERSY AND CONFUSION

The field of executive coaching is flourishing and continues to grow despite a challenging economic climate. However, the surge in interest and growth has led to a situation that has been described by the *Harvard Business Review* as a 'Wild West of Executive Coaching'. Despite the best efforts of an increasing number of professional associations, there is a reputational challenge facing the industry. We propose that some of the reasons for this are the confusion of terminology (e.g. executive coaching vs. consultancy vs. leadership mentoring), the ease of entry into the profession (i.e., anyone can call themselves a coach), and the fact that the 'brand' of coaching is seen as attractive. This has meant that some people and a number of consultancies have simply re-branded what they do as 'coaching'. This makes it difficult for:

- researchers to study the effects of coaching (as the interventions may vary);
- clients to know what they are buying;
- the profession of coaching to be seen as credible and trustworthy.

This book tackles some controversies head on. Firstly, there has been much debate about whether managers can act as coaches. An entire chapter is dedicated to this issue. Secondly, the status of academic research into coaching in organisations has been contested. This is also addressed directly in a chapter on the topic. There is no question that academic research is needed to generate relevant theories and inform practice within organisations. Of course, it is important that research and theories should be rooted in practice and also directly inform practice. Finally, throughout the book, there are a number of 'myth-busters' in which authors challenge some common misperceptions within the field.

WHAT IS COVERED IN THE CHAPTERS?

Chapter 1: The Importance of Understanding Professional Contexts

This chapter answers some questions that may be helpful to address straightaway. Key definitions are presented and a brief overview of every chapter is provided so that readers can make decisions about how to use this book to best effect.

Chapter 2: Coaching for Optimal Functioning

In this key chapter, Gordon Spence discusses ways that coaching can be used to support sustained high performance in organisations. He presents a new conceptual framework and this is further supported with practical tips for executive coaches to use with clients.

Chapter 3: Manager as Coach: The Challenge

Julia Milner and Alex Couley address a key question that has arisen within the field: is it possible for someone to both line manage and coach a direct report? This intriguing chapter explores an important issue by considering the complexities of merging the roles of coach and manager. The authors also present a new framework for practitioners and provide practical advice for those wishing to develop 'manager as coach' programmes.

Chapter 4: Coaching for Careers and Professional Development

In this chapter Julia Yates considers the use of career theory to inform coaching professionals about their careers and development. Three case studies ('Coaching using career theories', 'Coaching mid-life career change' and 'Coaching to "get back on track"') support this chapter.

Chapter 5: Coaching in the Financial Services Industry

Emma Fowler and John Ainley focus on the application of coaching within the financial services industry. The chapter is supported by three case studies: 'Executive coaching for top team members', 'Using a coaching approach with the executive team' and 'Leadership development in a multinational bank'.

Chapter 6: Coaching within Professional Services Firms

Caroline Flin and Ian McIntosh address the topic of coaching within professional services firms. The chapter is supported by two case studies: 'Preferred supplier list assessment and selection process' and 'Transition to partner programme'.

Chapter 7: Coaching in Local Government

Colin Williams and Samantha Darby explore current practice in the public sector. The use of executive coaching, coach training programmes and the creation of internal coaching resources will be covered. The chapter is supported by an in-depth case study of a public sector coaching pool ('West Midlands Coaching and Mentoring Pool').

Chapter 8: Coaching in Healthcare Settings

Vivien Walton and Julia Sinclair provide an overview of the use of coaching within the National Health Service (NHS). The chapter covers the application of coaching within healthcare settings and considers ways in which it can support medical careers. The chapter is supported by three case studies: 'Career coaching for a doctor', 'Coaching assistant directors within the NHS' and 'Coaching general practitioners'.

Chapter 9: Coaching Patients

Rachel Hawley discusses the use of coaching to support patients and explores the importance of dialogue between patient and clinician. The author proposes a new approach to the use of coaching with patients. The chapter is supported by two case studies: 'Coaching conversations, care and confidence' and 'Better conversations, better care'.

Chapter 10: Coaching in Schools

In this chapter, John Campbell provides a broad overview of the growth and development of coaching within schools in the UK, the USA and Australia. The use of coaching with school leaders, educators and students is explored and a new framework (Global Framework for Coaching in Education) is presented. The chapter is supported by two case studies written by educational practitioners: 'Opening the coaching portals' and 'Empowering our greatest resource'.

Chapter 11: Coaching in Higher Education

Three practitioners with experience of using coaching in higher education, Ioanna Iordanou, Agnieszka Lech and Veronica Barnes, share their thoughts about how coaching can be used within university settings. The use of coaching with staff and students is explored. The impact of teaching students to become coaches is also discussed in this chapter. The chapter is supported by a new 'Framework for Practitioners' on the topic of coaching for research supervision and three case studies: 'Developing coaches and coaching staff', 'Coaching PhD students' and 'A student's perspective'.

Chapter 12: Integrating Coaching and Positive Psychology in Education

In a ground-breaking chapter, Clive Leach and Suzy Green make a case for the integration of coaching and positive psychology within educational settings. The evidence-base for the use of positive education is surveyed and practical suggestions for the use of coaching and positive psychology are made. This chapter is supported by two case studies of the use of integrated approaches in schools: 'A strategic approach to enhance wellbeing' and 'A strength-based coaching programme'.

Chapter 13: The Current State of Research

In a timely and topical chapter, Tim Theeboom surveys the current state of play in relation to the research into coaching within organisational settings. A broad range of research into the field is presented and critiqued.

Chapter 14: Coaching for Wellbeing at Work

In this important chapter, a leading academic in the field, Lindsay Oades, argues for the inclusion of the concept of wellbeing in discussions about coaching. The concept of wellbeing at work brings together theories and practices from the fields of coaching psychology, positive psychology and health psychology. This chapter is supported by a case study entitled 'Coaching for wellbeing'.

Chapter 15: Supervision for Learning

Mary Watts, Esther Cavett and Sarah Dudney explore the role of supervision in supporting the development of coaches. In a thought-provoking and sometimes challenging chapter, they highlight the need for coaching supervision to support the use of coaching within professional settings. The chapter is supported by two case studies: 'Experience of coaching supervision' and 'Finding time to think'.

Chapter 16: Towards a Coaching Culture

This chapter considers the idea of 'coaching cultures'. Various approaches to 'creating coaching cultures' will be surveyed and discussed. Some practical ideas to support the development of coaching cultures will also be proposed. This chapter is supported by two 'Frameworks for Practitioners' and a 'Perspective from Practice'.

Chapter 17: Towards a Philosophy of Coaching?

The final chapter brings together the learning from this writing project. It explores what has emerged as unique within the various sectors. More importantly, it reflects on what has surfaced as consistent. This is explored provocatively as a 'philosophy of coaching' and questions are raised about 'coaching cultures' and the future of the coaching profession.

To the reader

On behalf of all of the contributors to this book, I would like to thank you for taking the time to reflect on the question of coaching in professional contexts. As the editor, chapter authors, case study contributors and writers of the frameworks for practitioners, we are all deeply committed to the effective use of coaching within our professional contexts. We hope that you will find useful insights, helpful experiences and thought-provoking questions within this text that will make a difference both to you and the contexts with which you engage.

REFERENCES

van Nieuwerburgh, C. (2014) *An Introduction to Coaching Skills: A Practical Guide.* London: Sage.

Whitmore, J. (2009) *Coaching for Performance: GROWing Human Potential and Purpose: The Principles and Practice of Coaching and Leadership* (4th ed.). London: Nicholas Brealey.

Willis, P. (2005) *EMCC Competency Research Project: Phase 2.* Watford: European Mentoring and Coaching Council.

2

COACHING FOR OPTIMAL FUNCTIONING

GORDON SPENCE

INTRODUCTION

The term 'performance' is arguably one of the most used but least examined concepts in the field of coaching. Whilst the literature is replete with definitions of coaching that refer in one way or another to the enhancement of performance, very few make any attempt to clarify just what *performance* means. According to Spence and Deci (2013) the term is often used in a rather generic way, primarily focused on gains made at behavioural levels. As they go on to argue however, focusing on 'what people can do and how well they can do it will yield an incomplete picture of their overall status' (2013: 87). In this chapter, the overall status of the performer will be kept very much in mind, as a performer cannot reasonably be separated from their accomplishments.

This chapter is about coaching for peak performance. Whilst it will most certainly be concerned with the demonstration of excellence and the accomplishment of remarkable feats, it will not be limited to these outcomes. Rather it will also consider how performance affects the performer; whether it leaves them enlivened or dispirited, enhanced or diminished, or to use more general terms, in a state of flourishing or languishing (Grant and Spence, 2010). Why? Because it is difficult to understand how performance can be considered 'peak' if its beneficial, in-the-world effects are not accompanied by pleasant subjective effects.

Within this framing of the concept, coaching is examined for its ability to support leaders, artists, players, managers, educators and a variety of other 'performers' to generate action that can achieve desirable outcomes in the world and within themselves. Given this broader perspective being taken on peak performance, the concept of optimal functioning is preferred from this point on, as this term captures aspects of not only doing well but also feeling well (Vitterso, 2013).

WHAT IS PEAK PERFORMANCE?

Before beginning, however, it is important to note that this concept can be thought about in at least two ways, delineated along temporal lines. The first is a relatively short-term, event-based notion of performance, one that seems to accord quite well with Privette's definition of peak performance as being:

> 'The prototype of superior use of human potential; it is more efficient, creative, productive, or in some way better than habitual behaviour … the full use of any human power.' (1983: 1362)

Whilst it would be a misrepresentation to suggest that Privette only construed peak performance in this way (as she recognised that it could be a single event, regular events, or in rare instances continuous events), the conventional way of understanding performance seems to be related to how well someone utilises their skills and talents to achieve a desired goal at a given point in time (Hays and Brown, 2004). This equates to a relatively common view that performances are discrete events, chained together by periods of non-performance.

A second way to understand peak performance is as a more enduring feature of human experience, a more holistic interpretation that extends beyond narrow behaviourally-focused conceptualisations of performance and is something more akin to the notion of optimal functioning. For Spence and Deci, optimal functioning represents a more appropriate goal for coaching and includes simultaneously seeking enhancements across the physiological, behavioural, cognitive, affective and meaning dimensions of experience. From this perspective, excellence in coaching would entail:

> 'The implementation of a set of interpersonal processes that lead to the coachee experiencing enhanced physical health (physiological), engagement in effective, purposeful actions (behavioural), the possession of sufficient attentional control to process information effectively (cognitive), an ability to encounter a wider range of emotional states with equanimity and poise (affective), and the conscious linking of personal goals and commitments to important beliefs, core values and/or developing interests (meaning)'. (2013: 87)

As such, coaching for optimal functioning is not simply about helping people to set stretching goals, maintain commitment towards them, and act in ways that facilitate their attainment. This is because, whilst such an approach may indeed result in impressive goal attainment for weeks, months and sometimes years, the quest for 'peak performance' is often associated with a range of dire consequences for those who seek it (such as burnout, social isolation, physical deterioration, or at its most extreme, suicide). Given the evidence that links workaholism (over-engagement in work) with a range of poor physical and mental health outcomes (Griffiths and Karanika-Murray, 2012; Van Gordon et al., 2014), there are compelling reasons for coaches to take a more holistic approach to thinking about and working with clients. Simply put, not thinking with coachees about the broader implications of their performance patterns potentially does them a disservice, by denying them opportunities to adopt patterns of behaviour that would support the sustainability of effort and eudaimonic wellbeing outcomes.

A MORE EUDAIMONIC VIEW OF PEAK PERFORMANCE

Whilst discussions about the nature of performance are not commonplace within the coaching literature, they do take place in related fields. For example, in a recent review of the relationship between human resource management (HRM) and performance, Janssens and Steyaert (2008) argued that members of the HR community have tended to conceptualise performance far too narrowly. More specifically, they contend that, in their quest to function more as strategic business partners and work with a variety of stakeholders, HR professionals have tended to preference the interests of the most powerful stakeholders. The result? A perspective on performance that disproportionately emphasises economic considerations (e.g. organisational productivity, profit maximisation) with scant consideration of 'the potential effects of high-performance practices on workers and society' (Janssens and Steyaert, 2009: 148).

This observation is offered here not as a criticism of HR practices, but to suggest that economics is the frame of reference that many professionals seem to internalise and use to construct personal notions of performance. However, given that most organisations are driven by economic and financial imperatives, this is hardly surprising. The difficulty is that this tends to translate into personal performance standards that are often associated with a strong drive to 'do things well, do them fast, then repeat the process'. When performers rigidly adopt this ethos it can put them in a perilous position as they may begin to prioritise these imperatives over more personally significant ones (e.g. self-care, nurturing key relationships etc.). Here the worst-case scenario is occupational sudden death or *karoshi*, which is on the rise in Japan and literally translated means 'death by overwork' (Kanai, 2009).

In situations where performer work patterns become excessive, coaches may assist by helping their coachees to:

- develop awareness of those patterns;
- consider the implications of those patterns;
- take action to change them in ways that will better support their long-term performance.

To restate the position, coaching for optimal functioning involves attempting to help a performer create a state of high-quality personal activation that is sustainable over long periods of time. Importantly, this perspective gauges 'peakness' by using criteria that reflect how well a person is doing across a variety of psychosocial dimensions. A wellbeing model that outlines a multidimensional understanding is Ryff's (1989) model of psychological wellbeing (PWB). Whilst previous models of the six PWB dimensions have included descriptions of individuals at the high and low end of each dimension (see Ryff, 1989:1072), only descriptions of high scorers have been provided in Table 2.1 due to the current focus on optimal functioning.

Table 2.1   Eudaimonic dimensions of optimal functioning

Dimension	Surface markers of an optimal functioning person
Autonomy	Is self-determining and independent; able to resist social pressures to think and act in certain ways; regulates behaviour from within, evaluates self by personal standards.
Environmental Mastery	Has a sense of mastery and competence in managing the environment; controls complex array of external activities; makes effective use of surrounding opportunities; able to choose or create contexts suitable to personal needs and values.
Personal Growth	Has a feeling of continued development; sees self as growing and expanding; is open to new experiences; has sense of realising their potential; sees improvement in self and behaviour over time; is changing in ways that reflect more self-knowledge and effectiveness.
Positive Relations with Others	Has warm, satisfying, trusting relationships with others; is concerned about the welfare of others; capable of strong empathy, affection and intimacy; understands the give and take of human relationships.
Purpose in Life	Has goals in life and a sense of directedness; feels there is meaning to present and past life; holds beliefs that give life purpose; has aims and objectives for living.
Self-acceptance	Possesses a positive attitude toward the self; acknowledges and accepts multiple aspects of the self, including good and bad qualities; feels positive about past life.

Source: Adapted from Ryff (1989)

One advantage of conceptualising performance in terms of optimal functioning and PWB is that it can cater for instances where goal attainment may not have occurred (e.g. a lost sales contract) but where one's cognitive, affective and/or behavioural responses have been highly adaptive, flexible and supportive of continuing attempts to pursue the same or similar goals into the future. In such a circumstance, whilst a stated goal may not have been attained, the experience might have been reflected upon in a way that led the performer to accept any mistakes they might have made without self-recriminations (self-acceptance), resulting in key on-the-job learning that will shape future efforts (environmental mastery) and leading to a re-commitment to important work goals that are personally meaningful (autonomy) and provide a strong sense of direction (purpose in life).

SUPPORTING OPTIMAL FUNCTIONING

So, how can coaches facilitate a process that can result in optimal functioning (or at least a move towards it)? According to numerous authors in the scholarly coaching literature (e.g. Grant and Cavanagh, 2011; Spence and Oades, 2011), use of relevant theory-guided models and evidence-based frameworks is a solid starting point. Fortunately, many such frameworks exist and whilst they share obvious conceptual overlap, each also offers something of value to the practising coach (as shown in Table 2.2).

Whilst all of the named frameworks in Table 2.2 will receive some attention within this chapter, the following discussion will focus on key elements of the Hays and Brown (2004) and Gardner and Moore (2007) frameworks, as these are the most comprehensive of those identified. When comparing the ideas presented by these authors, it becomes apparent that whilst they are organised differently, both emphasise the importance of developing in three related areas:

- Basic skills and abilities.
- Self-knowledge and personality coherence.
- Self-management and self-care.

For ease, these three aspects of performance will be elaborated upon below using the phrases 'Know thy Stuff' (basic skills and abilities), 'Know thy Self' (self-knowledge and personality coherence), and 'Know thy System' (self-management and self-care).

KNOW THY STUFF

This addresses perhaps the most obvious aspect of performance optimisation; the simple reality that it is extremely difficult to perform at high levels if we do not know what to do and how to do it. As such, the practising coach may wish to consider:

1. What task-relevant knowledge can the coachee consciously access? (*Explicit knowledge*)
2. What task-relevant knowledge might the coachee possess but not be able to ordinarily access? (*Implicit knowledge*)
3. What mental models or concepts might help the coachee better understand their performance? (*Psychoeducation*)
4. What constitutes the best form of preparation for the coachee, including specific practice exercises? (*Preparation and practice*)
5. How adept is the coachee at directing awareness and attention towards task-relevant information? (*Mindfulness*)

Table 2.2 Peak performance frameworks and practical value for coaches

Author(s)	Hays & Brown (2004) Hayes (2009)	Gardner & Moore (2007)	Csikszentmihalyi (1997; 2003)	Hanin (1997)	Loehr & Schwartz (2001) Schwartz (2010)
Concept	Peak Performance	Functional Performance	Flow	Individual Zones of Optimal Functioning	Ideal Performance State

Elements	1. Foundation
	  – Basic abilities
	  – Coherent sense of self
	  – 'Care of the instrument'
	2. Preparation
	  – Knowledge
	  – Active intentional learning
	  – Practising the delivery
	3. Mental skills
	4. Coping with stress
	5. Performance process
		Foundational factors:
		1. Instrumental competencies
		2. Environmental stimuli & performance demands
		3. Dispositional characteristics
		4. Behavioural self-regulation
		
		Performance phases:
		1. Pre-performance phase
		2. Performance phase
		3. Post-performance Response phase
			1. Balance of skill-challenge
			2. Clear short-term goals
			3. Immediate feedback
			4. Choiceful action
				1. Optimal positive emotions
				2. Optimal negative emotions
				3. Dysfunctional positive emotions
				4. Dysfunctional negative emotions
					1. Physical capacity
					2. Cognitive capacity
					3. Emotional capacity
					4. Spiritual capacity

Practical value	• Grounded in qualitative accounts of performers from four distinct performance domains. • Gives emphasis to the importance of a fully developing self, good self-care and the acquisition of good intrapersonal skills.	• Provides a comprehensive account of interdependent factors that shape human performance. • Offers an approach to case formulation and intervention, grounded in Acceptance and Commitment Theory and mindfulness training.	• An evidence-based account of pre-conditions associated with optimal performance. • Gives coachees a way of examining past, present and future performance events and finding ways to optimise them.	• Proposes best performances are preceded by blends of emotions that are unique to each person. • Sees positive and negative emotions as being both helpful and unhelpful to performance.	• Highlights importance of energy management via creation of optimal work-rest ratios (via oscillations). • Promotes the importance of preparing in same disciplined, structured way as professional athletes.

1. Explicit knowledge

This is knowledge that can be readily articulated and transmitted between people. It is a vital store of procedural and declarative knowledge that performers use to guide action and make decisions. In contrast to knowledge that derives from practical experience, explicit knowledge is usually gained from conventional forms of knowledge acquisition, like reading and classroom teaching. In coaching, the acquisition of explicit knowledge is relatively easy to support, through interactions that help people identify where knowledge gaps exist and explore different options for gaining access to such knowledge (e.g. reading matter, discussions with a mentor, short courses).

2. Implicit knowledge

This is a much subtler form of knowledge, also known as tacit knowledge (Polanyi, 1966), that is associated with seemingly simple actions yet is extremely difficult to articulate (e.g. how to successfully close a negotiation). Brockmann and Anthony (2002: 443) define tacit knowledge as 'work related practical know-how learned on the job', and argue that, given that it typically exists on the fringes of awareness, it can be effectively accessed through social processes that permit detailed reflection on past experiences. As coaching permits this type of reflection, coaches have the opportunity to help performers tap these stores of accumulated knowledge through the use of questioning techniques, journaling, and other forms of expressive writing. For example, exceptions questions are a solution-focused technique often used in coaching to help people explore past experiences in ways that permit a (re)connection with skills, abilities and knowledge, which may have previously contributed to positive outcomes but have either never been clearly articulated or simply forgotten (Berg and Szabo, 2005).

3. Psychoeducation

This is a good option for supporting optimal functioning (Gardner and Moore, 2007). Exposure to simple performance-related concepts and mental models can assist performers to learn more the mental states and processes that are associated with high performance. In this regard, psychology has much to offer. For example, flow theory (Csikszentmihalyi, 1997) offers an evidence-based account of moments of high absorption that are often associated with high levels of performance and personal satisfaction. Whilst the relationship between flow and high performance has not always been clear cut (Keller and Landhauber, 2012), the theory is useful as it gives some guidance on the conditions that need to exist for these states of highly focused motivation to emerge (see Table 2.2). Given the evidence that performers can influence the emergence of flow states (Jackson, 1995), this theory is potentially useful as it can encourage people to take more responsibility for their performance experiences (by attempting to create the pre-conditions for flow). Other useful models include the much-cited Inverted U hypothesis, or Yerkes Dodson law (Yerkes and Dodson, 1908), and the Individual Zones of Optimal Functioning (IZOF) model (Hanin, 1997). The Inverted U hypothesis is useful in coaching as it describes a basic curvilinear relationship between arousal and performance, where highest performance is predicted to occur at moderate levels of arousal (rather than at excessively low or high levels). The IZOF model supports a more nuanced view of performance-relevant emotional states, with Hanin (1997) arguing that performers have a specific optimal pre-performance zone of idiosyncratic emotion intensities in which best performance is *most likely* to occur. Using specific emotion profiling methods, the IZOF is built by identifying which emotional states (both positive and negative) are facilitative or inhibiting of best performance (see Hanin, 1997). As such, the use of either the IZOF or Inverted U models in coaching can help performers become more aware of their ideal performance states and design strategies to support the creation of these optimal pre-performance states.

4. Preparation and practice

These are vital for high-level performance (Hays and Brown, 2004). Whilst natural talent, giftedness and other innate abilities (such as IQ) were long thought to be what separated the great from the good performers, other positive qualities like grit (i.e. perseverance and passion for long term goals) appear to be important differentiators of success in a variety of performance arenas (Duckworth et al., 2007). Such findings seem to lend some support to the popular idea that expertise develops somewhere beyond 10,000 hours of practice (Gladwell, 2008) and suggest that coaches might be able to assist their clients towards optimal functioning by helping them maintain a sustained commitment to important preparatory activities. As Brown (2009: 312) points out, whilst 'active intentional learning' is vital to the mastering of one's craft, it 'does not necessarily feel good because it is full of mistakes and attempts at tasks that surpass one's current abilities'. As such, coaches have an important dual role to play during any performance preparation phase, namely to encourage an adequate investment in all forms of preparation including what might be gained from the five conventional psychological skill training (PST) areas: relaxation, self-talk, imagery and visualisation, goal setting and concentration (see Andersen, 2009, for detailed descriptions and guidance). As noted above by Brown (2009), given these will be periods of conscious incompetence for many performers, supporting their resilience during these periods of developing competence and mastery will be important.

5. Mindfulness

This is considered a special topic within the context of this discussion as it has been consistently associated with adaptive self-regulation and elevated wellbeing (K.W. Brown et al., 2007). Whilst the concept has been defined in a variety of secular and non-secular ways (for discussions see Cavanagh and Spence, 2013; Dane, 2011), mindfulness represents a basic ability to give one's full attention to present moment events and experience (K. W. Brown and Ryan, 2003). Whilst more will be said about mindfulness in the following sections, all that needs to be noted here is that human attention can be developed much like any other acquired skill (through committed training and practice), with various forms of meditation found to be particularly effective (Slagter et al., 2007). Given the body of evidence that now supports the cultivation of mindfulness in a variety of life domains (K. W. Brown and Holt, 2011), there is much to recommend the use of mindfulness practices within the context of a coaching relationship, for both for the coach and the coachee (Hall, 2013). However, when it comes to the enhancement of performance, coaches should be careful about how they promote the virtues of 'living in the now'. As will shortly be discussed, the relationship between mindfulness and performance is not as simple as it is sometimes made out to be.

Know thy Stuff – Practical tips

- Conduct a skills audit to identify knowledge and skill gaps, including formal feedback procedures such as 360-degree surveys.
- Encourage reflective processing (through discussion or written narratives) to surface tacit knowledge.
- Familiarise yourself with three or four performance models that relate to important aspects of common performance experiences.
- Encourage clients to explore a variety of mindfulness training practices, both formal and informal. For example, consider beginning coaching sessions with a short guided breathing space exercise (for a script see Williams et al., 2007) or recommending more structured, formal mindfulness training (e.g. Mindfulness-Based Stress Reduction; Kabat-Zinn, 2013).

KNOW THY SELF

In their qualitative analysis of elite performers, Hays and Brown noted the following:

'Excellent performers exhibited a coherent sense of identity. They showed confidence in their abilities and expressed a sense of purpose and direction, self-knowledge, a clear sense of identity, and, for some, even a sense of destiny.' (2004: 83)

Another way to express this is that these high performers seemed 'comfortable in their own skin', a notion that is highly compatible with the eudaimonic perspective on performance being taken in this chapter. That is, this observation reflects elements of autonomy, environmental mastery, personal growth, purpose in life and self-acceptance (see the descriptions in Table 2.1). Presuming that these performers also enjoy good physical health, adequate positive emotion and strong social connections, then their overall status should be close to optimal. The issue being introduced here relates to self-knowledge and personality development. This is of course no small matter, having dominated the work of preeminent psychologists such as Freud, Rogers, Bandura, and numerous others over many decades. Whilst a detailed discussion is not warranted within the context of this chapter, it is useful to continue exploring the concept of mindfulness as it is highly relevant to both.

Mindfulness reflects a particular quality of consciousness, one typified by relaxed, non-judgmental awareness of moment-by-moment experience. As many authors have pointed out (K.W. Brown and Holt, 2011; Cavanagh and Spence, 2013; Hall, 2013), an important consequence of cultivating this wakeful, open state of mind is that one becomes more sensitive to important aspects of the self (e.g. values, interests, intuitions), which represent a form of intrapersonal attunement. Writing on the challenge of finding one's 'voice' in dialogue with others, Isaacs states:

> 'My voice is not simply something that reveals my thought, or even parts of myself; it literally can bring forth a world, conjure an image. But this kind of speaking requires that I learn to listen for the distant thunder that may ultimately turn out to be my own voice waiting to be spoken … Suddenly I have the sense that everyone is waiting for me, that it is somehow my turn, that I have something for others that must come out. Often I find people who have this experience look around anxiously for someone else to fill their shoes, to do this job for them. 'They can't have meant me.' Yet this inner call can only be answered by you, and in answering it one finds one's own voice and one's own authority.' (1999: 165)

What Isaacs so eloquently describes is a form of intrapersonal attunement. That is, being able to bring open awareness and attention to internal events allows a person to better detect their 'distant thunder' – free of distortions or automatic reactions – and opens up opportunities to respond with more congruence and authenticity (Niemiec and Ryan, 2013). Thus mindfulness provides a foundation for healthy personality development, insofar as it allows people to glimpse core aspects of the self more vividly.

According to Cavanagh and Spence (2013) the benefits that flow from mindfulness and intrapersonal attunement include values clarification and more autonomous (congruent) goal-setting. Whilst these effects can be (and often are) achieved in coaching, this developmental work generally needs to occur at a slower pace because coachees need time to question themselves, slow down, still mind and body, and better listen to (notice) what is happening within. It is important to note that this is not the typical approach in performance coaching, where the emphasis is often on moving the goal-striving process on as efficiently as possible. More developmental forms of coaching tend to take more time, require great patience and move towards outcomes that are often difficult to predict, as people will often change the way they make meaning and sense of themselves and the world (Garvey Berger, 2012). As such, this style of coaching might not be for everyone. However, the deep developmental potential of coaching is mentioned here because it can help to enhance several aspects of PWB (e.g. purpose in life, personal growth, autonomy, self-acceptance), which make it highly supportive of optimal functioning.

There are other ways that mindfulness can assist performers to Know thy Self. For example, according to Dane (2011) mindful states help to improve access to intuitions (or gut feelings), which can be useful in loosely structured tasks (such as strategic decision making; see Brockmann and Anthony, 2002). Whilst conventional wisdom recommends that intuitions should always be challenged or questioned (to guard against bias or inaccuracy), Dane (2011) contends that the utility of any intuition depends on the task expertise of the performer. That is, research suggests that the intuitions of experts tend to enhance task performance, whilst the intuitions of novices tend to inhibit task performance (Kahneman and Klein, 2009).

Another common claim made about mindfulness is that it supports purposeful, adaptive self-regulation, which means that people are able to behave in ways that are flexible, sensitive to current conditions, and that ultimately serve the person well (Wrosch et al., 2003). According to Gardner and Moore's (2007) Mindfulness-Acceptance-Commitment (MAC) approach, a critical step for achieving this flexibility is to assist performers to defuse from unhelpful thoughts and beliefs, through the mindful observation of thoughts as mere thoughts, rather than literal truths or facts about events, objects or people (that may elicit automatic, habitual responses). This is pertinent to the current discussion because knowing about these processes provides performers with an important form of knowledge about the workings of the mind and the attachments of the self.

Examples of fused thinking would be the belief that one must always act independent of others (i.e. never accept help) or that one should never give up on a goal. Held firmly, these beliefs are likely to act as a powerful source of motivation but also be associated with considerable pressure and tension, which might lead to rigid behavioural responses. Consider the concept of mental toughness. In essence mental toughness represents the ability to successfully manage adversity, such that one remains committed to and engaged with important personal goals (Clough and Strycharczyk, 2012). For some, remaining 'committed to and engaged with important goals' easily translates to highly controlling self-beliefs such as 'I must do this myself' and/or 'I must never give up'. Of course, it is possible to imagine many situations where acting in accordance with these beliefs is completely legitimate and carries little risk for the performer (beyond the cognitive and emotional challenge of continuing effort). However, it is also possible to imagine how the rigid adoption of such beliefs (i.e. cognitive fusion) might incline performers to 'stay the course' when it might be more beneficial to either suspend their effort or seek help from others (as doing so would preserve their physical health, reduce stress, allow social reconnection, etc.).

In such situations, the MAC approach uses mindfulness training and acceptance techniques to help performers notice that they have fused with these beliefs, that this fusion comes with some challenging cognitive effects that do not have to be acted on (e.g. uncompromising self-talk; 'Asking for help is a sign of weakness'), and that the best action to take is the one that accords well with the values that underlie performance activities (Gardner and Moore, 2007). Whilst in some circumstances this may lead people to decide to disengage from specific goals, such decisions would not necessarily be considered failures of mental toughness. For example, if such a decision in some way preserves a client's ability to perform consistently at a high level over time, then it would align well with Gucciardi and Gordon's (2010) definition of the construct. In a similar vein, it has been argued that the disengagement from goals is a highly adaptive thing to do at times (Wrosch et al., 2003), and rather than being seen as a sign of weakness (as 'quitting' is generally frowned upon in many achievement-orientated, western cultures) such decisions would in fact convey great strength.

Know thy Self – Practical tips

- Encourage people to explore a variety of mindfulness training practices, both formal (e.g. meditation) and informal (e.g. body scans, mindful eating).
- Encourage people to spend time in quiet reflection.
- Recommend regular journaling or other narrative/expressive writing (such as Reflected Best Self; see Roberts et al., 2005).
- Encourage discussion of these exercises when completed.

KNOW THY SYSTEM

Assuming that a performer possesses the necessary skill and abilities to competently engage in tasks (*Know thy Stuff*), and is developing in a way that feels congruent and authentic (*Know thy Self*), then it is likely that they will feel well equipped to perform at a high level and quite comfortable with the direction they are heading. Whilst these feelings of confidence and congruence are likely to be highly energising and stimulate prolonged high-quality effort, this will be difficult to sustain if performers are not actively attending to their self-care. Simply stated, performers need to be able to regularly 'check in' with themselves and take whatever action is required to keep functioning as well as possible. This will now be explored in relation to attentional restoration, sleep and energy management.

Attentional restoration

It is hard to imagine anyone not acknowledging (at least at some level) the importance of taking a break from work and investing in some 'downtime'. Yet recent research suggests that workers are not accomplished at taking breaks (Berman and West, 2007), and even when they do, many seem to direct attention back into work in ways that do not lead to the positive outcomes associated with taking breaks (such as increased effectiveness and feeling restored). When considered alongside Attention Restoration Theory (ART; Kaplan, 1995) these findings are not surprising. In short, ART argues that restoration occurs when controlled attention is allowed to rest and involuntary attention is activated. The theory suggests this is often accomplished in nature, provided the natural setting: (a) can take a person into a private and secluded psychological state (Being away); (b) provide a coherent other world (Extent); (c) evoke involuntary or effortless attention (Fascination); and (d) achieve a match between what typically occurs in the new environment and one's purpose or inclinations (Compatibility). Importantly, empirical explorations of ART have shown that natural settings are not only perceived as more restorative (Felsten, 2009), they also facilitate recovery from mental fatigue and bolster performance on cognitive tasks (Berto, 2005). Of course, the beneficial impact of natural settings will depend on how much of the environment is truly noticed, as a failure to do so is unlikely to result in feelings of fascination or psychological seclusion. As such, mindfulness is considered to be a vital part of restorative experiences, and when in nature, a wide external attentional breadth (Dane, 2011) seems the appropriate orientation if one is to gain from the experience.

Sleep

It is harder again to imagine anyone disputing the importance of sleep to optimal performance. Indeed, there is an overwhelming amount of evidence that attests to the positive impact of sleep on performance on a wide variety of cognitive and motor-based tasks, and for successful mood regulation (Lim and Dinges, 2010; Pilcher and Huffcutt, 1996). Despite this, sleep durations of less than six and a half hours ('short sleep') are being increasingly reported by people in Australia and North America (Magee et al., 2009). The challenge for coaches is not what needs to be done to improve sleep (assuming that no clinical condition exists, such as sleep apnea). Detailed lists of sleep hygiene practices are both easily accessible (for an example see NSF, 2014) and relatively consistent. Rather, the challenge is what might compel a performer to want to change their sleep patterns? Whilst this is a natural starting point for any behaviour change, sleep has special importance for optimal functioning as the fatigue created by sleep deficiency compromises one's ability to think efficiently, inhibits physical activity (which impacts overall general health in myriad ways), and makes it harder to regulate emotions and mood (which can adversely impact relationships and mental health). Given that people do not get adequate sleep for many reasons (e.g. having young children, environmental noise, work stress, financial concerns, faulty beliefs about the amount of sleep required), creating improvements in this area will require a good understanding of the client and decent exploration of their ambivalence about letting go of old patterns of sleep behaviours.

Energy management

According to Loehr and Schwartz (2001: 122), the enemy of high performance is the constant, linear expenditure of effort and 'the absence of disciplined, intermittent recovery'. They argue strongly for the importance of energy management, which is seen as a rhythmic alternation between energy expenditure (stress) and energy renewal (recovery). Referred to as oscillations, stress-recovery transitions are promoted by rituals – specific, purposeful behavioural routines that offer performers short periods of time to replenish physical, emotional, cognitive or spiritual capacities. Whilst there are many things that can be done to bolster capacities at each level (see Loehr and Schwartz, 2001; Schwartz, 2010), the behaviours associated with sleep and attentional restoration are ideally suited to the creation of rituals. For example, physical capacity can be enhanced by creating rituals that support better sleep, such as beginning to wind down 30 to 45 minutes before trying to sleep (e.g. by reading a book, avoiding computer use, etc.). Similarly, cognitive capacity can be enhanced by creating rituals around encounters with nature, such as maintaining a regular lunchtime visit to a public garden, or a morning run along a beach. Another related activity is the completion of an Energy Audit (Spreitzer and Grant, 2012) as this can give people some visibility of how their energy levels vary across the course of a day and what they might like to do to better manage that energy.

Know thy System – Practical tips

- Help clients generate compelling reasons for maintaining good self-care.
- Create (and discuss) a list of environments that clients find most restorative.
- Discuss the importance of engaging in those environments with a wide attentional breadth, free of intentions and devices that might control attention.
- Provide (and discuss) a detailed list of sleep hygiene principles.
- Help clients build a self-management plan, complete with restoration strategies and positive sleep behaviours.
- Encourage clients to undertake an Energy Audit.

CONCLUSION

In this chapter an expanded notion of peak performance has been presented, one that considers both the actions of a performer and the subjective consequences of those actions. It has been argued that coaching is uniquely positioned to assist with the creation of optimal functioning, where simultaneous enhancements may be sought across the physiological, behavioural, cognitive, affective and meaning dimensions of experience. The development of performers (coachees) was then explored in three related areas. The first, 'Know thy Stuff', focused on the acquisition and consolidation of basic skills and abilities. The second, 'Know thy Self', focused on the importance of self-knowledge and personality coherence. The third, 'Know thy System', focused on the importance of self-care and rituals that would assist with the management of energy. The material has been organised in this way to help show that *doing well* does not have to come at the expense of *feeling well*. Rather both can be achieved simultaneously, and when they are, individuals are able to sustain high levels of functioning without suffering unduly for their efforts.

REFERENCES

Andersen, M.B. (2009) 'The "canon" of psychological skills training for enhancing performance'. In K.F. Hays (ed.), *Performance Psychology in Action: A Casebook for Working with Athletes, Performing Artists, Business Leaders, and Professionals in High-Risk Occupations.* Washington, DC: APA. pp. 11–34.

Berg, I.K. and Szabo, P. (2005) *Brief Coaching for Lasting Solutions.* New York: Norton.

Berman, E.M. and West, J.P. (2007) 'The effective manager …takes a break', *Review of Public Personnel Administration, 27*(4): 380–400.

Berto, R. (2005) 'Exposure to restorative environments helps restore attentional capacity', *Journal of Environmental Psychology, 25*: 249–59.

Brockmann, E. and Anthony, W. (2002) 'Tacit knowledge and strategic decision making', *Group and Organization Management, 27*(4): 436–55.

Brown, C.H. (2009) 'The consultant as a performer'. In K.F. Hays (ed.), *Performance Psychology in Action: Casebook for Working With Athletes, Performing Artists, Business Leaders, and Professionals in High-Risk Occupations.* Washington, DC: APA. pp. 309–27.

Brown, K.W. and Holt, M. (2011) 'Experiential processing and the integration of bright and dark sides of the human psyche'. In K.M. Sheldon, T.B. Kashdan and M.F. Steger (eds), *Designing Positive Psychology: Taking Stock and Moving Forward.* New York: Oxford University Press. pp. 147–59.

Brown, K.W. and Ryan, R.M. (2003) 'The benefits of being present: Mindfulness and its role in psychological well-being', *Journal of Personality and Social Psychology, 84*: 822–48.

Brown, K.W., Ryan, R.M. and Creswell, J.D. (2007) 'Mindfulness: Theoretical foundations and evidence for its salutary effects', *Psychological Inquiry, 18*(4): 211–37.

Cavanagh, M. and Spence, G.B. (2013) 'Mindfulness in coaching: Philosophy, psychology, or just a useful skill?' In J. Passmore, D. Peterson and T. Freire (eds), *The Wiley-Blackwell Handbook of the Psychology of Coaching and Mentoring.* New York: Wiley-Blackwell. pp. 112–34.

Clough, P. and Strycharczyk, D. (2012) *Developing Mental Toughness: Improving Performance, Wellbeing and Positive Behaviour in Others.* London: Kogan Page.

Csikszentmihalyi, M. (1997) *Finding Flow in Everyday Life.* New York: Basic Books.

Csikszentmihalyi, M. (2003) *Good Business: Leadership, Flow and the Making of Meaning*. London: Hodder & Stoughton.

Dane, E. (2011) 'Paying attention to mindfulness and its effects on task performance in the workplace', *Journal of Management*, 37(4): 997–1018.

Duckworth, A.L., Peterson, C., Matthews, M.D. and Kelly, D.R. (2007) 'Grit: Perseverance and passion for long-term goals', *Journal of Personality and Social Psychology*, 92(6): 1087–101.

Felsten, G. (2009) 'Where to take a study break on the college campus: An attention restoration theory perspective', *Journal of Environmental Psychology*, 29: 160–7.

Gardner, F.L. and Moore, Z.E. (2007) *The Psychology of Enhancing Human Performance: The Mindfulness-Acceptance-Commitment (MAC) Approach*. New York: Springer.

Garvey Berger, J. (2012) *Changing on the Job: Developing Leaders for a Complex World*. Stanford, CA: Stanford University Press.

Gladwell, M. (2008) *Outliers*. New York: Little, Brown and Company.

Grant, A.M. and Cavanagh, M. (2011) 'Coaching and positive psychology'. In K.M. Sheldon, T.B. Kashdan and M.F. Steger (eds), *Designing Positive Psychology: Taking Stock and Moving Forward*. Oxford: Oxford University Press. pp. 293–309.

Grant, A.M. and Spence, G.B. (2010) 'Using coaching and positive psychology to promote a flourishing workforce: A model of goal-striving and mental health'. In P. A. Linley, S. Harrington and N. Garcea (eds), *Oxford Handbook of Positive Psychology and Work*. New York: Oxford University Press. pp. 175–88.

Griffiths, M.D. and Karanika-Murray, M. (2012) 'Contextualising over-engagement in work: Towards a more global understanding of workaholism as an addiction', *Journal of Behavioral Addictions*, 1(3): 87–95.

Gucciardi, D. and Gordon, S. (eds) (2010) *Mental Toughness in Sport: Developments in Theory and Research*. London: Routledge.

Hall, L. (2013) *Mindful Coaching: How Mindfulness can Transform Coaching Practice*. London: Kogan Page.

Hanin, Y.L. (1997) 'Emotions and athletic performance: Individual zones of optimal functioning model', *European Yearbook of Sport Psychology*, 1: 29–72.

Hays, K.F. (2009) *Performance Psychology in Action: Casebook for Working with Athletes, Performing Artists, Business Leaders, and Professionals in High-Risk Occupations*. Washington DC: APA.

Hays, K.F. and Brown, C.H. (2004) *You've On: Consulting for Peak Performance*. Washington, DC: APA.

Isaacs, W. (1999) *Dialogue and the Art of Thinking Together*. New York: Doubleday.

Jackson, S.A. (1995) 'Factors influencing the occurrence of flow in elite athletes', *Journal of Applied Sport Psychology*, 7(2): 135–63.

Janssens, M. and Steyaert, C. (2009) 'HRM and performance: A plea for reflexivity in HRM studies', *Journal of Management Studies*, 46(1): 143–55.

Kabat-Zinn, J. (2013) *Full Catastrophe Living: Using the Wisdom of Your Body and Mind to Face Stress, Pain, and Illness*. New York: Bantam.

Kahneman, D. and Klein, G. (2009) 'Conditions for intuitive expertise: A failure to disagree', *American Psychologist, 64*: 515–26.

Kanai, A. (2009) 'Karoshi (Work to Death) in Japan', *Journal of Business Ethics, 84*: 209–16.

Kaplan, S. (1995) 'The restorative benefits of nature: Towards an integrative framework', *Journal of Environmental Psychology, 15*: 169–82.

Keller, J. and Landhauber, A. (2012) 'The flow model revisited'. In S. Engeser (ed.), *Advances in Flow-research*. New York: Springer. pp. 51–64.

Lim, J. and Dinges, J.M. (2010) 'A meta-analysis of the impact of short-term sleep deprivation on cognitive variables', *Psychological Bulletin, 136*(3): 375–89.

Loehr, J. and Schwartz, T. (2001) 'The making of a corporate athlete', *Harvard Business Review, 79*(1): 120–8.

Magee, C.A., Iverson, D.C. and Caputi, P. (2009) 'Factors associated with short and long sleep', *Preventive Medicine, 49*: 461–7.

Niemiec, C.P. and Ryan, R.M. (2013) 'What makes for a life well lived? Autonomy and its relation to full functioning and organismic wellness'. In S. David, I. Boniwell and A.C. Ayers (eds), *Oxford Handbook of Happiness*. Oxford: Oxford University Press. pp. 214–226.

NSF (2014) 'Sleep Hygiene'. Retrieved 21st August 2014, from http://sleepfoundation.org/ask-the-expert/sleep-hygiene

Pilcher, J.J. and Huffcutt, A.I. (1996) 'Effects of sleep deprivation on performance: A meta-analysis', *Sleep, 19*(4): 318–26.

Polayni, M. (1966) *The Tacit Dimension*. London: Routledge & Kegan Paul.

Privette, G. (1983) 'Peak experience, peak performance, and flow: A comparative analysis of positive human experiences', *Journal of Personality and Social Psychology, 45*(6): 1361–8.

Roberts, L., Dutton, J., Spreitzer, G., Heaphy, E. and Quinn, R. (2005) 'Composing the reflected best self portrait: Building pathways for becoming extraordinary in work organizations', *Academy of Management Review, 30*(4): 712–36.

Ryff, C.D. (1989) 'Happiness is everything, or is it? Explorations on the meaning of psychological well-being', *Journal of Personality and Social Psychology, 57*(6): 1069–81.

Schwartz, T. (2010) *The Way We're Working Isn't Working*. New York: Free Press.

Slagter, H.A., Lutz, A., Greischar, L.L., Francis, A.D., Nieuwenhuis, S., Davis, J.M. and Davidson, R.J. (2007) 'Mental training affects use of limited brain resources', *PLoS Biology, 5*(6): e138.

Spence, G.B. and Deci, E.L. (2013) 'Self-determination with coaching contexts: Supporting motives and goals that promote optimal functioning and well-being'. In S. David, D. Clutterbuck and D. Megginson (eds), *Beyond Goals: Effective Strategies for Coaching and Mentoring*. Padstow: Gower. pp. 85–108.

Spence, G.B., and Oades, L. G. (2011) 'Coaching with self-determination theory in mind: Using theory to advance evidence-based coaching practice', *International Journal of Evidence Based Coaching and Mentoring, 9*(2): 37–55.

Spreitzer, G.M. and Grant, T. (2012) 'Helping students manage their energy taking their pulse with the energy audit', *Journal of Management Education*, 36(2): 239–63.

Van Gordon, W., Shonin, E., Zangeneh, M. and Griffiths, M.D. (2014) 'Work-related mental health and job performance: Can mindfulness help?', *International Journal of Mental Health and Addiction*, 12(2): 129–37.

Vitterso, J. (2013) 'Functional well-being: Happiness as feelings, evaluations, and functioning'. In S. David, I. Boniwell and A.C. Ayers (eds), *The Oxford Handbook of Happiness*. Croydon: Oxford University Press. pp. 227–44.

Williams, J.M.G., Teasdale, J.D., Segal, Z.V. and Kabat-Zinn, J. (2007) *The Mindful Way through Depression: Freeing Yourself from Chronic Unhappiness*. New York: Guilford.

Wrosch, C., Scheier, M.F., Miller, G.E., Schulz, R. and Carver, C.S. (2003) 'Adaptive self-regulation of unattainable goals: Goal disengagement, goal reengagement, and subjective well-being', *Personality and Social Psychology Bulletin*, 29(12): 1494–508.

Yerkes, R.M. and Dodson, J.D. (1908) 'The relation of strength of stimulus to rapidity of habit-formation', *Journal of Comparative Neurology and Psychology*, 18: 459–82.

3

MANAGER AS COACH: THE CHALLENGE

JULIA MILNER AND ALEX COULEY

INTRODUCTION

The 'manager as coach' concept is gaining momentum within industry and academic circles. In recent years, there has been an increase in expectations for managers to use coaching skills at work. As a result of this, more managers are reporting that they are 'coaching' their employees. Due to the increased emphasis on value for money, the high costs of external coaching and the desire to develop internal coaching capacity, the demand for 'manager as coach' is increasing. The 'manager as coach' role is however different from other coaching roles such as the external or internal coach. We do not view 'manager as coach' as a substitute to these latter roles but rather as an addition, capitalising on the opportunities that coaching can bring to organisations.

Notwithstanding its popularity, the concept of 'manager as coach' is not the simple panacea that organisations may have hoped for. It is more complex than it seems initially and managers often face challenges specific to the 'manager as coach' role (McCarthy and Milner, 2013; Milner and Couley, 2014). If it is seen to be beneficial, organisations should invest in training opportunities for managers. With the appropriate organisational support mechanisms, coaching can add value to a manager's leadership toolbox. Despite the global imperative to adopt coaching as a management tool there has been little research into its efficacy within the particular context of 'manager as coach'. Although the pool of research evidence for coaching as a methodology is rapidly growing (Theeboom et al., 2013) not enough attention has been paid to the particular use of 'manager as coach' skills (see Chapter 13: Current State of the Research). In this chapter, we shed light on the practice of the 'manager as coach' concept, share insights about the creation of appropriate training opportunities as well as the inevitable challenges, and conclude with some practical suggestions for successful implementation of the 'manager as coach' concept.

DEFINING THE 'MANAGER AS COACH' CONCEPT

Different phrases are being used for the concept of the 'manager as coach' (Ellinger et al., 2010) such as 'managerial coaching' (Ellinger and Bostrom, 1999; Hagen, 2012; McCarthy and Milner, 2013; Milner and McCarthy 2013) and 'leader as coach' (Grant and Hartley, 2013). This chapter will use the term 'manager as coach'. In short, this term relates to the use, by managers, of coaching skills in the workplace. For the purposes of focus, this chapter will not differentiate between the roles of 'manager' and 'leader'.

There are some variations in the way the idea of 'manager as coach' is being translated into practice. A manager (as coach) can use coaching skills one-on-one with an employee (coachee) or with several employees (coachees) in a group context. Another opportunity for using coaching skills is for managers to coach people *outside* their team. This application can be considered an extension of the internal coaching role. Our chapter will focus on managers and leaders using coaching skills *within* their own teams. It is important at the outset to distinguish between using coaching skills in an informal way (using a coaching style) and having formal coaching sessions (undertaking coaching conversations). When implementing a formal coaching session, a certain timeframe will be agreed upon where the manager and coachee come together to discuss an issue. Informal coaching conversations can occur without this prescribed frame and can be, for example, a quick exchange whilst walking back from a meeting.

Coaching can happen face to face, but also through other communication channels such as phone, video conference or email (Filsinger, 2014). It is no longer unusual for managers to find themselves leading geographically remote teams. In these instances, alternatives to face-to-face meetings should be considered. The benefits of coaching have been documented (Grant et al., 2009). A manager using a coaching style can be empowering for employees, allowing them to come up with their own solutions. For many, this is more motivational than the common (mis)perception of being micro-managed. It has been suggested that positive outcomes of 'manager as coach' engagements are increased self-awareness, ownership, development and confidence of coachees (Milner and McCarthy, 2013) as well as increased employee performance (Kim, 2014; Pousa and Mathieu, 2014).

Coaching seems especially effective when it is used as a process to enhance learning and development. One way to conceptualise this is the idea described by Jim Collins (2001) of moving from 'good to great'. Coaching may be a useful tool for managers as they assist a direct report to challenge themself and grasp opportunities to grow beyond their current space. Accepting that concept, the list of specific situations where coaching is an appropriate intervention becomes quite large. Examples of situations where a manager may wish to use a coaching style or engage in coaching conversations would be:

- the coachee has just performed well in a given task and could benefit from exploring what they have learnt from this;
- the coachee is new to a leadership role and wishes to explore where they need to grow;
- the coachee is in the process of career planning and is unsure of potential options.

In recent times we have come across a debate about the 'manager as coach'. On one side of this are those who would argue that managers can coach their own team effectively. On the other side are those who would say that the role of a manager is not a comfortable fit with that of a coach. This chapter will shed light on key issues that arise from this debate and suggest strategies as a way forward for managers and organisations.

WHAT IS UNIQUE ABOUT THE ROLE OF 'MANAGER AS COACH'?

In an environment of ever-increasing complexity, those in leadership roles are expected to expand their repertoire in many directions. Coaching is only one of these additional roles. It is with this increased complexity in mind that we must explore the uniqueness of the 'manager as coach' concept. It would be easy to argue that the dual role of the 'manager as coach' is unique compared to other coaching roles, but this is in fact understating the challenges faced by managers in today's global environment. Managers have to lead their teams and have responsibilities when it comes to outcomes and results of the team that are expected to occur within an environment that is widely described as 'VUCA' – volatile, uncertain, complex and ambiguous (Bennett and Lemoine, 2014). To complicate matters further, they have pre-existing working relationships with their direct reports, which may be based upon a completely different leadership style. From a coaching perspective, managers are helping their employees to explore questions for themselves and to draw upon their own internal resources to find solutions. At the same time, managers often already know the context and might be aware of issues that an employee wishes to discuss during coaching conversations. Hence, it could be argued that the manager's internal view lacks the impartial perspective that might be helpful when asking unbiased questions.

Thus we reach our first real challenge for the 'manager as coach'. The internal knowledge that managers are likely to have due to their proximity to the team may make it more difficult to withhold answers and instructions instead of supporting the team with questioning techniques and other coaching skills. Therefore the manager, as opposed to an internal or external coach, has to distinguish between situations where coaching skills might be helpful as a leadership style and those situations where a more directive approach is needed. For example, direction would be helpful in an emergency situation, or when people are new to their roles. Table 3.1 provides further examples.

Another key challenge relates to the ability of the 'manager as coach' to promise confidentiality. Gyllensten and Palmer (2007) describe confidentiality as being vital in the coaching relationship. An agreement of complete confidentiality between coach and coachee can seem almost impossible in some 'manager as coach' situations (e.g., when the coachee is disclosing something that the manager needs to discuss further with the team, or when the coachee talks about an issue where the manager has knowledge that cannot be disclosed). A possible confidentiality conflict needs to be addressed early on – especially for formal coaching sessions

Table 3.1   Examples for different situations and styles

	Coaching style	Formal coaching sessions	Directive approach
Emergency situation			✓
Performance managing someone			✓
Next career move	✓	✓	
When a team member is taking on a new responsibility	✓	✓	
Facilitating a team meeting in a more collaborative way	✓		
Giving a team member some quick feedback after a presentation	✓		
A team member asking you to solve an issue for them, but you think they could arrive at their own answer	✓		
Reflections on key learning from a project	✓	✓	
As you are walking in the corridor a team members stops for a quick update on a new project	✓		
A team member lacks specific knowledge or a specific skill			✓

and when boundaries have to be agreed upon. With this in mind we would recommend that when the manager contracts with the coachee, the issue of confidentiality is raised immediately. The manager should identify situations in which confidentiality cannot be maintained. There should be an agreement outlining how the coach will alert the coachee that something has arisen that needs to be taken elsewhere. This could be as simple as saying 'Do you remember in our first session we talked about the possibility of me needing to share information with the HR department? Well, I think this is one of those times.' Having such an agreement in place early makes this conversation much easier.

Questions you could should consider discussing in the first coaching session

- What can we agree to keep confidential and what might need to be shared with others?
- How can the coach or coachee signal to the other party if something needs to be kept confidential?
- Are there currently any conflicts of interest that should be highlighted?
- What will we do if a conflict of interest arises during a coaching conversation?

The next challenge that managers often face is a perception of lack of time. The increasing complexity of the business environment can lead to a sense of time poverty. The thought of adding coaching sessions to a busy schedule can pose a hurdle. However, using coaching in a number of different interactions might be one way of reducing time pressure in the long term.

Myth:	If I don't have time for formal coaching, I can't coach.
Myth buster:	You can employ an informal coaching approach and use coaching skills throughout your interactions with your team.

Studies indicate a relationship between short-term time investment versus long-term time saving when it comes to managers coaching (e.g. Milner and McCarthy, 2013). When learning new coaching behaviours and trialling new skills, more resources are needed. If ownership is transferred to employees through effective coaching and managers have room to work on other issues instead of micro-managing, then time can be saved (Milner and McCarthy, 2013). In addition to the challenges mentioned above, this can be further complicated by unrealistic expectations from the parties involved in the coaching process (i.e. the coachee, the organisation and the managers themselves). One example of these unrealistic expectations is that managers are sometimes expected to be 'fully fledged coaches' after a two-day training programme. They are also expected to have access to sufficient additional time when this is increasingly a key barrier to the successful implementation of coaching interventions. In some situations, there are unrealistic expectations that everything will run smoothly and no challenges will be encountered. In the scenario where managers do encounter implementation issues it is often assumed that they can solve these for themselves. Moreover, the manager who has undertaken a coach training course and eagerly looks forward to bring enlightenment to those they are working with can be disappointed when employees are not as keen!

Ellam-Dyson and Palmer (2011) explored some of the reasons that impact upon the coachees' willingness to be coached. Their findings suggest that the coachees' self-perceptions are more significant than their views of the coaching process. In essence, what they found was that the biggest barrier to people accepting coaching was not a belief about the efficacy of coaching but a greater level of conditional self-acceptance, i.e. 'I am only worthy if I succeed'. This group of people will not engage in coaching for fear of failure.

The above named expectations from different parties involved in the coaching process are not only diverse but also emotional and powerful. Expectations therefore need to be discussed openly in order for realistic results to be sought rather than the occasionally inflated claims that are presented. Both clients and providers of coaching services should avoid fuelling such exaggerated claims.

DIFFERENT APPROACHES TO 'MANAGER AS COACH'

Given the reported benefits of coaching employees such as increased engagement, lower levels of attrition and improved teamwork, coaching has become a very attractive management tool (PricewaterhouseCoopers, 2013). It is not surprising that with these reported benefits and the high cost of external coaches some organisations have forged ahead and implemented a coaching style of management trying to replicate the reported success of external or internal coaching methodologies.

This chapter is based upon the firsthand experience of the authors of working with organisations, teams and individual managers to translate the current scientific knowledge base into practical pathways to leverage the benefits associated with coaching. Furthermore, the authors have been involved in research studies exploring the 'manager as coach' concept from the manager as well as employee perspective. Although there are limitations to what the current scientific knowledge-base can demonstrate, there are indications of successful implementation to encourage those wishing to become 'manager as coach' practitioners. Given these complexities and the lack of a scientific base for organisations to reference, a number of different approaches have been evolving. Some of these applications have become more widespread than others and some more or less successful. As with most fields, it seems that there is no one-size-fits-all answer.

Organisations have looked for an evidence base that does exist and tried to adhere closely to the coaching methodologies described in the literature. One way this has become manifest is that some organisations have striven to maintain fidelity to what they perceive to be 'true' coaching. In a strong desire to offer this type of 'true' coaching they have tried to replicate the external coaching framework (e.g. through organisations attempting to adopt a structure where managers coach non-direct reports). This can become complex and creates multiple reporting pathways that could potentially lead to miscommunication. Even though the sincere intention is to closely model the dynamic of the external coaching agreement, in reality coachees remain very aware of the organisational dynamics and there is a possibility of creating more problems than this resolves.

An alternative approach to implementing coaching has been to split formal appraisal, supervision and coaching, with the same manager appraising as well as supervising an employee's performance, and then on separate occasions setting aside time for formal coaching sessions. To achieve this, organisations have often established a new coaching structure within a team, department or organisation. The time-poor nature of management in the current climate has been highlighted earlier in this chapter. It is clear that time becomes the obvious barrier to implementing a new structure within any team or organisation. Managers should not allow themselves to be trapped into thinking that coaching can only be successful if they are able to organise formal coaching sessions with every direct report. Formal coaching sessions are extremely powerful interventions that can generate significant growth for individuals. However, there will be many opportunities that arise to utilise coaching approaches in day-to-day interactions with direct reports and teams. The conversation over the water cooler, the chat in the lift or a discussion over lunch can often provide opportunities to increase the exposure of coaching skills within a team.

As the benefits of coaching in the workplace have become more widely understood there is another, less effective way in which coaching is being approached. In some organisations the management team has been simply told that they are now expected to coach. No training or guidance is provided and the individual manager has to come to their own conclusions about how to make this work. In the experience of the chapter authors, this often leads to the implementation of activity termed 'coaching' which could, in fact, be one of a number of other types of interventions. We would argue strongly for a need for effective coaching training that is provided at an appropriate level of depth.

Coaching does involve the use of a range of skills. Some people assume that managers will already possess all of the core skills of coaching, for example listening, asking questions, paraphrasing, summarising and giving feedback (van Nieuwerburgh, 2014). Even skilful leaders and managers however will benefit from refining and sharpening these coaching-related skills. Furthermore, without the appropriate training, it is easy to fall into the trap of coaching sessions becoming deficit focused. Coaching works well when it draws upon the strengths of the individual and uses those strengths to address current challenges. Focusing on strengths is not a new concept. In his seminal work *The Effective Executive*, Peter Drucker proposed making strengths productive as early as 1967. However, using coaching as a mechanism to leverage strengths is a skill and needs to be learned.

Myth:	As a 'manager as coach' I won't encounter any challenges because it's only a small part of what I do.
Myth buster:	Challenges might be even more likely due to the multiple roles of the manager. Therefore training courses should prepare for these challenges of the 'manager as coach' role.

DEVELOPING 'MANAGER AS COACH' CAPABILITY WITHIN ORGANISATIONS

Considerations for training programmes

Whilst there is evidence of benefits arising from training managers in coaching skills, consideration should be given to assisting organisations to gain the traction and the quality that they would like from such programmes. The operating environment that makes the 'manager as coach' role unique has been discussed earlier in the chapter. It is imperative that training opportunities are adjusted for the context of 'manager as coach'. Most coach training programmes, however, are not designed for use in this unique arena. When choosing a training programme it is essential to ensure that the trainers have experience of working with 'managers as coaches' and the associated complexities.

In addition, the issue of training does not stop with the initial introduction to coaching skills. It is important that managers not only receive training in coaching, but also have the opportunity for continuous support from their organisation. In these training courses and catch-up sessions, the challenges of the 'manager as coach' should be addressed to better support managers (McCarthy and Milner, 2013).

Myth: If I have attended a two-day training programme, I am a professional coach.
Myth buster: A two-day programme does not make you a professional coach. However you can learn some valuable basic coaching skills.

SOME HELPFUL TRAINING CONSIDERATIONS FOR HR PROFESSIONALS OR COMMISSIONERS OF COACHING

Tailor the training to the managerial coaching context: It is important to tailor the training to the specific needs of the manager. We suggest below the LEADER model (Milner and Couley, 2014: 55) that can assist managers to decide if a coaching approach is useful and apply it accordingly.

Make it practical: Whilst it might be relatively easy to understand good coaching skills on an intellectual level, it is important to actually put these skills into practice and to receive feedback on them. Feedback from others is necessary in order to gain insights and notice 'blind spots'.

Address challenges: Many training programmes assume ideal circumstances when discussing practice. Usually participants are eager to learn and 'clients' often played by other fellow participants are positive, supportive and easy to work with. Once participants return to their workplaces they are often faced with several challenges, such as the time pressures previously discussed, uncooperative coachees, and having to decide whether coaching is the right approach for various situations. Thus implementation barriers should be addressed in training programmes to increase the likelihood of participants integrating their newly learned skills in the workplace even when presented with obstacles.

Establish peer support: Peer support could be one way to overcome the implementation barriers mentioned above. This should be established early on, ideally already within the coaching training programme. Peers can get together after the training programme to exchange challenges they encounter, brainstorm strategies, and receive feedback from like-minded people in similar situations.

Create a 'coaching-point-of-contact': Once the individual manager or organisation has established a good grounding in coaching skills through the training programme, there also needs to be consideration given to creating a 'coaching-point-of-contact'. As mentioned above, it is likely that managers will encounter challenges along the way when implementing any coaching efforts. Having a person who coordinates questions around coaching and helps to streamline coaching efforts could be beneficial in demonstrating that organisations are investing in and supporting 'manager as coach' efforts.

BEYOND TRAINING

Once people have completed a training programme, the evidence suggests that they then struggle to integrate new skills into their existing work practices. This applies to coaching training programmes just as much as any others. Indeed it is reported that only 30% of all training is translated into the workplace (Stolovitch, 2000). The good news is that coaching itself can become part of the answer. If people are coached around implementing the particular skill-set in question, application rates can increase (Bright and Crockett, 2012). Over time, as the manager meets barriers to implementation, it is not unusual for people to default to a more directive approach. This suggests that there is a need for long-term support structures such as the peer coaching mechanisms described above. It is, however, necessary to clearly distinguish between 'managers as coaches' using a peer coaching support process and 'managers as coaches' receiving coaching supervision. As Rogers (2004) argues, these are very distinct skill-sets. If coaching becomes a large part of what a manager does, they may wish to consider receiving formal coaching supervision (see Chapter 15: Supervision for Learning for a full discussion).

As a manager moves forward with coaching it is not necessarily about becoming a coach in every interaction but more about using coaching techniques to enhance the opportunities for their team members to attain optimal performance levels. It is important to recognise that adopting coaching skills does not mean that a manager abandons their existing skill-sets. The new skills of coaching enhance the pre-existing toolkit. In practice, the advantage of the 'manager as coach' approach is the opportunity for managers to ask themselves 'Will this person benefit from a coaching conversation at this point?'.

Table 3.2   Issues to consider at the start with some suggestions based on experience

When searching for the evidence, consider a range of terms	Some terms to search are: 'manager as coach', 'leadership coaching' and 'managerial coaching'
Be realistic about expectations	Despite many very big claims, coaching is not a process that will solve every challenge experienced by organisations
When considering engaging trainers, look for professionals with experience in the 'manager as coach' arena	Most training is tailored to fit the external or internal coaching market. Very little is developed specifically for the unique challenges of 'manager as coach'
Make sure the training contains a practical element	Many of the coaching skills are practical in nature. Without practising them and receiving direct feedback, blind spots and bad habits can develop

(Continued)

Table 3.2 (Continued)

Develop a peer support network	Managers and organisations should expect implementation barriers to arise. Sharing with others is one useful way to address these barriers
When introducing coaching, a blend of formal and informal coaching sessions may be practical	For time-constrained managers it is possible to use a 'coaching approach' whilst not engaging in 'formal' coaching sessions
The 'manager as coach' will have to clearly distinguish between times when coaching is appropriate and times when it is not	External coaches do not have the duality of being both manager and coach

Furthermore, managers need to be aware that adopting a coaching style can have other effects that can go beyond the impact upon the coachee. Mukherjee (2012) reports that managers trained to become coaches develop as part of the interaction. The study suggests that 'managers as coaches' showed improvement in leadership skills, interpersonal skills and work–life balance as they became competent coaches.

Helpful questions to ask before implementing coaching into an organisation

- What are we attempting to achieve with the coaching?
- Which model will we use?
- How much time can be devoted to the implementation of this coaching initiative?
- How will we support our newly-trained coaches?
- How will we measure the success (or otherwise) of the coaching?
- What training will be needed?
- Is the trainer experienced in the context of 'manager as coach'?
- Is the training designed for our context?

Helpful questions to ask before starting to coach someone

- Have I undertaken appropriate training?
- Do I feel confident enough to coach others?
- Am I the right person to coach in this scenario?
- Is coaching the right approach?
- Am I prepared to invest more time initially?

CONCLUSION

The American Management Association (2008) predicted that coaching would continue to grow and expand as a process of development within organisations. The 'manager as coach' concept is an important contribution to this expansion. If managers use key coaching skills in the right situations with people who are open to this approach, this can then have a significant positive impact on all involved. The way forward for 'managers as coaches' could be to encourage organisations to include basic coaching skills into their leadership development programmes. Here, appropriate training is a vital cornerstone. For formal coaching sessions, issues of the dual role of the 'manager as coach' need to be carefully reflected upon. Challenges as outlined in this chapter need to be taken into consideration. Then the trend to train managers in coaching skills could contribute to transforming leadership and the sociability of the workplace. We do not see the 'manager as coach' concept as a replacement for the professional external or internal coach. We see it as an addition to other coaching roles and one that might help organisations to create flourishing coaching cultures (see Chapter 16: Towards a Coaching Culture for further discussion of this concept).

REFERENCES

American Management Association (2008) *Coaching a Global Study of Successful Practices*, available at amanet.org

Bennett, N. and Lemoine, G.J. (2014) 'What VUCA really means for you', *Harvard Business Review*, 92 (1/2).

Bright, D. and Crockett, A. (2012) 'Training combined with coaching can make a significant difference in job performance and satisfaction', *Coaching: An International Journal of Theory, Research and Practice*, 5(1): 4–21.

Collins, J. (2001) *Good to Great: Why Some Companies Make the Leap … and Others Don't.* New York: Harper Business.

Drucker, P. (1967) *The Effective Executive.* New York: Harper & Row.

Ellam-Dyson, V. and Palmer, S. (2011) 'Leadership Coaching? No thanks I'm not worthy', *The Coaching Psychologist*, 7(2): 108–17.

Ellinger, A.D., Beattie, R.S. and Hamlin, R.G. (2010) 'The manager as coach'. In E. Cox, T. Bachkirova and D. Clutterbuck (eds), *The Complete Handbook of Coaching*. London: Sage. pp. 257–70.

Ellinger, A.D. and Bostrom, R.P. (1999) 'Managerial coaching behaviours in learning organizations', *Journal of Management Development*, 18(9): 752–71.

Filsinger, C. (2014) 'The virtual line manager as coach: Coaching direct reports remotely and across cultures', *International Journal of Evidence Based Coaching and Mentoring*, 12(2): 188–202.

Grant, A. and Hartley, M. (2013) 'Developing the leader as coach: insights, strategies and tips for embedding coaching skills in the workplace', *Coaching: An International Journal of Theory, Research and Practice*, 6(2): 102–15.

Grant, A.M., Curtayne, L. and Burton, G. (2009) 'Executive coaching enhances goal attainment, resilience and workplace wellbeing: a randomised controlled study', *The Journal of Positive Psychology*, 4(5): 396–407.

Gyllensten, K. and Palmer, S. (2007) 'The coaching relationship: An interpretative phenomenological analysis', *International Coaching Psychology Review*, 2(2): 168–77.

Hagen, M. (2012) 'Managerial coaching: A review of the literature', *Performance Improvement Quarterly*, 24(4): 17–39.

Kim, S. (2014) 'Assessing the influence of managerial coaching on employee outcomes', *Human Resource Development Quarterly*, 25(1): 59–85.

McCarthy, G. and Milner, J. (2013) 'Managerial coaching: Challenges, opportunities and training', *Journal of Management Development*, 32(7): 768–79.

Milner, J. and Couley, A. (2014) *Coaching: How to Lead*. Calwell: Inspiring Publishers.

Milner, J. and McCarthy, G. (2013) 'Positive and negative events in managerial coaching', 27th Annual Australian and New Zealand Academy of Management conference, December, Hobart, Australia.

Mukherjee, S. (2012) 'Does coaching transform coaches? A case study of internal coaches', *International Journal of Evidence Based Coaching and Mentoring*, 10(2): 76–87.

Pousa, C. and Mathieu, A. (2014) 'The influence of coaching on employee performance: Results from two international quantitative studies', *Performance Improvement Quarterly*, 27: 75–92.

PricewaterhouseCoopers (2013) *ICF Organizational Coaching Study*, available at coachfederation.org

Rogers, J. (2004) *Coaching Skills: A Handbook*. Maidenhead: Open University Press.

Stolovitch, H.D. (2000) Human performance technology: Research and theory to practice. *Performance Improvement*, 39(4): 7–16.

Theeboom, T., Beersma, B. and van Vianen, A. (2013) 'Does coaching work? A meta-analysis on the effects of coaching on individual level outcomes in an organizational context', *Journal of Positive Psychology*, 9(1): 1–18.

van Nieuwerburgh, C. (2014) *An Introduction to Coaching Skills: A Practical Guide*. London: Sage.

4

COACHING FOR CAREER AND PROFESSIONAL DEVELOPMENT

JULIA YATES

INTRODUCTION

This chapter addresses the specialism of coaching for career and professional development and explains some of the contexts in which career coaches work. The chapter examines the key issues facing those managing their career paths in the 21st century, introduces the theory of Life Design, explores the use of a narrative approach to career conversations, and presents a model for coaching clients in the process of a career transition. The chapter ends with a brief discussion of the subjectivity of 'career success'.

CAREER COACHING

'Having a job' is linked to a range of positive outcomes. The physical, psychological and financial benefits of employment over unemployment are striking, and include a range of mental and physical health benefits, from minimising minor and short-term ailments through to a clear link with reduced chances of mortality (Costa et al., 1987) and suicide (Yur'yev et al., 2012). These benefits are conferred on people with a job. Those in a 'good' job benefit from an additional array of advantages. A fulfilling working life has a knock-on impact that goes far beyond the normal working day, enhancing many aspects of our personal and social lives. As Rath and Harter (2010: 16) explain 'those who are thriving in their careers are twice as likely to be happy in their lives overall'.

Career coaching therefore has enormous potential to make a real difference to clients' professional and personal lives. Before moving on to exploring the topic in more detail it is worth pausing to consider what is meant by 'career coaching'. For the purposes of this chapter the definition below will be used.

> 'Career Coaching is one or a series of collaborative conversations with a trained professional who operates within an ethical code. The process is grounded in evidence-based coaching approaches, incorporating theories and tools, and career theory and **aims to lead to a positive outcome for the client regarding their career decision, work and/or personal fulfilment.'** (Yates, 2013: 2, emphasis added)

The essence of the practice lies in the final phrase, which emphasises the focus on career decisions, and highlights the aim of enhancing work or personal fulfilment. One could be tempted to argue that career coaching is no different from any other kind of coaching. Coaching of any kind will aim to lead to a positive outcome for work and/or personal fulfilment, so if the only difference lies in the nature of the topic, then does it really deserve a specialism of its own and a chapter in this book? On the surface this view makes some sense – it may be fair to assume that any coach would be able to support a client making a career decision and use their professional skills and coaching models to enable clients to reach their own conclusions. But there is a significant benefit that a career coach can offer over and above an executive or life coach, and that is a real understanding of the complexities and subtleties of careers, career paths and career transitions.

WHAT IS UNIQUE ABOUT COACHING FOR CAREER AND PROFESSIONAL DEVELOPMENT?

Coaching for career and professional development can take place in a range of different environments and with a range of different types of clients. A career coach might specialise in one group of clients (e.g. career changers, women returning after a career break, or people facing redundancy), might focus on one part of the process (e.g. making career decisions, professional development or interview coaching), or could specialise in different kinds of contracts (e.g. in-house, outplacement or private clients). For some practitioners the 'career' aspect is their specialism; for others, it is a topic that comes up once in a while alongside a range of other professional development issues.

The particular context in which a coach works will influence the kinds of issues that clients most commonly bring. More often than not, career coaching clients are thinking about a job or career change. Often the change is entirely driven by the client and the discussion might then centre around identifying and evaluating the client's options. Other changes might be beyond the client's control and quite at odds with their wishes – those facing redundancy or other job loss may fall into this category. In these circumstances the conversations may need to focus on the emotional aspect of the change before considering the future. Usually, however, the drivers behind the career decisions are more complex, incorporating perhaps a tension between what the individual wants for themself and what they feel is right for their family or organisation. At other times, the complexity may emerge from a contradiction of values where, for example, one option would make them 'happy' and another would make them wealthy.

Professionals will sometimes choose to see a coach for some support with their career development. Individuals can be content in the role and the organisation in which they work, but may want to ensure that they make the most of their skills, expertise and opportunities. Conversations would centre on identifying development needs, making the most of training courses or generating ideas to prepare for future changes. Although the specific topics that tend to be covered in these conversations can be different from more traditional 'career coaching' conversations, the process is similar: coaches need to work with clients to identify what they need to do in order to achieve what they want to achieve.

Three of the most common contexts for career and professional development coaching will be discussed below.

1. Career coaching consultancies

Many career coaches are employed by consultancy firms whose services are requested by organisations needing occasional input to support their employees' careers. Career coaches can be employed to work on a wide variety of projects ranging from selection through to managing redundancies. There is a growing awareness that employees' careers need to be managed and nurtured, and career consultants are often brought in to train managers on how to have productive career conversations with their staff. Contracts with organisations vary. Consultancies might be employed to deliver a single workshop, or undertake one-to-one meetings with members of staff, or to develop long-term strategic partnerships.

2. Private client work

Many career coaches are self-employed and will work with individual, private clients. The nature of the work will vary from one coach to another. Many coaches will choose to specialise in one client group: recent graduates, women returning to employment after a career break, clients approaching retirement, or entrepreneurs setting up their own businesses. Developing this kind of specialist expertise can help to establish credibility. Coaches often offer a range of workshops as well as formal coaching sessions and can use a variety of tools, models and assessment tests to support the career coaching process. One of the major challenges in this arena is self-promotion. Career coaching relationships tend to last for only a few sessions – that is, for as long as it takes the client to identify and find themselves a suitable role. This contrasts with executive coaching where coach/client relationships can last for longer periods of time. Career coaches therefore need to find ways to promote themselves effectively to a wide range of potential clients, or to combine private client work with other activities.

3. In-house career coaching

Some organisations will employ their own 'in-house' career coaches. For the most part this tends to happen in organisations where career change is a common or inevitable part of their employees' careers. For example, the Houses of Parliament and the Ministry of Defence (MoD) in the UK have their own teams of career coaches, employed to support outgoing Ministers of Parliament (MPs) and their teams or military personnel leaving active service. Other organisations will train a member of the Human Resources (HR) team to understand the processes involved in career coaching in order to support employees as they progress through their careers. These coaching roles will often involve a focus on professional development within the organisation, supporting their internal clients as they make choices about training and development and put new learning into practice. Educational establishments too will employ teams of career coaches to help support their graduating students. Universities and business schools in particular are keen to provide career coaching alongside academic courses to ensure their students are able to make the most of their new qualifications.

HOW CAN COACHING BE USED FOR CAREER AND PROFESSIONAL DEVELOPMENT?

Career management in the 21st century is unique. People have opportunities and options available like never before, and although this is a fortunate position to be in, this new paradigm for careers brings particular challenges with it. Before a coach is in a position to make use of their classic coaching skills and models, an understanding of some of the key issues that face the contemporary workforce is needed. There are theories, models and frameworks about career decision making to help a wide range of groups of workers (e.g. young people, career changers, women or older workers). This literature provides evidence which can help coaches and their clients identify and transition to their ideal jobs.

There is a range of concepts which are useful for coaches working within more or less all contexts and with most types of clients. Four will be discussed here. Emerging features of career paths in the 21st century will be presented as a context for Savickas's model of Life Design, conceptualised as a way of building careers for the 21st century. Savickas proposes narrative coaching as an approach that complements the Life Design model. This will be followed with

Barclay's model for coaching clients experiencing professional change. Finally the concept of 'career success' will be considered.

CAREER PATHS

Prospects for careers and career paths these days look and feel quite different from those our parents and grandparents experienced. These shifting expectations are, in part, a response to the dramatic changes in the labour market over the last generation. Technology, globalisation, flexible working hours and a shift in the kinds of jobs people do (with the dramatic reduction in the manufacturing industry and the rise in service roles in the West) are some of the key differences (Kidd, 2008). More significant, perhaps, is the increase in the pace of change that has been witnessed across all industry sectors.

Accompanying these changes in the nature of work are changes in attitudes. One widely-seen change in attitude is the understanding of the notion of a 'job for life' (Woods, 2011). People now expect to face a number of changes of organisation, job or career during their working lives. In reality, labour market data do not quite support the attitudinal change. Job tenure (i.e. how long someone stays in a job) has remained fairly consistent over the last 50 years, with year-on-year changes generally accounted for by economic cycles (ONS, 2013).

The expectation that employees will change jobs, organisations and careers numerous times during their working lives is perhaps overstated, but the expectation that change will be experienced is not. Whilst the chances of resigning from one job and applying to another have only marginally increased, experiencing change of some sort in a career has become more or less inevitable. Even if individuals never move organisation, they may find themselves working for several different employers throughout their lives through mergers and takeovers. And even if they never resign from their jobs, they will probably find that their day-to-day work patterns will have changed, often beyond recognition, within 15 years.

The career theories that were developed to allow practitioners to support their clients in the 20th century workplace are no longer as useful as they once were, and a new generation of theories has been generated to support coaches as they support the new workforce.

The main distinction between 20th century career theories and those generated more recently is around the notion of agency (Savickas, 2002). The 1950s' stereotype of a career path was one that was owned and controlled by the employer. The worker was committed to the organisation for the duration of their working life, and the organisation made decisions about the training required, eligibility for promotions and the opportunities available to them.

These days, the threat and fear of redundancy and the expectation of change throughout careers have placed the responsibility for career planning firmly at the door of employees. It is now up to each employee to judge whether they are in the right job, whether they are getting the right experience and the right training, when they should move and where they should go to next. It is down to the individual to plan and monitor their career, to ensure that they remain fulfilled and employable, so that whatever changes comes their way, there are options open to them.

LIFE DESIGN

One interesting theory which has emerged as a result of these new patterns of working is Savickas et al.'s (2009) Life Design. Responding to the new psychological contracts in the workplace and acknowledging the challenges that the pace of change brings to employees, the Life Design model offers a framework for career development that emphasises flexibility, adaptability and lifelong learning. The authors propose that career coaching should respond to the challenges of contemporary working life with one-to-one interventions which have a 'dynamic approach that encourages individuals' imaginative thinking and exploration of possible selves' (2009: 241).

A key tenet of this approach is an acknowledgement of the holistic nature of careers: work is invariably situated within clients' lives, and coaches must understand both the impact that work has on lives and that lives have on work. Savickas et al. (2009) suggest that rather than asking what job clients want to do, coaches should be encouraging clients to ask themselves 'What am I going to make of my life?'. Rather than thinking about what kind of job role might match their employment skills, the question should be 'How may individuals best design their own lives in the human society in which they live?'. Employees need to consider how they develop their skills in the workplace in order to respond to and anticipate change, and to cope with the boundary-less career paths that are commonplace these days (Arthur and Rousseau, 1996). Career decisions will now occur more frequently and will be based on the interplay of the self-concept and the environment. Career coaching conversations therefore need to focus on lifelong learning, holistic design and contextual environments, and also need to be preventative (i.e. not just focused on transition points, but on strategic planning for the future).

This represents a significant change from the career conversations of a generation ago which were often focused quite narrowly on a matching system to link skills and experience to local job opportunities. Career coaches now need to employ new approaches which can allow clients to consider their careers within the context of their broader lives, and to acknowledge, respond to and anticipate change. Narrative career coaching is seen as an excellent mechanism for this (Savickas, 2012). A narrative approach to career coaching will allow individuals to recognise that they can tell their stories in different ways. This understanding of the nature of the past will allow clients to see that their future too can be written in different ways. This allows individuals to believe that they are in control of their own career plans.

CAREER STORIES

A useful approach for an initial coaching session is to ask a client to give an account of their career story. Narrative coaching aligns with post-modern constructivist approaches. At its core is the belief that there is no single truth. Instead, there are multiple realities, each of which is as valid and as real or 'true' as another. These realities will vary depending on the angles from which the scene is viewed, the way they are interpreted, and the mood or perspective that is present when the event is recalled. Narrative career coaching is a way to allow clients to identify their own realities within their own experiences, past, present and future. The narrative approach encourages them to see their experiences as 'stories'. Telling these stories allows clients to understand their experiences (past, present and future) with more depth and insight.

A client's CV, for example, might suggest to a reader that the client has had a varied, interesting and successful career. When given the opportunity to talk it through, the client might tell a different story. They might talk about a lack of meaning, and explain that rather than making strategic and positives moves from one role to another, their job changes were not considered and it felt more as though they was moving from one terrible position to another.

The client may tell their own story from two perspectives, and sharing this distinction with a client can lead to further understanding. The first perspective is that of client as narrator. The story is told from the perspective of someone watching it, and the narrator can talk about things they were not aware of at the time (e.g. 'Whilst all this was going on, the management behind closed doors were planning a whole series of redundancies') or from a longer-term perspective (e.g. 'Of course at the time it was devastating, but looking back, it was the best thing that could have happened to me'). Alongside the role of narrator, the client telling their story is also the protagonist – the hero or main character in the story. The story is an account of their life and they are the key player. They are both constructing the story and enacting it.

Narrative career coaching can help the coaching relationship in a number of ways. It helps to ensure that the coaching session is client-centred and non-judgmental. In accepting that the story is written by the client, the coach automatically adopts a non-judgmental attitude: a coach would not fall into the trap of assuming that the threat of redundancy is upsetting for the client, because the client is telling the story, and as the author, they are clearly the one who knows what their reaction is. Narrative coaching also offers great insights to clients. There is something about framing their experiences as a story that encourages people to think about their history from a range of perspectives and this can generate new insights.

CAREER TRANSITIONS

Most career conversations are about change or its possibility. It is encouraging to learn that career changers are generally happier, better paid and work shorter hours than those who have stayed put (Carless and Arnup, 2010). But the path to a new role is not always straightforward, and it can be helpful for a coach working with these clients to have an understanding of how individuals experience these changes. Barclay et al. (2011) have mapped the stages of a career change onto Prochaska et al.'s (1992) transtheoretical model of change. They have identified five stages to the process and suggested coaching approaches that may be particularly helpful at each stage (see the box on p. 48).

The stages of career change

Stage 1: Pre-contemplation

The client is feeling disenchanted with work, although not always able to articulate what the difficulties are. They might be beginning to put some distance between themself and their current work identity.

The coach at this stage will be focused on relationship building, empathic listening, and will be helping the client to explore their own emotions towards work and identity. Humanistic coaching and motivational interviewing can be fruitful at this stage.

Stage 2: Contemplation

The client is becoming increasingly aware of their dissatisfaction with the current situation and is gaining an understanding of the reasons for those feelings. They have started thinking seriously about a career change, but are not yet ready to commit.

The coach is supporting the client as they identify the problem and start thinking about options for the future. The coach may use a narrative style to help the client identify life themes, and encourage them to explore a range of different identities.

Stage 3: Preparation

At this stage, the client begins to plan a change. Motivation is high, and the client is open to exploration, considering a number of options and wanting to learn more. One or two options start to emerge as particularly desirable and the client can begin to think about what they would need to do to make the change happen.

The coach here is supporting the client in their exploration. The coach might help the client think about their own strengths, values and skills, and the discussions might centre on generating and researching job options.

Stage 4: Action

The client is determined and has committed to a course of action. They are assuming a new identity and redefining their self-concept to incorporate the new role.

The coach may help build resilience in the client, and support them with the practical tasks needed to secure a new position.

Stage 5: Maintenance

The client has moved on and is settling into their new role.

The coach is now supporting the client as they develop their new identity and start to develop in their new role. Discussions might focus on the expectations and behaviour required in the new position.

(Adapted from Barclay et al., 2011)

Their theory holds that every career changer will go through each of these stages in sequence. Many will move from one stage to the next with ease, but some will seek the support of a coach if they feel that their movement has become stilted. This model can be shared with clients to help them towards a deeper understanding of their own experience, or can be used as an *aide memoire* for coaches, to give suggestions as to the kind of coaching behaviour that might be particularly productive at that stage.

The stages of change and the positive outcomes mentioned above apply equally to those whose job or career changes are not of their own choice. In fact, those who are made redundant often encounter something known as 'post job-loss career growth' (Eby and Buch, 1995), which describes the experiences of those who did not choose to leave their jobs, but ended up much more fulfilled in their careers as a direct result of their forced transition. It is important to remember though that the process of redundancy is often difficult and those coping with an involuntary job loss often need to progress through various stages of grief before they are in a position to engage with a new working identity.

The stages of grief were identified by Kubler Ross (1969) and applied to job loss by Nicholson and West (1987). There are five psychological stages which individuals work through in response to grief: denial ('I can't believe this is happening to me'); anger ('I'm furious with the organisation for doing this to me'); bargaining ('If I do x or y, the organisation should let me stay'); depression ('I often feel close to tears when I think about this'); and acceptance ('I think I'll be okay') (Blau, 2007). Individuals usually work through the stages in sequence, although they can grind to halt at any point and perhaps find themselves stuck in a loop as they go from depression back to bargaining and back to depression again.

If you have a client who is facing redundancy, it can be useful to share this information with them. It can validate their current feelings and make them feel that they are reacting in a very 'normal' way; it can lead them to the realisation that they are trapped in a particular stage, or it may encourage progression to the next stage. It can help them understand where they are now, and allow them to feel hopeful about the future.

CAREER SUCCESS

The assertion that career coaching aims to support clients in making positive decisions which lead to work and/or personal fulfilment is clearly entirely predicated on what a particular client sees as a 'positive' decision and what 'fulfilment' means to them. One of the first tasks, therefore, in almost any career coaching relationship is to develop a shared understanding of what these terms mean for that particular client. These conversations can be challenging because it is often the first time that a client has conceptualised their goals in this way, but the discussion can be empowering for a client as they accept the idea that they can define their own concept of 'success'.

The career guidance literature tends to divide the concept into subjective and objective success. Subjective success is, in essence, job satisfaction. It is how an individual feels about their work, and therefore is a subjective measure – two people in exactly the same job in the same organisation might have quite different levels of job satisfaction because they are motivated, stimulated and fulfilled by different things. Despite this subjectivity, there are, however, some common themes that can be seen in the careers of those who report high levels of career satisfaction (Roelen et al., 2008). These can be of great interest to clients who are hoping to increase their chances of identifying a fulfilling role. At the top of almost every list of work factors is task variety. What constitutes a varied job may differ from one individual to another, but feeling that a job is different from hour to hour, day to day, or from one season to the next, seems to be an important factor. Linked to this is the notion of autonomy, which as well as being desirable in itself, tends to allow an individual to ensure they have varied days. It comes as no surprise to find that having good colleagues is high on the list of factors that lead to job satisfaction. Having a group of colleagues with a shared purpose is important, as is having a 'best friend' in the work place (Rath and Hartner, 2010). The work environment itself plays a part. Firstly, a nice office space (own desk, a window, a convenient location) is appreciated, and people are more likely to thrive in an organisation which has a strong reputation and is more focused on creativity than competition. Finally, the opportunity to learn, whether through new challenging projects or formal training or education, seems to keep people motivated (Roelen et al., 2008).

Objective success, on the other hand, is more easily measured from the outside. Signs of objective success are a high salary, seniority, and a job within a high status occupational area (Zhou, 2005). A meta analysis gives some indication of the factors that predict objective success, concluding that salary tends to be a result of an individual's intelligence, their education, and their political awareness (Ng et al., 2005). The ability to get a promotion is linked to a person's social capital – i.e. how well networked they are, the number of hours worked (the more the better), and the amount of training they get access to.

The interaction between these objective and subjective measures of success is interesting. Objective success has a negligible impact on subjective success: a higher salary and promotions do not lead to greater job satisfaction (Jacobson, 2010). This might seem a little counterintuitive, but the explanation seems to be that whilst climbing the management ladder tends to lead to a higher degree of autonomy and task variety, it also gives rise to lower satisfaction from colleagues. Subjective success, however, does appear to have an impact on objective success: the more a person enjoys their work, the more likely they are to get promoted.

The values that society and individuals place on these two measures of success are complex and interesting, and conversations with clients around their own opinions and values can be revealing. Social pressures often lead clients to pursue financial reward at the expense of job satisfaction. A conversation which highlights the differences can cause a client to reflect on their own values, helping them come to fulfilling decisions.

CONCLUSION

Work takes up a significant proportion of our lives, but its impact on people and their everyday lives goes far beyond the pleasure that can be achieved during the normal working week. A career that works for someone can be a badge of identity that gives meaning to their whole life and satisfies the basic human desire for purpose. Finding or creating this niche is tough and it gets no easier as people work their way through their careers. The nature of the 21st century workplace and the pace of change means that no one can afford to stand still. Even if a person ends up staying in the same job in the same organisation for the best part of their working life, the job and the organisation will not be static. Careers need to be managed throughout to make sure that people are employable and in control throughout their lives. A career coach with a wealth of insightful empathy and a clear understanding of the world of work can ease a client's passage to a satisfying working life.

Practical suggestions for those coaching in this sector

1. Consider whether you and your expertise are most suited to work with career coaching consultancies, private clients or in-house.
2. Immerse yourself in the literature about careers. Anyone can read a newspaper's perspective on the state of employment in the country. A good career coach will go beyond the headlines to understand what is actually happening, and what can be done about it.
3. Network. One of the challenges for the self-employed career coach is that if they are doing their job well, they are not likely to develop ongoing client relationships. Career coaches should get involved in as many networks as possible.
4. Consider finding a niche. Experience suggests that having a particular specialism is the key to freelance success. It gives a person instant credibility and also gives potential clients a clearer understanding of a career coach's specialism.
5. For coaches specialising in professional development coaching, the three-way contract between the coach, the client and the organisation is crucial. It may appear to the employer that the role of the coach is to increase the productivity of the organisation, but the most effective coaching conversations will only be possible with the assurance of a confidential, client-centred relationship.
6. Take advantage of external tools or resources that clients can work on independently in between coaching sessions. There are numerous free career-related web tools and clients could be asked to work on paper and pencil exercises, or bring along a copy of their internal review to aid discussions and to make the most of their time with the coach.

Visit the companion website, https://study.sagepub.com/coachingcontexts, to read the case studies that accompany this chapter:

- Case Study 1: Coaching using career theories
  Michelle Pritchard

- Case Study 2: Coaching mid-life career change
  Julia Yates

- Case Study 3: Coaching to 'get back on track'
  Julia Heynat

REFERENCES

Arthur, M.B. and Rousseau, D.M. (eds) (1996) *The Boundaryless Career: A New Employment Principle for a New Organizational Era*. Oxford: Oxford University Press.

Barclay, S.R., Stoltz, K.B. and Chung, Y.B. (2011) 'Voluntary midlife career change: Integrating the transtheoretical model and the life-span, life-space approach', *The Career Development Quarterly, 59*: 386–99.

Blau, G. (2007) 'Partially testing a process model for understanding victim responses to an anticipated worksite closure', *Journal of Vocational Behavior, 71*: 421–8.

Carless, S.A. and Arnup, J.L. (2010) 'A longitundinal study of the determinants and outcomes of career change', *Journal of Vocational Behaviour, 78*: 80–91.

Costa, P.T., McCrae, R.R. and Zonderman, A.B. (1987) 'Environmental and dispositional influences on well-being: Longitudinal follow-up of an American national sample', *British Journal of Psychology, 78*: 299–306.

Eby, L.T. and Buch, K. (1995) 'Job loss as career growth: Responses to involuntary career transitions', *The Career Development Quarterly, 44*: 26–42.

Harter, J.K. and Gurley, V.F. (2008) 'Measuring well-being in the United States', *Association for Psychological Science, 21*(8): 23–6.

Jacobsen, M. (2010) 'Positive psychology for career counsellors', *Career Planning and Adult Development Journal, 26*(1): 26–39.

Kidd, J. (2008) 'Mental capital and wellbeing: Making the most of ourselves in the 21st century', *State-of-Science Review: SR-C10 Careers at Work*. London: The Government Office for Science.

Kubler-Ross, E. (1969) *On Death and Dying*. New York: Macmillan.

Littman-Ovadia, H. and Davidovitch, N. (2010) 'Effects of congruence and character-strength deployment on work adjustment and well-being', *International Journal of Business and Social Science, 1*(3): 138–46.

Ng, T.W.H., Eby, L.T., Sorensen, K.L. and Feldman, D.C. (2005) 'Predictors of objective and subjective career success: A meta-analysis', *Personnel Psychology, 58*: 367–408.

Nicholson, N. and West, M.A. (1987) *Managerial Job Change: Men and Women in Transition*. Cambridge: Cambridge University Press.

Office for National Statistics (2013) *Labour Market Statistics*. London: Office for National Statistics.

Prochaska, J.O., DiClemente, C.C. and Norcross, J.C. (1992) 'In search of how people change: Applications to addictive behaviors', *American Psychologist, 47*: 1102–14.

Rath, T. (2007) *StrengthsFinder 2.0*. New York: Gallup.

Rath, T. and Harter, J. (2010) *Well Being: The Five Essential Elements*. New York: Gallup.

Roelen, C.A.M., Koopmans, P.C. and Groothoff, J.W.(2008) 'Which work factors determine job satisfaction?', *Work, 30*: 433–9.

Savickas, M. (2002) 'Career construction: A developmental theory of vocational behaviour'. In D. Brown and associates (eds), *Career Choice and Development*, 4th edn. San Francisco, CA: Jossey-Bass. pp. 149–205.

Savickas, M. (2012) 'Life Design: A paradigm for career interventions in the 21st century', *Journal of Counseling and Development, 90*: 13–19.

Savickas, M.L., Nota, L., Rossier, J., Dauwalder, J-P., Duarte, M.E., Guicharde, J. Soresi, S., Van Esbroeck, R. and van Vianen, A.E.M. (2009) 'Life designing: A paradigm for career construction in the 21st century', *Journal of Vocational Behavior, 75*(3): 239–50.

Woods, D. (2011) 'No such thing as a job for life for young people', *HR Magazine*, 20 September 2011, available at www.hrmagazine.co.uk/hro/news/1020164/no-job-life-young-people-hr-staff-hyphen

Yates, J. (2013) *The Career Coaching Handbook*. Hove: Routledge.

Yur'yev, A., Värnik, A., Värnik, P., Sisask, M. and Leppik L. (2012) 'Employment status influences suicide mortality in Europe', *International Journal of Social Psychiatry, 58*(1): 62–8.

Zhou, Q. (2005) 'The institutional logic of occupational prestige ranking: Reconceptualization and reanalyses', *American Journal of Sociology, 111*(1): 90–140.

5

COACHING IN THE FINANCIAL SERVICES INDUSTRY

EMMA FOWLER AND JOHN AINLEY

INTRODUCTION

As the coaching market expands, little has been written specifically for the financial services industry. This chapter surveys what already exists across the sector, provides viewpoints of industry experts and discusses specific requirements of the industry.

Financial services (FS) are economic services provided by companies that manage money, including banks and building societies, mortgage providers and credit card companies, insurance companies, accountancy firms, stockbrokers, investment funds and public sector organisations such as the Bank of England. We focus primarily upon banks and insurance companies in this chapter. To give an idea of scale, financial and insurance services in the UK in 2011 contributed £125.4 billion to the country's economy. Further, 3.6% of all jobs in the UK came from this sector (Maer and Broughton, 2012) with the UK insurance industry employing around 320,000 staff (ABI, 2013).

It is also interesting to note that this already dominant sector is growing: following the impact of the financial crisis, a CityUK Employment Survey report has shown optimistic growth figures of around 2% for the FS industry in London in 2014 (TheCityUK, 2014) and predicts continued expansion. This trend offers growing opportunities for coaches and consultants offering services to the industry.

CURRENT FOCUS OF FINANCIAL SERVICES COMPANIES

According to a 2014 Deloitte report, six key issues currently influence banking: competition and markets; clients and products; governance, risk and compliance; financial management; technology dynamics; and organisational effectiveness.

This last element, organisational effectiveness, includes how the industry is responding to issues regarding processes, business operations and talent. Since the start of the 2008 financial crisis the FS market has been a challenging place in which to work and cost-cutting measures have been implemented across the industry. This is coupled with other factors such as a multi-faceted global talent crisis, including:

- organisations making staff redundant in countries with high overheads, strategically offshoring staff to cheaper destinations;
- other organisations near-shoring employees, or building multi-location talent incubators and hubs;
- not enough highly skilled individuals locally available for multinational organisations;
- skilled staff reluctant to move during crisis times and their current companies fighting for them, creating 'salary bubbles';
- in the USA, the norm for staff to change company every 4.6 years (Bureau of Labor Statistics, 2012) and in Asia at just under 4 years (PwC, 2012) creates a significant flux especially when it comes to senior succession planning.

These issues lead to an industry under pressure, with leaders stretched to capacity and development of staff sometimes forgotten. Similarly, staff are being asked to 'lead' in this changing landscape rather than simply manage, often with limited support as they transition into leadership roles, which creates pressure upon the performance not just of the individual but the whole team.

According to Deloitte, the banks likely to succeed in future are those who employ agile minds. In other words, banks that are able to create teams that learn rapidly and shift focus dynamically will be more likely to thrive. With such fast-paced change being presented as a competitive differentiator for FS firms, there has never been a better time for coaching to offer value and support to this highly-pressured industry.

COACHING IN FS

So what already exists in FS? Coaching tends to be offered to employees as one of a number of interventions (including assessments, training and mentoring) and sometimes in conjunction with these. Standard Bank describe staff coaching as 'a short term intervention used to support learning through increasing self-insight such as learning new behaviours and attitudes' (Standard Bank, 2013a). They do not divulge their annual coaching spend, but in 2013 they allocated 2.4% of total staff costs to training, totalling R638 million (£35.6 million; US$59.6 million). There is clearly a significant market to be considered here.

Who delivers the coaching?

There are three options: an internal coach (not involved in the line management of the coachee), an external coach and the line manager.

Internal coaching solutions

Internal coaches differ from external coaches simply because they are a 'fellow employee of the same organization' (Frisch, 2001). The recent, significant rise of the prevalence of internal coaching services could be linked to cost-saving initiatives driven from the financial crisis, or perhaps it is due to increased awareness of the advantages of training staff to become coaches, or both. Nowadays, experienced internal coaching experts exist in large FS firms – many will have a Head of Learning and Development who is a qualified coach, for example. Banks like Standard Chartered have a network of 200 'strength coaches' across their global business, with 34 'team coaches' providing supervisory support for this team (CIPD, 2007) which they describe as critical to their leadership development strategy. They report higher staff engagement, stronger business performance and lower employee turnover as a result of this initiative.

The credit card company Capital One has an in-house executive coaching capability, operating as part of the leadership development function. In the late 1990s, their HR division recognised a need in their executives for an external perspective on leadership and business. From this, a coaching programme was designed and the internal function was developed to support this, embedding it firmly into the framework of the organisation (Corporate Leadership Council, 2003).

Internal coaching services tend to be accessed more frequently by middle management rather than the Board and Executive. Possible reasons for this include the fact that some of the internal coaching solutions offered may not be as relevant for the executive and top-level leaders who have had experience of coaching before. Perhaps senior leaders wish to speak with someone external who is experienced in organisational development and understands the intricacies of the politics of leadership (Deans et al., 2007).

When are external coaches used?

Recently, the notion of coaching has been seen more positively within FS organisations. Earlier ideas that receiving coaching may have been perceived that the coachee was doing 'something wrong' have been replaced with recognition that coaching can enhance a coachee's productivity and effectiveness. In fact, parallels are being drawn with the outstanding performance of sportspeople who achieve extraordinary results with the support of coaches. The possibility that coaching can increase resilience has also improved its image in an environment where high levels of stress and associated burnout are relatively common.

Companies hire coaches to develop the leadership capabilities of their executives (Underhill et al., 2007), especially as they transition into more senior roles, as well as for newly appointed CEOs and senior executives. Coaching is provided for individual executives and leaders, as well as for teams (see Case Study 4). Of course, access to coaching can be provided for anyone in any team. In particular, there is a trend to equip the manager of the team to become a coach themselves in order to support ongoing coaching (see Chapter 3, Manager as Coach). We discuss this phenomenon in the performance and sales coaching section below.

COACHING INTERVENTIONS PREVALENT IN FS FIRMS

Performance and Sales coaching

A survey found that in 79% of cases, coaching was deployed for an employee by an organisation to improve their performance or productivity (American Management Association, 2008), both of which are subject to close scrutiny and are of paramount importance across the industry. A recent McKinsey paper, providing guidance for the corporate and investment banking (CIB) arena, highlighted the tough market facing sales teams in Western economies. They suggest relationship managers and their teams must undergo transformational change in order to stay ahead of competition and achieve higher sales performance. The paper states, '90% of classroom training is lost within one month. The key to successful talent management is to embed new skills and behaviors into both individuals and the bank's culture as a whole. Formal training should be paired with innovative adult learning tools such as experiential exercises ("field & forum") and coaching' (McKinsey, 2011). They go on to say that sales managers should 'spend less time reacting to ad hoc requests and more on coaching, identifying and deploying best practices'. This recommendation from a leading consultancy for banks to move towards creating a coaching culture amongst their CIB sales divisions offers a clear opportunity for coaches to support improvements within the sector.

Also interesting to consider are results from a 2014 Canadian bank study, which demonstrated that coaching from bank managers to financial advisor (FA) staff members on the 'frontline' created a significant positive variation in these employees' performance – as well as developing their customer orientation – which can be translated as developing an all-important level of trust between the FA and the customer (Pousa and Mathieu, 2014).

Note of caution

A banking executive revealed to us that in his multinational bank, if a senior individual was noted for non-performance, was relatively new and was expensive, rather than addressing the issues through performance management, a coach was usually allocated. If and when the individual was eventually exited from the company, it was easier to justify because they had been 'given a chance' with coaching and the exit was rarely queried. Coaches should be mindful of involvement in similar situations.

Maternity/paternity coaching

Coaching for new parents is an emerging and growing trend in the FS industry. In a 2011 article in *HR Magazine*, coaching in a variety of organisations was covered, including at Deutsche Bank where one-to-one maternity coaching is made available for senior female executives, with group workshops for more junior female staff. An associated programme for line managers of the employees taking maternity leave is also delivered. According to the Head of Talent and Development of Deutsche Bank UK, 'We are seeing the success of this programme, as we have a return rate from maternity leave of 90%'. Mothers may be the first to receive this type of coaching, but we predict a need for paternity coaching over time as the benefits are recognised for employees.

Retention

Retaining top talent is a key agenda issue for FS companies. A recent PwC study on human capital trends highlighted that the most significant legacy from the financial crisis is employee engagement, with younger employees hit particularly hard, as opportunities in general are scarce and routes upwards in organisations are blocked by older workers who cannot afford to – or don't wish to – retire (PwC, 2012). In fact the study found 55% of business leaders in Western economies rate recruitment and retention of high potential employees as a key challenge. In China, the paper reported that from a survey of 2,200 managers, two thirds had received a competing job offer in the previous 18 months. It also found that 19.2% of new hires in China resigned within their first year of tenure – staggering when you consider not only the cost of replacing these individuals, but also the strategic impact of losing this talent.

Coaching can be offered as a tool to help embed talented individuals securely into the organisation, to engage them and generate pride and loyalty (Axmith, 2004). If a coach is working with an individual to help plan for their future within their current organisation, the experience may increase that individual's commitment to the company and this in turn can reduce the likelihood of their leaving: the 10:9 rule suggests that every 10% improvement in commitment decreases an employee's probability of leaving by 9% (Council, 2004).

Coaching can also be used to help executives avoid derailment (the failure to deliver on performance objectives which would have a negative impact on current or future employment) although it is difficult to identify potential derailment circumstances (Levenson, 2009). However, if such a situation is identified and coaching deployed, it seems that it could lead to a reduced risk of derailment. A 2009 study of a United Arab Emirates Bank that suffered a 50% attrition of its highly-prized Emirati staff and in response partnered with a Canadian company to implement an in-house career coaching solution, saw positive preliminary results in terms of retention (McDermott and Neault, 2011). However, the effects were limited and the conclusion was that more research (with a larger sample size and longer reporting timeline) was required. Still, we believe this is a valuable contribution to our understanding of the benefits of coaching and the study provides a useful starting point and framework for further research into the efficacy of coaching within this sector.

Onboarding

Coaching is becoming a routine part of many organisations' onboarding processes (Park, 2007) and companies coach new members of staff to help them settle in and navigate in their new environment. In addition, to support the new member of staff, organisations recognise that coaching may allow them to get the best out of the newly hired talent as quickly as possible. In fact, a lack of feedback and coaching is identified by Branham (2005) as one of seven reasons employees leave an organisation. He goes on to highlight that intensive feedback and coaching for new hires is critical, especially in their first week. Onboarding coaching will also achieve the most for the surrounding team as the new hire becomes comfortable navigating and networking swiftly, resulting in business benefits such as a rapid dissemination of expertise, skills and innovation amongst the team. A study by Mellon financial services found external hires took twice as long as internal movers to reach full productivity, with nearly half of internal hires rapidly reaching a relatively high level of productivity, versus a fifth of external hires (Williams, 2003). They concluded that lost productivity due to learning curves could be translated as a loss of 1% to 2% of total revenue. This presents a significant opportunity for coaching to add tangible value by supporting external hires in their new roles in order to become productive as rapidly as possible. Furthermore, employees can be let go in their probationary period – or early on in their career with a new company – for a number of reasons, but particularly if they do not fit into the company culture, or because of inappropriate reactions to new, high stress situations. By careful selection of the right staff, coupled with coaching and training, these outcomes can be avoided (Wagner and Rieves, 2009).

Promoting diversity

The issue of diversity within FS has recently taken an even higher profile. Key concerns include an ageing population, the case for quotas for women on Boards, building multicultural teams, fulfilling regulatory requirements in certain countries, or companies addressing the enablement of staff with disabilities in the workplace. Most banks have created a Diversity and Inclusion division within their HR department in order to spread the positive message of these values across their businesses.

Certainly there seems to be a requirement in FS to promote diversity: according to a US and Europe-wide study by McKinsey, listed firms with diversity in their executive team delivered 53% higher returns on equity during the volatile years of 2008–2010 compared with their less diverse competition (Barta et al., 2012). However, a study into the diversity of the FTSE100 companies in the banking and finance sector revealed that only 22% of the top 20 most senior positions in organisations were occupied by women (Green Park, 2012).

One way of responding to this could be the provision of coaching for female executives stepping into a first Board position to build confidence and help them embed and navigate in their new roles, particularly if the Board is predominantly male.

Leadership development

In the American Management Association's (AMA) 2008 coaching survey, 63% of respondents reported that they purchased coaching services in order to address leadership development or succession planning, the second highest response after performance improvement (AMA, 2008). Executive coaching is 'the one to one development of an organizational leader' (Underhill et al., 2007) and these services are usually purchased by an FS organisation in a tripartite setting. The main objective is primarily for an established or up and coming leader to quickly develop to the next level of their career. In fact, depending upon the seniority and the situation, more than one coach can be used to support the executive (see Case Study 5).

Professional Insight

Andy Rear, CEO, Africa, Asia Pacific, UK and Ireland Life, Munich Re

'FS is fast-paced and above all, complex. The complexity sometimes gets in the way of your vision. As a leader you occasionally need to stop and think broadly about what you are trying to achieve personally, how and why. In my career I have used coaching to give me the time and the techniques for that big think. Seriously undertaken, you come out a better leader than you went in. I believe that is true of me, and I have seen it in some of my executive team.'

In-house talent management and succession planning

Career management coaching services are designed 'to help individuals assess where their career is now and where they want to go next' (AMA, 2008). Career coaching can be offered as a 'bonus' by companies to help employees feel valued, or to prevent top talent being headhunted by rivals. It may also be offered in response to initiatives in competitor organisations. If rising talent in an organisation has 'nowhere to go' because their technical capability limits them to a specific discipline or silo, talent management coaching may be offered to develop other, more personal capabilities, allowing them to network efficiently internally and ultimately helping them to identify and achieve an internal move (see Chapter 4, Coaching for Careers and Professional Development).

Career coaching may be used when an individual first steps into a management role, or when a leader takes their first executive committee (ExCO) or board position. As the individual's responsibilities and priorities shift, supporting that person to successfully embrace this change – and understanding how the move fits into the wider context of their long-term career plan – can help determine that person's success.

Managing succession planning is a key priority for FS companies and this is clearly demonstrated in situations such as the plans made after the exit of HSBC's Chairman Stephen Green in 2010 (Corrigan, 2010). In fact in a recent White Paper on behavioural risks from MWM Consulting, one chairperson is quoted as saying 'managing succession is the most important task that a Board has; it has to be a regular discussion item' (MWM Consulting, 2012). Providing coaching for executives can open discussions which lead to new career goals – for example, a CFO or Chief Actuary in an insurance company may identify a desire to develop their marketing skills, which over time leads them to move across into a Chief Marketing Officer position. This in turn equips them to be a more rounded candidate for CEO when the role becomes available, as they understand the way the business interacts with the customer, as well as the financial decisions that underpin and drive product and investment choices. Coaching is invaluable in supporting these exploratory conversations.

Facilitated executive committee meetings

The importance of the executive team in developing and implementing business strategy is often secondary to addressing the day to day management needs of the organisation. However, when an ExCO truly takes accountability for the future of the enterprise and performs quickly and efficiently, business outperformance follows. With the impact of the financial crisis still affecting the international FS industry, business performance is critical and this outperformance is always strived for. Unfortunately, some executive teams are slow to act and riven with internal politics and ego. A growing need, identified by forward-looking CEOs, is to work with the ExCO to develop an effective team through the use of a coach. Much of the coach's work here is to build trust, the willingness to challenge and the suspension of individual power for the good of the whole. For many in the executive team who manage jobs of some significance and are masters of their own fiefdoms, this may not come naturally. A skilled and effective coach can work with such a team to highlight the value of working together effectively. In such meetings the CEO needs to be a participating member of the team and not the leader. The role of the coach is to create an environment where the current norms are challenged and so a new, more effective way of working together is the result.

The coach's competency here is many faceted and includes having a true appreciation of the pressures upon – and responsibilities of – the top team, plus previous experience of helping to create the right conditions for facilitating team interventions, and the gravitas to deal with challenging situations. The potential outcomes can be significant (see Case Study 5).

Wellness

There is a perception that the FS industry is characterised by stress, pressure and illness. This should certainly be a key issue for consideration. Exacerbated by a combination of company, industry and personal performance pressure, we have seen many executives require a break from work for health reasons over the past few years (including high profile names such as Hector Sants, Executive at Barclays, and Antonio Horta-Orsorio, Lloyds Banking Group CEO). It certainly seems to be a lonely job at the top with CEOs and chairpersons of the UK's largest companies reporting feeling isolated and unsupported (Ainley, 2013).

Many financial companies are facing a significantly increasing impact of employee stress, which not only affects the bottom line but the culture of the organisation as well. In fact in 2013 the UK City Mental Health Alliance (CMHA) was formed and is comprised of banks, insurance organisations and associated firms (including Goldman Sachs, Bank of America, Merrill Lynch, Lloyds Banking Group, Aon, Morgan Stanley and the Bank of England). Their initial research indicates that mental ill health costs UK organisations £26 billion a year (an average of more than £1,000 per employee) and that one in five employees had taken a day off work for stress in the previous year (CMHA, 2013).

So what are companies doing to combat the impact of stress? Certainly coaching seems to be part of the solution and we have regular conversations with clients regarding wellness, resilience and mindfulness. We predict 'coaching for wellbeing' is a trend that will be called upon more frequently to help FS companies search for a solution to a growing problem (see Chapter 14, Coaching for Wellbeing at Work, for an in-depth discussion).

Coaching to change culture

Working in an FS company is not always the fast-paced, cut-throat environment we see sensationalised in films such as *The Wolf of Wall Street* but there may be similarities. With the relentless focus upon revenue and profit, investment in people can become secondary. This has been exacerbated by the impact of the recent financial crisis, with organisational spend on learning and development down by approximately 4% between 2009 and 2010 (O'Leonard, 2011). Personal financial gain is certainly a focus for many who are drawn to work in the banking sector. In a recent Employee Outlook survey (CIPD, 2013) 32% of respondents said salary was the factor that attracted them to banking, with career opportunities coming second (31%). In the same survey, 46% of senior managers said that if regulations limited how much they could earn in banking, they would leave the sector.

Other findings from the survey include respondents' answers to the question of whether the senior executives in their organisation had instigated or led initiatives to change the culture over the past 12 months: less than 40% said 'yes', with 45% saying 'no' and 16% saying 'don't know'.

As the survey states, 'this is set against a backdrop of an ongoing public debate about the need to change culture in banking and financial services' following the financial crisis.

To refer back to the CIPD survey, it seems there is a very present opportunity for coaching to help with the 'tone from the top' in an organisation, which could drive the cultural change that may be required. As the Governor of the Bank of England, Mark Carney, discussed in his recent speech at the Conference of Inclusive Capitalism, cultural change 'begins with boards and senior management defining clearly the purpose of their organizations and promoting a culture of ethical business throughout them. Employees must be grounded in strong connections to their clients and their communities. To move to a world that once again values the future, bankers need to see themselves as custodians of their institutions, improving them before passing them along to their successors' (Carney, 2014).

So what does this mean for coaches? The coach is often asked to help support the development of company-wide cultural change, or even to facilitate the internal development of a coaching culture for FS organisations, although the complete development of this solution may be some way off. We suggest a model could exist whereby coaches could work with a partner who carries out an assessment of the cultural position of a team or a firm before commencing an assignment (see the Framework for Practitioners 3: Supporting the Development of Coaching Cultures).

Now more than ever, there is a spotlight upon the culture prevalent in FS firms. For Barclays, following a difficult few years including hundreds of millions of pounds worth of fines associated with the rigging of interest rates, attempting to fix commodity prices and mis-selling protection products, there seems to be a strong incentive to consider ways of changing the organisational culture. Arguably, the public's trust in banks is at a low ebb because of perceived deficiencies in the cultures of FS organisations. In a letter to staff, Barclays CEO Antony Jenkins (2013) unveiled a new 'Purpose and Values' blueprint, with the bank's five values listed as Respect, Integrity, Service, Excellence and Stewardship. The letter suggested that banking had 'lost its way, and ... lost touch with the values on which reputation and trust were built'. He describes the fifth value, stewardship, as 'being determined to leave things better than we found them, so we constantly strive to improve the way we operate ... and the impact we have on society' (Jenkins, 2013). Radically changing the culture of an organisation with 140,000 employees is no simple task. It is important to note that Barclays are by no means alone in this journey. Many other global, national and local banks are re-writing their values and considering culture change. These industry-wide challenges would surely benefit from the support of coaches who are well-versed in facilitating large-scale cultural change (see Chapter 16: Towards a Coaching Culture, for a further discussion).

WHAT COACHING SOLUTIONS ARE APPROPRIATE FOR FS CLIENTS?

There is little question that being highly-qualified and technically adept will increase your chances of employability in the FS industry. For example, you are unlikely to be employed in the underwriting department of an insurance company without having actuarial qualifications.

Similarly, obtaining an influential position within a finance function of a bank is unlikely without an accountancy background. However, three types of intelligence have been identified as important: IQ, expertise and emotional intelligence (Burgess, 2005). The first, IQ, is the poorest predictor of success in the workplace (between 4–25%) and expertise is a baseline competence rather than a differentiator between average and outstanding performance (Goleman, 1998). So emotional intelligence (EQ) is clearly key in the FS industry. Staff may well have been hired – and promoted – according to technical and transactional capability, but EQ and soft skills could be the differentiator that pushes them towards great leadership and achievement. Perhaps it would be interesting to consider Alban-Metcalfe and Alimo-Metcalfe's (2002) view of transformational leadership and the challenge and opportunity this may present for coaches: 'The real skill is being transactional (i.e. setting objectives, planning, providing feedback, etc) in a transformational way. But perhaps the greatest challenge is, how willing will those in the most senior positions – who may well have been appointed precisely because of their transactional strengths – be to adopt a transformational style?'.

So what does this mean for coaches? Different coaching solutions can be employed according to a client's needs. The most common form of coaching within the sector is a solution-focused, cognitive-behavioural (SF-CB) approach. This type of approach is appropriate for performance improvement, skill development and stress reduction. SF-CB solutions are well suited to the sector. They are well researched and validated and tend to be relatively easy to understand and apply. Importantly, they have been shown to be effective (Grant et al., 2009). The ultimate goal for CB coaching is for coachees to become self-reflective and self-motivated. It has been shown that teaching others is a great way of maintaining these learned skills (Neenan and Palmer, 2001). If we refer back to the focus of FS organisations wanting to change culture, this 'coaching cascade' underpinned by a SF-CB framework may be a solution that coaches can present to their clients.

However, if the issues requiring resolution revolve around unconscious motives or conflict, the SF-CB framework may be insufficient (Ducharme, 2004). Some coaches are employing alternative approaches within the sector. Fifth Third Bancorp in Michigan ran a leadership development course that incorporated coaching, as well as focusing upon the development of emotional intelligence, social intelligence and visioning (Boyatzis et al., 2013). The coaching was varied and included 'coaching with compassion'. Emotional and social intelligence of individuals were assessed through questionnaires and the results discussed with participants during the programme. Personal visioning and hope for the future were established, then the programme moved to engage others in these conversations. After almost three years of these programmes, the bank's CEO Kevin Kabat feels that, 'the entire team (is) participating in a very, very different way, in a great way … it really does show through … it really has made a difference'.

MARKETING COACHING SERVICES TO THE FS INDUSTRY

If you are a coach presenting your organisation's services to the ExCO and board, bear in mind that CEOs and the top team want to work with a 'peer', someone with real-world business credentials who knows what it is like to operate at a similar level (Axmith, 2004). This is not to say that the coach necessarily needs to have come from the same industry, although one might hypothesise that an understanding of terminology, jargon and the complexity of the business could help a coach develop rapport with a coachee more rapidly than if they had not. It is also worth noting that presentation, polish and gravitas are highly regarded by the FS industry and these traits in coaches could increase the chances of success. Whether the coach has presented successfully to a business leader, or someone in the talent, HR, learning or procurement divisions, unless you are coaching the board the route to delivering coaching services in FS firms will often be through the means of a coaching panel.

Coaching panels

A panel is often in place in larger FS organisations, made up of a range of coaches with different experience and skill sets in order to provide volume, diversity, choice and expertise according to the requirements of the situation. A panel is useful in order to provide a choice of external coach for an employee. This overcomes the problem of a mismatch between coach and coachee, and is something which is employed by Harford Financial Services Group where an employee who requests coaching gets to select the coach they prefer from a choice of three offered from the panel (AMA, 2008). This model is also employed by the West Midlands Coaching Pool (see Case Study 9).

An internal representative such as a Head of Learning and Development or sometimes the HR Director will decide who makes up the panel. In other instances an intermediate third party is retained to manage the panel on behalf of the organisation. More often than not, panels will consist of individuals running personal, boutique coaching companies who have been recommended to the firm, or have existing professional relationships with senior members of the organisation's staff. Coaches will be expected to demonstrate their previous relevant coaching experience in the field. They should also have appropriate coach training qualifications and be a member of a professional association (e.g. the Association for Coaching, the European Mentoring and Coaching Council or the International Coaching Federation). Evidence of coaching supervision is also a requirement. However, it is interesting to note from a recent study that purchasers of executive coaching services did not select their coach because of their education, certification or coaching qualifications: they selected according to the coach's business experience and ability to establish a rapport (Underhill et al., 2007).

MEASURING SUCCESS: COACHING AND ROI

For people working in financial organisations, it is not surprising that a key question will relate to the return on investment (ROI) of a coaching intervention or service. ROI is the language used to evaluate capital projects (Levenson, 2009). A 2014 study of executive coaching demonstrated that the ROI formula is only used by 11% of executive coaches as a preferred method of measurement: 28% of coaches tend to favour the Goldsmith method of measurement, which is to run a 360° assessment before and after the intervention (Sherpa Coaching, 2014).

Note of caution

It is worth noting that using ROI as a measure of success for a coaching intervention will distil the result down to very basic numerical data and perhaps ignore benefits which are not easily quantifiable (Levenson and Cohen, 2003). Unsurprisingly, purchasers in the FS industry use financial language and measures to determine the 'success' of a provided service, whereas providers of coaching often use an assessment framework which is less financial and more subjective.

International FS coaching diversity

There is a broad difference in service offered depending on which continent – and country – you are operating in as a coach.

Professional insight: Executive coaching in Asian contexts

Gautam Dev, Chief HR Officer, Eastspring Investments

Determining whether coaching is or is not successful in a broader Asian context is often complicated by different pre-conceptions and perceptions about the role of a coach on the part of many Asian executives. Most notably:

- *The Guru Syndrome* Coaching in many parts of Asia can often be viewed as a relationship where the coach is expected to impart great wisdom and knowledge to the coachee. Therefore the perceived 'success' or 'value' from coaching can be heavily contingent on the extent to which the coachee perceives that a coach has provided profound insights and/ or breakthrough solutions rather than the extent to which the coachee has been helped to better understand (and seek out answers) for themselves.
- *The Facilitator of Promotions* In many Asian cultures, the drive for personal success and achievement (and highly visible acknowledgement of such success through promotions, pay rises, etc.) is a dominant behavioural driver. Within a coaching context, I've observed that this often manifests itself in the coachee measuring coaching value based on the extent to which a coach has contributed to the tangible career progression of that coachee.

(Continued)

(Continued)

- *The Complex Problem Solver* I've also observed that many coaching relationships across Asia are defined by the coachee's belief that a coach should be able to provide specific solutions to complex business issues currently confronting the coachee. I have lost count of the number of times an Asian coachee will ask for a coach that has deep industry and/or technical expertise, purely driven by the expectation that a coach should be able to advise on specific business/industry/technical issues from a position of expertise.

Therefore the value (or lack of value) of a coach in many parts of Asia is heavily influenced by the perception on the part of coachees (and often their sponsors) of how well a coach has performed as a guru/career-promoter/technical expert. This view is of course at odds with the Western paradigm of a coach as one who uses expertise and methodologies to make a coachee more self-aware and better prepared to reach their own conclusions on operating more effectively.

OPPORTUNITY FOR COACHING

Considering the range of significant change agendas currently being addressed, coaching clearly has an opportunity to expand its reach across the FS industry, both internally and externally. More research is required to support the efficacy of coaching (see Chapter 13: The Current State of Research, for a further discussion) and this is especially true in the FS arena. Some great examples of the impact of coaching do already exist. For nearly a decade, Middelfart Sparekasse Bank in Denmark has been recognised as one of the best small- to medium-sized enterprises (SMEs) in Europe to work for by the Great Place to Work Institute. This is in no small part due to the fulfilling culture they have created, using a combination of coaching, self-directed leadership, training and personal growth (Gargiulo, 2011).

So, does a coaching solution differ when presented to the FS industry, in comparison with other sectors – or if not currently, should it? How does a coach make themselves 'FS ready'? Certainly the way the service is first presented must be culturally aligned, with polish, gravitas, efficiency and professionalism. Perhaps this presentation style sits at one end of a continuum, with other more relaxed styles being more suited to different client segments. The coach might take an active interest in the organisation – its goals, strategy, market sector and competitors – in order that conversations with key decision makers are aligned with the experience they have when purchasing other professional services, where 'client partners' are viewed as subject matter experts. Regardless of whether this information is of use during the coaching sessions conducted, presenting in this manner when initially pitching a solution will aid the credibility of the coaching profession broadly across the sector, as well as presenting the coach as a capable, knowledgeable and interested professional.

Secondly, demonstrating success needs to be considered carefully. Linking one's coaching to a specific client product launch, new market sector penetration or change programme may allow for an assessment of success as part of this project as useful data will perhaps be made available to the coach (including a capability to determine the client's ROI from the service). As such, if it is possible, the coach should make it their priority to work with the business more broadly than the individual they are coaching, in order to take advantage of such data. A welcome by-product of such behaviour is that other coaching opportunities may present themselves, as the coach networks across the organisation.

Finally, broadening one's service outside the coaching arena could perhaps be the competitive differentiator that allows for both personal success and client satisfaction. A coach should consider presenting a range of services with other professionals, as a multi-faceted solution may be more relevant and have a far greater impact for the client than coaching alone. Other professional services firms do this for FS clients – they will manage audit work, tax matters, transactional services projects and restructuring programmes simultaneously and multi-jurisdictionally, in order to provide a client with the best and most appropriate, joined-up solution. We suggest coaches need to consider how their services fit into a broader context of talent management, employee engagement and wellness.

CONCLUSION

Does coaching have a place in the current FS industry? With the financial crisis still fresh in the minds of the public and many associated cultural issues at the forefront of leaders' minds, the answer is definitely 'yes'. We might also consider the potential of another financial crisis in future, and the role coaching might play in helping FS leaders avert the next downturn. Is coaching 'fit for purpose' as regards this challenge? One might argue it is not quite there yet: ' … from a critical perspective, it is debatable whether coaching in its current form, and internal coaching provision in particular, is powerful and challenging enough on its own to stave off a future disaster such as we have experienced with the banking crisis' (Du Toit and Sim, 2010). So the opportunity for coaching is clear: the current and future need for change across the FS industry is very real, and coaches are primed and ready to help financial industry leaders, but effort is required to design and present frameworks, interventions and solutions which will provide FS organisations with exactly what they need.

Visit the companion website, https://study.sagepub.com/coachingcontexts, to read the case studies that accompany this chapter:

- Case Study 4: Executive coaching for top team members
  Andrew Sheridan

(Continued)

(Continued)

- Case Study 5: Using a coaching approach with the executive team
  John Ainley

- Case Study 6a: Leadership development in a multinational bank
  Case Study 6b: Maternity returner at a large global bank
  Emma Fowler

REFERENCES

Ainley, J. (2013) 'The loneliness of the CEO, and the dangers for their businesses', *The Independent*. Available at www.independent.co.uk/news/business/comment/john-ainley-the-loneliness-of-the-ceo-and-the-dangers-for-their-businesses-8777267.html

Alban-Metcalfe, B. and Alimo-Metcalfe, J. (2002) 'Leadership: Time to debunk the myths', Cabinet Office report. Leeds: Leadership Research and Development, 3.

American Management Association (AMA) (2008) *Coaching: A Global Study of Successful Practices. Current Trends and Future Possibilities 2008–2018*. Available at www.opm.gov/WIKI/uploads/docs/Wiki/OPM/training/i4cp-coaching.pdf

Association of British Insurers (ABI) (2013) *Insurance and Savings Statistics*. Available at www.abi.org.uk/Insurance-and-savings/Industry-data

Axmith, M. (2004) 'Executive coaching: A catalyst for personal growth and corporate change', *Ivey Business Journal*, 68(5): 1–5.

Barta, T., Kleiner, M. and Neuman, T. (2012) 'Is there a payoff from top – team diversity?', *McKinsey Quarterly*, April. Available at www.mckinsey.com/insights/organization/is_there_a_payoff_from_top-team_diversity

Boyatzis, R.E., Smith, M.L., Van Oosten, E. and Woolford, L. (2013) 'Developing resonant leaders through emotional intelligence, vision and coaching', *Organizational Dynamics*, 42(1): 17–24.

Branham, L. (2005) *The 7 Hidden Reasons Employees Leave*. New York: Amacom.

Bureau of Labor Statistics, US Dept. of Labor (2012) *Employee Tenure in 2012*. Available at www.bls.gov/news.release/pdf/tenure.pdf

Burgess, R.C. (2005) 'A model for enhancing individual and organisational learning of "Emotional Intelligence": The drama and winner's triangles', *Social Work Education*, 24(1): 97–112.

Business Wire (2001) 'Executive coaching yields return on investment of almost six times its cost'. Available at www.thefreelibrary.com/Executive Coaching Yields Return On Investment Of Almost Six Times...-a068725844

Carney, M. (2014) Speech on 'Inclusive Capitalism: Creating a sense of the systemic', at the Conference of Inclusive Capitalism, London. Available at www.bankofengland.co.uk/publications/Documents/speeches/2014/speech731.pdf

CIPD (2007) *Coaching Supervision: Maximising the Potential of Coaching*. Available at www.cipd.co.uk/NR/rdonlyres/5EBC80A0-1279-4301-BFAD-37400BAA4DB4/0/coachsuperv.pdf

CIPD (2013) *Focus on Rebuilding Trust in the City*, Employee Outlook Report. Available at www.cipd.co.uk/binaries/6214%20EO%20Focus%20Rebuilding%20trust%20(WEB).pdf

CMHA (2013) *City Mental Health Alliance: Mental Health is Everyone's Business*. Available at www.hrmaturity.com/wp-content/uploads/2013/11/CMHA.pdf

Corrigan, T. (2010) 'HSBC succession: not pretty but it's the result that counts', *Telegraph Online*. Available at http://blogs.telegraph.co.uk/finance/tracycorrigan/100007741/hsbc-succession-not-pretty-but-its-the-result-that-counts/

Corporate Leadership Council (2003) Maximizing returns on professional executive coaching. Washington DC. Sourced from: http://integratedleadership.com/wp-content/uploads/2011/09/CLC_Maximizing_Returns_on_Professional_Executive_Coaching.pdf

Council, C.L. (2004) *Driving Performance and Retention through Employee Engagement*. Washington, DC: Corporate Executive Board.

Cowlett, M. (2011) 'Coaching and mentoring: doing more with less training budget', *HR Magazine*. Available at www.hrmagazine.co.uk/hro/features/1019491/coaching-mentoring-doing-training-budget#sthash.BPqMJT02.dpuf

Deans, F., Oakley, L., James, R. and Wrigley, R. (2007) *Praxis Paper 14: Coaching and Mentoring for Leadership Development in Civil Society*. Available at www.intrac.org/data/files/resources/371/Praxis-Paper-14-Coaching-and-Mentoring-for-Leadership-Development.pdf

Deloitte Center for Financial Services (2014) *Banking Industry Outlook: Repositioning for Growth: Agility in a re-regulated world*. Available at www.deloitte.com/assets/Dcom-UnitedStates/Local%20Assets/Documents/FSI/us_fsi_DCFS2014BankingIndustryOutlook_111113.pdf

Ducharme, M.J. (2004) 'The cognitive-behavioral approach to executive coaching', *Consulting Psychology Journal: Practice and Research*, 56 (4): 214–24.

Du Toit, A. and Sim, S. (2010) *Rethinking Coaching: Critical Theory and the Economic Crisis*. London: Palgrave Macmillan.

Frisch, M. (2001) 'The emerging role of the internal coach', *Consulting Psychology Journal: Practice and Research*, 53(4): 240–50.

Gargiulo, S. (2011) 'CNN: Route to the Top: How one small bank keeps its staff among the happiest in Europe'. Available at http://edition.cnn.com/2011/09/30/business/gargiulo-route-to-the-top-middelfart-sparekasse/

Goffee, R. and Jones, G. (1996) 'What holds the modern company together?', *Harvard Business Review*, November. Available at http://hbr.org/1996/11/what-holds-the-modern-company-together/ar/1

Goleman, D. (1998) *Working with Emotional Intelligence*. London: Bloomsbury.

Grant, A. (2006) 'A personal perspective on professional coaching and the development of coaching psychology', *International Coaching Psychology Review, 1* (1): 12–20.

Grant, A. (2010) 'It takes time: A stages of change perspective on the adoption of workplace coaching skills', *Journal of Change Management, 10*(1): 61–77.

Grant, A., Curtayne, L. and Burton, G. (2009) 'Executive coaching enhances goal attainment, resilience and workplace well-being: A randomised controlled study', *Journal of Positive Psychology*, 4: 396–407.

Green Park (2012) 'Diversity: A ten minute guide for the busy executive'. Available at www.green-park.co.uk/wp-content/uploads/2014/02/GP-Diversity-Guide.pdf

International Coaching Federation (2012) *Global Coaching Study*. Available at www.coachfederation.org/coachingstudy2012

International Coaching Federation (2014) *Hiring a Coach*. Available at www.coachfederation.org.uk/find-a-coach/hiring/

Jenkins, A. (2013) *Barclays Purpose and Values Letter*. Available at www.telegraph.co.uk/finance/newsbysector/banksandfinance/9808042/Antony-Jenkins-to-staff-adopt-new-values-or-leave-Barclays.html

Kilburg, R.R. (1996) 'Toward a conceptual understanding and definition of executive coaching', *Consulting Psychology Journal: Practice and Research*, 48(2): 134–44.

Levenson, A. (2009) 'Measuring and maximizing the business impact of executive coaching', *Consulting Psychology Journal: Practice and Research*, 61(2): 103.

Levenson, A. and Cohen, S.G. (2003) 'Meeting the performance challenge: Calculating ROI for virtual teams'. In C.B. Gibson and S.G. Cohen (eds), *Virtual Teams that Work: Creating Conditions for Virtual Team Effectiveness*. San Francisco, CA: Jossey-Bass.

Maer, L. and Broughton, N. (2012) *Financial Services: Contribution to the UK Economy*. Available at www.parliament.uk/briefing-papers/sn06193.pdf

McDermott, D. and Neault, R.A. (2011) 'In-house career coaching: An international partnership', *Journal Of Employment Counseling*, 48(3): 121–8.

McKinsey Working Papers on Corporate & Investment Banking, No. 2 (2011) *Sales Transformation in Mid-Market Corporate Banking*. Available at www.mckinsey.com/~/media/mckinsey/dotcom/client_service/Financial%20Services/Latest%20thinking/Corporate%20and%20investment%20banking/CIB_Working_Paper_2_Sales_Transformation.ashx

MWM Consulting (2012) *Taming Narcissus: Managing Behavioural Risk in Top Business Leaders*. Available at www.mwmconsulting.com/wp-content/uploads/2012/07/Electronic-version-Behavioural-Risks.pdf

Neenan, M. and Palmer, S. (2001) 'Cognitive behavioural coaching', *Stress News*, 13(3): 15–18.

O'Leonard, K. (2011) *The Corporate Learning Factbook*. Oakland, CA: Bersin & Associates Research Report.

Park, A. (2007) 'Making the most of your coaching program', *Harvard Management Update*, 12(9): 1. Available at www.vital.co.kr/harvard/hmmplus/hmm11_kr_quickpath/coaching/base/resources/MakingtheMost_CoachingProgram.pdf

Peterson, D.B. (2007) 'Executive coaching in a cross-cultural context', *Consulting Psychology Journal: Practice And Research*, 59 (4): 261–71.

Pousa, C. and Mathieu, A. (2014) 'Boosting customer orientation through coaching: a Canadian study', *International Journal of Bank Marketing*, 32 (1): 60–81.

PwC (2012) *Key Trends in Human Capital 2012: A Global Perspective*. Available at www.slide-share.net/hrtecheurope/key-trends-in-human-capital-management

Segers, J., Vloeberghs, D., Henderickx, E. and Inceoglu, I. (2011) 'Structuring and understanding the coaching industry: The coaching cube', *Academy of Management Learning & Education*, 10: 204–21.

Sherpa Coaching (2014) *Executive Coaching Survey '14, Evidence & Interaction*. Available at http://sherpacoaching.com/pdf%20files/2014%20Executive%20Coaching%20Survey%20-%20Public%20report.pdf

Smith, S. (2014) *How Maslow's Hierarchy of Needs influences Employee Engagement*. Available at www.hrzone.com/blogs/employee-engagement-staff-surveys/how-maslow%E2%80%99s-hierarchy-needs-influences-employee-engagement

Standard Bank (2013a) *Talent Management Global Reporting Initiative*. Available at http://sustainability.standardbank.com/people/talent-management/

Standard Bank (2013b) *Learning and Development Global Reporting Initiative*. Available at http://sustainability.standardbank.com/people/talent-management/learning-and-development/

TheCityUK (2014) *London Employment Survey*. Available at www.thecityuk.com/assets/Uploads/Employment-survey-Feb-2014.pdf

The Coaches Training Institute (2012) *Being an Internal Coach*. Available at www.thecoaches.com/learning-hub/fundamentals/res/FUN-Topics/FUN-Being-an-Internal-Coach.pdf

Turner, A. (2011) Mansion House Speech. Available at www.fsa.gov.uk/library/communication/speeches/2011/1020_at.shtml

Underhill, B.O., Koriath, J.J. and McAnally, K. (2007) *Executive Coaching for Results: The Definitive Guide to Developing Organizational Leaders* (1st edn). San Francisco, CA: Berrett-Koehler.

Wagner, W.H. and Rieves, R.A. (2009) *Investment Management: Meeting the Noble Challenges of Funding Pensions, Deficits, and Growth*. Hoboken, NJ: Wiley.

Williams, R. (2003) *Mellon Learning Curve Research Study*. New York: Mellon Corp.

6

COACHING WITHIN PROFESSIONAL SERVICES FIRMS

CAROLINE FLIN AND IAN McINTOSH

INTRODUCTION

This chapter discusses professional services firms (PSFs), looking at the obvious professions (lawyers and accountants) but also firms in other professional services sectors. Professional Services is a diverse area, with businesses of different sizes, from the very large accounting-based firms, with significant experience of using coaches and defining their coaching needs, to much smaller businesses which may be less familiar with coaching. The chapter draws out some features of professional services that are distinctive, particularly the professional ethos and the partnership model. Following this, there is an explanation of how these features contribute to the development challenges that face professional staff in these firms, especially the move beyond technical expertise to wider leadership and client relationship roles. This leads to an examination of the different ways coaching is used in PSFs, where it is sometimes directed towards promotion points but can also be part of a wider ongoing staff development programme. Further discussion of how the features of PSFs impact on the coaching process and the needs of coachees follows. Finally, this chapter explores how PSFs are expanding coaching in their businesses and provides some practical suggestions for coaches working in this sector.

PROFESSIONAL SERVICES

The word 'professional' is used traditionally to describe an occupation involving a particular skill and role-specific qualifications that are covered by the regulatory powers of a professional body. More recently the word has been used in a wider sense, describing behaviours or environments that are 'businesslike', with high levels of personal commitment and standards. In this chapter, the term 'PSF' will refer to firms in specific professional sectors. Most obviously, this includes law firms and accounting practices, the classic PSFs, not least because these two sectors use coaching significantly (18% of respondents to the Ridler Report 2013 were from these two sectors). However, the contents of this chapter also apply to PSFs in the following sectors:

- Intellectual property firms – patent attorneys and trademark agents.
- Real estate-based advisers – architects, surveyors, environmental consultants and consulting engineers.
- Newer business areas, like management consultants and IT consultancies.
- Financial services-related advisers such as actuaries.

Clearly, these businesses are very diverse in terms of their cultures and professional skills. At the same time, they have important characteristics in common, which are explored below, with particular emphasis on their implications for coaching in those PSFs.

PSFs are diverse not only in occupational terms, but also in their origins and scale. Some have long histories, beginning as small partnerships but expanding greatly in recent years, especially since the abolition in the UK of the 20 partner size limit in the 1960s. Professional services is a strong sector for the UK and the largest PSFs are now both very large (PWC generated UK revenues of over £2.6 billion from its national office network in 2012/3) and global (in 2013 Deloitte had some 200,000 employees worldwide). Some, especially the 'Big Four' accounting-based firms, have expanded their service ranges so they are a combination of several different professions and practice areas. However, many, in all sectors, are much smaller, trading in just one market from a single UK location, with revenues in single millions or less.

Defining key terms

The language used in this chapter illustrates some features of PSFs:

- 'Firm' (rather than 'company') is how people refer to the organisation, reflecting previous partnership structures.
- 'Clients': Firms have 'clients' rather than 'customers'.
- 'Partner' is the most senior level in a firm.
- 'Director', 'Manager', 'Associate' and 'Assistant' refer to the descending levels of professional staff below 'Partner'.
- 'Practice' describes the nature and amount of client work undertaken by a firm.

What is unique about coaching in this context?

Von Nordenflycht (2010) and Empson (2010) suggest several characteristics that make PSFs distinctive and we discuss each of the features below.

A firm's people are its key asset

PSFs sell advice and guidance. That advice and guidance are sometimes packaged into some kind of deliverable (a presentation, legal documents, architectural drawings), which in turn supports a client objective (a strategy, a transaction, a building). In each case advice and communication are the core PSF products, and they are created and delivered exclusively by the firm's staff. The quality of that product is largely a function of the qualities of the PSF's staff who deliver it – the product is their analysis, their exposition, and its cost is a function of their time. As PSFs compete on the quality and price of their product, the people undertaking the delivery are fundamental to their competitive strength.

High levels of expertise

The advice of PSFs is based on high levels of expertise (a combination of knowledge, skill, experience and know-how). In large PSFs, that expertise can be very specialised and narrow. High levels of expertise matter to PSF staff as well as clients; they are important in promotion decisions at all levels, and they can make the difference between winning and losing client work.

Professionalised workforce

The occupations of PSFs often have high social status and can be highly remunerative, so the competition for jobs can be intense and attract some of the best graduates with very strong academic records. This can lead to strong individual self-perceptions (and firm cultures) of high achievement. When combined with demanding formal professional qualifications and prominent professional standards, these factors can create a shared professional identity, particularly amongst partners.

Partnership structure

Historically, PSFs were set up as partnerships. Partners knew each other well, and (unlike limited companies) shared unlimited personal legal responsibility for their firm's debts and liabilities (and hence their fellow partners' work). While many old style partnership structures have been replaced by newer more effective legal forms (e.g. Limited Liability Partnerships and Swiss Vereins), many PSFs, particularly smaller PSFs, still have a sense of a 'partnership' culture, with an emphasis on collegiality. Partnership is therefore the key status in a PSF, and 'making partner' is the defining professional aim for many. That does not mean that all partners are of equal status. In fact they are often less likely to be. There can be wide variations in partners' performance, status, influence and remuneration. Many partnership legal structures reinforce these variations, with senior partners being equity partners (fully sharing in the firm's profits and investing capital in the firm) and more junior partners being quasi-equity or fixed share partners, with fewer rights and lower levels of remuneration. These issues tend to be hidden from clients by the apparent equality of partnership.

Implications of working within PSFs

Against these formal features some cultural themes emerge. Each is discussed below as a way of providing you with a sense of what may be different within this sector.

Progression and leverage in PSFs

Two themes are key here. Firstly, PSFs, especially the larger ones, aim to operate a pyramid structure with relatively large numbers of non-partners working for smaller numbers of partners. This reflects a leverage model in which revenue and profitability are significantly increased by staffing client work with larger numbers of junior staff, supervised by partners and senior staff. The consequence of this is that relatively few people make partner. The pyramid structure can be represented diagrammatically by pyramids showing the different hierarchies in a PSF and their roles (see Figure 6.1).

These pyramids illustrate the changing roles that individuals perform at different levels as they progress through a PSF hierarchy. Adapting to the different needs of each role, particularly

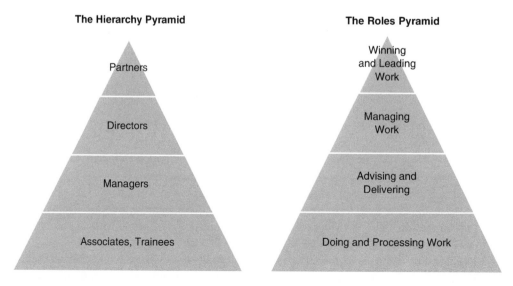

Figure 6.1   Pyramids Diagram

partner roles, is often a significant driver of coaching in PSFs, as individuals begin to understand for themselves at each stage what is expected of them, and that 'what got you here won't get you there' to use Marshall Goldsmith's (2008) phrase.

The importance of client success

Winning work, doing client work well and being valued by clients are important. Being successful with clients is a motivator for individuals, setting and shaping their professional self-esteem and self-definition. It also gives high status within the firm, where the 'heroes' are often the people who win really good work, do the particularly hard or large assignments, or hold the key client relationships. Not only is client success important for self- and peer-esteem, it has harder aspects too. At junior levels it is a key factor in promotion decisions, and for senior staff it evolves into a vital and highly sensitive performance metric: billings for work won and work done. Having said this, being good at doing work for clients is important but it is not enough.

Growing importance of client skills

Coaching in PSFs often involves working with individuals wishing to build their client relationship skills which become increasingly important with greater seniority. All PSFs need their client relationship partners to have the credibility and other personal skills to build strong relationships with the firm's clients for a number of reasons. First, in an increasingly competitive world, the quality of the client relationship is often the main defence against losing work to competitors, a reason for a client to stay with the firm it knows. Correspondingly, an in-depth understanding of a client is essential for another aspect of PSF partner roles: 'cross-selling' effectively. This means introducing clients to other services provided by the firm, thereby increasing the breadth, depth and value of the relationship. That in turn may involve a client partner being more entrepreneurial and having the imagination and confidence to see and exploit opportunities for providing services to clients. For some clients, the lead partner is also expected to be a 'trusted business adviser', valued beyond their practice area for experience, wisdom and well-judged general advice. All these slightly different aspects are fundamentally similar. They are all client relationship skills that need different qualities from the technical and intellectual skills so important at more junior levels.

Ability to manage teams

Another category of 'soft skills' (as they are called within PSFs) is team management. Individual expertise is essential for all PSF client work, but higher value and more complex client work will invariably involve partners leading teams drawn from several practice areas. Leading fellow partners and large teams of junior staff requires very different skills from core client work skills. While promotion processes in large PSFs emphasise these team leadership skills, they are not equally well developed in all PSF partners and senior staff.

5. Changing delivery skills

Delivering client work also demands slightly different skills as individuals become more senior. Some may be expected to supplement their technical expertise (which by this stage is almost taken for granted, and often referred to as 'a given') with specialist knowledge in the market and business sector in which they operate so that their advice reflects wider commercial and strategic imperatives in their clients' markets. For others, it may be a matter of changing how the work is done, making more use of technology and standardisation, and having the vision and confidence to lead that change. And many PSFs face a strengthening regulatory and risk environment, so individuals sometimes have to demonstrate skilful judgments and tact to address a client's wishes whilst adhering to their firm's internal risk procedures. Again, these may not be the same skills that helped the individual reach their current position, and addressing those changing demands is often an area where PSFs find coaches most valuable.

On top of these themes is change in the wider world: technology, speed of communication, client expectations and ever-increasing competition. All of these simply compound the changes that professionals in PSFs are experiencing in their own worlds. So the management of change is an overarching theme in PSF coaching, as we will discuss below.

HOW IS COACHING TO BE USED IN THIS CONTEXT?

As outlined previously, the PSF sector is broad, far-reaching and diverse. The precise nature of coaching in the PSF context may vary according to the size of the firm, the importance it attaches to people development, and the level of sophistication of its people development systems. This section therefore addresses the unique quality at the heart of this sector, coaching within the partnership model and coaching partners and aspiring partners. Some recent interventions, predominantly made by larger PSFs, such as coaching for senior female professionals and the development of a coaching culture as a Learning and Development (L&D) strategy, are discussed later in the chapter.

Routes into coaching in PSFs are usually via Human Resources (HR) or L&D functions, although partners may also request coaching directly for people in their teams. Partners and directors may also seek out coaches for themselves.

Typical occasions for coaching in PSFs include the following:

- Key transition points or promotion milestones.
- Development or assessment centres.

- Leadership development.
- Business development training programmes.
- Behavioural development needs.

Irrespective of how a coach is introduced into a PSF, a key factor in their success in this sector will be their professional ability to consult or advise. In other words, the ability to deliver coaching services with skill and credibility, judged by the same standards by which the firm judges its own services. Even the most sophisticated procurers of coaching in the professional services sector require their coaches to use a broad range of advisory and consultancy skills whilst engaging with the organisation, in addition to demonstrating the highest levels of coaching capability. Even exceptional coaches may not find a place within PSFs if they are unable to prove themselves using a skill-set that is a core part of the work of PSFs themselves.

Procurers of coaching in the PSF sector place an emphasis on the business benefits of coaching and robust measurement of such interventions. Regular reporting on the efficacy of learning interventions and the impact on the bottom line is commonplace. As such, PSFs value interventions that can be measured and evaluated. Each PSF may have its own preferred method of evaluation, involving feedback from the coachee, their business sponsor (usually the line manager or an HR manager), and even from the coach. The firm may in addition ask its coaches to provide support and guidance around coaching evaluation methods.

Coaches may also be required to provide feedback to a sponsor from the PSF so the firm can evaluate the status of a particular development topic within the firm from the coaches' external perspective. This raises obvious confidentiality issues, as it would be unethical to disclose to the firm the content of coaching sessions themselves or indeed the progress of individual coachees. As a result, this organisational learning is usually presented in aggregate and anonymised form. This is made possible by ensuring that coaches work with sufficient numbers of coachees that they are positioned to make general observations about development trends across that coachee group. Alternatively, it is possible to arrange for a group of coaches to pool their perspectives to present collective themes to the PSF.

Note of caution

The issue of using information from coaching conversations to inform organisational development priorities is one that is being explored within the coaching industry. There is little doubt that organisational clients can see the advantages of collecting information in this way. However, such arrangements can undermine the coaching process and raise questions about the confidentiality of individual coaching sessions. Such doubts are likely to impact negatively on coaching relationships, so coaches and procurers of coaching should proceed with caution.

COACHING PARTNERS

As discussed earlier, the unique factor that differentiates PSFs from other sectors is the partnership model itself and the distinction between partners and 'non-partners' within the firm. Along with the partner title comes the impact of the individual power and authority that are awarded to 'owners' of the business. As with other leadership roles partnership can be a lonely place, with a more explicit focus on financial performance and building external relationships with clients replacing a more junior professional's sense of belonging to a team. As such, coaches are often engaged to support individual partners as part of their ongoing development. In such situations, the coaching may not be 'issue-led' but more general and wide-ranging, reflecting the complexity of the partner role. Taken together, these factors can call for the coach to take on the role of a close confidante, in which it is important to be able to demonstrate empathetic understanding of the partner and business environment.

The amount of support and role-modelling offered by senior partners may vary from firm to firm, depending on their size and culture, and even across service lines within the same firm. In smaller PSFs, where greater individual autonomy is often granted, individual practising styles may be less homogeneous than in larger, more corporate PSFs. This can present various challenges to a coach, particularly in PSF environments that do not have well-established people development and performance management systems. The coach may find that individual development issues have not been addressed with the coachee prior to the coach's involvement, so the issues may be new to the coachee. And, for some coachees, discussing these topics with a coach may be the first time in their academic and professional life that a coachee is not simply being regarded as 'top of the class'.

Another potential challenge is the attitude of partners coming to coaching for the first time. In an environment where individuals are used to giving advice and knowing the answer, coaching may seem out of tune. The importance of their buy-in to the coaching process and readiness for coaching cannot be underestimated. In this context, the coach's ability to demonstrate quickly professional credibility is essential. Understanding the preconceptions with which partners approach coaching may be helpful. Although all individuals, teams and PSFs are different, themes that may affect attitudes to coaching include:

- high levels of ambition and self expectation;
- a keen results orientation;
- an appreciation of directive learning approaches;
- primacy awarded to the clients, business and profitability;
- time pressures.

Myth:	PSFs view coaching positively and coaching is widely used by PSFs (Ridler & Co., 2013).
Myth buster:	This does not necessarily mean that all coachees, or their colleagues, view coaching positively, or give it the same priority as the client work they really value.

In addition, becoming a partner is no longer the final destination. It is now just the first step in a new partnership hierarchy. Typical partner coaching challenges might therefore include helping coachees establish themselves in their partner role and maintain or grow levels of professional success. In the case of new partner coachees coaches may observe the following priorities, along with other individual competency-based or behavioural development needs:

- The requirement to build their own profitable client portfolio rather than receiving this from others in the firm.
- An increased focus on building teams to service this new portfolio.
- Establishing and maintaining relationships with other partners.
- Time management and prioritisation challenges.
- Maintaining a work-life balance.
- Building resilience to cope with the pressurised and ever-changing environment.

So, what coaching approaches tend to work well with partners? We are reminded by Bachkirova et al. (2007) that overusing certain tools and techniques, or adhering to fixed views of 'right' and 'wrong' in coaching, can prove detrimental to the process. Indeed this may be important advice for those coaching in PSFs. Partners will expect to be treated as unique, so it is crucial that the coach can be flexible and adaptable, meeting the specific needs of the individual, in the moment. Partners' business experience, operating on the expert consultant side of the table, may make them keen judges of the service they receive. Although a coach needs to be adept and flexible in their approach to gaining buy-in, building rapport and establishing professional credibility, partners within the PSF context will generally show their willingness to explore personal and professional development areas with their coach. Indeed, in an environment where partners are used to having to persuade, influence and win others over, highly reflective approaches such as Nancy Kline's (2009) 'Time to Think' coaching approach may work well. In contrast to the challenging dialogue situations normally experienced by partners, needing to persuade a client or win the argument on behalf of a client, these approaches provide a space where partners can use their well-developed thinking skills to explore issues safely, with little direction from a coach.

COACHING BELOW PARTNER

In PSFs, coaches are frequently engaged to support change, notably the transition to partner (see Case Study 8). This can involve a significant change, i.e. from doing and advising to managing and leading. Here, individuals may experience seismic shifts in expectation, bringing about significant challenges in managing this adaptive change. Where individuals may have been valued for their academic and perceived technical ability, this transition can bring immediate requirements for individuals to build relationships with clients, develop other people, and grow their own leadership capabilities. In this situation, individuals will find that emphasis is placed on competencies and skills that their technical training has not prepared them for.

Instead of being judged simply on their own abilities, they are now evaluated more on the overall effectiveness of their teams. Individuals are also likely to start receiving feedback about their personal or leadership qualities, possibly for the first time. This transition is business and client-led; individuals are required to move up through the leverage model to become leaders, becoming the firm's public face and embodying the competitive differentiation that it seeks from its competitors.

Coaches are often engaged to support individuals during this transition. It may be a time that is difficult, emotional and disorientating. For some, it may even be a time to accept the fact that the priorities of the new role are different from the reasons why a coachee chose their career path. Indeed, this transition may mark a move away from the technical work that the coachee enjoyed the most. Individuals may come to coaching at this transition demonstrating either a lack of awareness of, or willingness to adapt to, these new requirements. In certain professional services contexts, this transition may be a significant step up in personal working style, from one where success can be achieved largely through simply responding to internal and client demands, to one where individuals need to make choices about how they can best deliver the firm's priorities.

Coaches can also usefully explore with new and aspiring partners the nature of their motivation to achieve their firm's goals. It is not axiomatic that those goals will be self-con-cordant and aligned with the coachee's motives, and if they are not (and cannot be re-framed to be so) the coachee can find it harder to achieve their goals, and then sustain the effort of doing so over time. Exploring these issues with coachees, helping them understand what kind of appeals and motivations are most effective for them, and their derailers, can be very powerful in helping coachees become more effective.

ISSUE-LED OR REMEDIAL COACHING

Issue-led or remedial coaching in the professional services sector is a complex picture. Many larger PSFs will suggest that they are moving away from remedial coaching (in the sense of coaching those who are perceived to be generally underperforming). These firms prefer to address general underperformance through performance management, preserving the coaching budget for higher performers. Notwithstanding this situation, individuals may be put forward for coaching who, although not under-performing overall, have a particular behavioural development issue, often identified against an objective benchmark such as a competency framework. These may be highly technical or 'niche' individuals, who have high market value or hold key account relationships. Coaches may find that, sometimes due to the highly technical and specialised nature of their role, these individuals lack focus on the people aspects of their role and have limited leadership experi-ence, despite their seniority. These issue-led coaching situations can be challenging with a specialist and highly marketable coachee being invited to make significant behavioural shifts to meet the firm's business objectives. Coaches may also find that in some firms, the sponsor and others in the firm may shy away from delivering the direct and constructive feedback required to establish the context for coaching, for fear of alienating a high-value member of their team.

TALENT DEVELOPMENT

One of the biggest challenges facing the professional services sector is what is sometimes termed the 'war for talent' (Michaels et al., 2001), i.e. the focus on recruiting and retaining the best people in the market, across challenging economic times. PSFs face competition not only from direct competitors but also from other industries (including their own clients) recruiting their staff, and offering wider opportunities, attractive packages and a change in working style. Therefore, a number of PSFs currently include coaching as part of their talent development programmes. Here a coach may be engaged as a motivator or reward for such talented individuals, building in them an interest in their own personal development.

COACHING FOR FEMALE PROFESSIONALS

A number of PSFs, particularly the medium and large firms, have introduced coaching programmes for female professionals. This is typically driven by a desire to increase the number of females reaching senior leadership positions or to decrease rates of female attrition. Whilst most PSFs recruit broadly equal numbers of male and female graduates, the number of females reaching partner level is far reduced when compared with that of their male counterparts. *The Public Accounting Report 2010* studied the 'Big Four' accounting-based firms and found that, despite an average of 47.3% of employees being female, women accounted for only 18.1% of all equity partners. Similarly it was reported in 2013 that, averaged out across virtually all the UK's largest 20 solicitors' firms, only 18.6% of partners were female (*The Lawyer*, 2013).

Coaches may be engaged to assist female professionals seeking to build their own leadership style in a context where the predominant leadership approach may be quite masculine in nature. Some larger PSFs have also introduced coaching for women around maternity leave, the transition point at which attrition rates are typically elevated. PSFs will often engage external coaches who specialise in transition coaching for women to provide support before, during and after maternity leave. Much of this coaching may be focused on a work–life balance or building the flexibility required for women to reconcile the demands of work with the needs of their family. In an environment where long hours are common, travel is frequent and client demands are unpredictable, achieving this balance can be extremely challenging. The coaching may also include a specific focus on the changes and challenges women will experience as they become mothers.

COACHING SUPPORT FOR TEAMS

Another recent introduction, particularly in larger PSFs, is 'team coaching' where coaches work with existing internal teams that need to work together more effectively.

Here, coaches use a facilitative style to support learning in 'real work' contexts, such as a client meeting. Although termed 'team coaching', this is more akin to action learning.

Coaches may be also be engaged with teams to facilitate learning to support change and the development of objectives, align goals and build leadership capability. PSFs have found that team interventions provide a forum in which to explore dynamics and raise awareness of the diversity of working styles. This, in turn, serves to build understanding and trust, sometimes even mediating ongoing conflicts within teams. PSFs have found that such interventions can benefit cross-functional teams, bringing them together and assisting them to present a coherent picture to new and existing clients.

DEVELOPING COACHING CULTURES

With the aim of developing people as their biggest asset, many PSFs have taken coaching beyond one-to-one relationships towards a more business-wide method of improving organisational performance (Hawkins, 2008). A number of PSFs have a stated aim of creating a 'coaching culture' in their businesses, where coaching techniques are core skills for working with others (see Chapter 16: Towards a Coaching Culture, for a further discussion).

Many PSFs, sometimes in the stated pursuit of a coaching culture, have introduced or developed internal, professionally trained coaches. These internal coaches may carry out that role full-time or they may be HR professionals allocating a percentage of their time to coaching. Many PSFs require these in-house coaches to be trained to a comparable professional level as their external counterparts, and the Ridler Report (2013) suggests that this is at least to the professional coaching certificate level.

PSFs describe the key benefits of internal coaches as their deep knowledge of and connection with the business and the internal political environment, as well as their availability at the point of need. The business case for developing in-house coaches may also be financially driven, reducing the dependency on external coaches, particularly for more junior coachees. However, a general trend across PSFs is for internal coaches to be used below partner level, and they are rarely used to coach the most senior partners. This may be due to the challenges of confidentiality, or a perception that external coaches have greater expertise and experience, or provide greater objectivity and an ability to provide effective challenge. Where PSFs have internal coaches, external coaches may also be responsible for their training and development or ongoing supervision.

APPLYING COACHING SKILLS MORE WIDELY

For many PSFs, a key step in the journey towards a coaching culture is developing coaching skills across the organisation. So, for example, managers are encouraged to build a toolkit of coaching skills and approaches for use with their internal teams. However, PSFs have found that developing such skills carries the additional benefit of enhancing relationships with clients. The cornerstone skills of active listening, questioning, paraphrasing, summarising, and giving (and receiving) feedback (van Nieuwerburgh, 2014) may be valuable in building a deeper understanding of a firm's clients, and their needs, likes and dislikes. That, in turn, can assist the PSF's experts to communicate more effectively, with both their current and prospective clients. PSFs have also found that building coaching skills across the business offers further commercial opportunities. For example, where the predominant culture advocates listening and a curiosity about others, people are more likely to cross-sell the work of others, thereby expanding the range of services offered to clients.

Finally, PSFs have found that developing a coaching culture has been a good way to bring balance to the predominant organisational culture. PSF culture has traditionally been relentlessly client-, business- and revenue-focused, and this enhancement to organisational culture serves to steer some attention back towards the businesses' key asset, i.e. its people.

CONCLUSION

It is difficult to generalise about the state of coaching in professional services firms and the overall benefits derived from coaching so far. The themes discussed in this chapter – changing markets and increasing professional pressures, individuals progressing and expanding their skill-sets beyond the analytical and technical, building leadership, strategic and relationship-based skills – certainly lend themselves to a coaching approach. Anecdotal market-based evidence, as well as publicly available data such as the Ridler Report (2013), suggest that coaching is widely used in larger PSFs. The benefits of coaching are also motivating the larger firms to seek to embed coaching more deeply in their businesses. So, as this chapter has discussed, PSFs are building internal coaching capabilities and exploring the wider use of traditional coaching skills (particularly active listening) in helping their staff to develop team leadership skills and build stronger client relationships.

There is less evidence that coaching is as widely used in the small- and medium-sized PSFs. This may of course simply be a question of the evidence being hard to find. Certainly the themes that drive coaching needs in the larger firms apply to small- and medium-sized PSFs. Indeed, in some respects the need for coaching may be greater in smaller firms where the impact of individual behaviours may be more powerful than in larger practices with well-established brands. But other factors – most obviously cost pressures and looser management structures with less well-developed people development systems – could explain why coaching has been less widely taken up by these firms.

It will be interesting to see whether, in the future, these small- and medium-sized firms are prompted to use coaching more widely. That would provide opportunities, not only for coaches with strong track records and experience of working with larger PSFs already, but also perhaps for those who are newer to this sector and have the right mix of qualities to succeed.

Practical suggestions for those working in this sector

Ensure goals and expectations are clear and shared

Expect to spend time in three-way meetings, agreeing the coaching objectives, ensuring they are clear, with a shared understanding and buy-in from the coachee and other stakeholders. In larger PSFs the coaching may start with an experienced coaching/HR lead briefing the coach. In smaller PSFs, with less experience of coaching, the coach may find the coaching brief is less clearly articulated and requires more effort at the outset to define it properly. In PSFs of all sizes the various parties involved can approach coaching issues with very different perspectives. These differences may simply be around the terminology of 'coaching', or they may be more significant, revealing divergent views about the issues and a coachee's needs. When combined with the unclear line management structures sometimes found in PSFs, these factors make it vital for a coach to clarify the goals at the outset.

The coachee and their environment

Does the coachee have an understanding of coaching and what it requires of them? Levels of knowledge may vary across PSFs. How does the coachee view this coaching? As a badge of honour indicating star quality, or an embarrassing indication of weakness? How do the coachee's colleagues see this coaching? All these issues can affect a coachee's attitude to the coaching conversations and their willingness and ability to implement any development actions.

Persuasion and proof

A core PSF skill is articulating and packaging advice, to persuade and convince clients. So coachees in PSFs, often subconsciously, will expect their coach to have these skills, and be able to convince them of the issue. This may be particularly important where there is resistance to a coaching issue, perhaps because it is uncomfortable or new to the coachee. In such circumstances 360-degree feedback can be persuasive evidence. Psychometric tools can also be helpful (Passmore, 2012) and can be more engaging to the analytical thinkers that are common in PSFs.

Make it relevant and resonant

Coaches should help coachees (especially skeptical ones) to frame the coaching topics in terms that are relevant to their daily work life. For almost all PSF coachees this means being more successful with clients, a key measure of personal success and credibility. Another driver is becoming a more effective manager and team leader. The aims of being better with clients and with colleagues are not only powerful motivators, they often relate closely to the original coaching need.

Decision making can be slow

Coaching decisions in PSFs can be connected with a range of HR processes and are often only taken after discussions with a range of senior people. Coaches may need to be patient in these phases, recognising that the delays are unlikely to carry across into the coaching relationship.

Visit the companion website, https://study.sagepub.com/coachingcontexts, to read the case studies that accompany this chapter:

- Case Study 7: Preferred supplier list assessment and selection process
  Caroline Flin

- Case Study 8: Transition to partner programme
  Lucy Mair

REFERENCES

Bachkirova, T., Cox, E. and Clutterbuck, D. (eds) (2007) *The Complete Handbook of Coaching*. London: Sage.

Clutterbuck, D. and Megginson, D. (2005) 'How to create a coaching culture', *People Management*, *11*(8): 44–5.

Empson, L. (2010) *What Are Professional Service Firms and Why Do We Study Them?* Available at www.cassknowledge.com/research/article/what-are-professional-service-firms-and-why-do-we-study-them?page=0,0 (last accessed on 15 July 2014).

Goldsmith, M. (2008) *What Got You Here Won't Get You There: How Successful People Become Even More Successful*. New York: Hyperion.

Grant, A.M. (2006) 'An integrative goal focused approach to executive coaching'. In D.R. Stober and A.M. Grant (eds), *Evidence Based Coaching Handbook: Putting Best Practices to Work for Your Clients*. London: Wiley.

Hawkins, P. (2008) 'The coaching profession: Some of the key challenges', *Coaching: An International Journal of Theory, Research and Practice*, 1: 28–38.

Hawkins, P. and Smith, N. (2006) *Coaching, Mentoring and Organisational Consultancy: Supervision and Development*. Maidenhead: Open University Press.

Kline, N. (2009) *More Time To Think: A Way of Being in the World*. Poole-in-Wharfedale: Fisher King.

The Lawyer (2013) 'Diversity efforts fail to pay off at top end of profession'. Available at www.thelawyer.com/analysis/the-lawyer-management/management-news/diversity-efforts-fail-to-pay-off-at-top-end-of-profession/3008182.article (last accessed 15 July 2014).

Michaels, E., Handfield-Jones, H. and Axelrod, H. (2001) *'The War for Talent'*. Watertown, MA: Harvard Business Review Press.

Passmore, J. (ed.) (2012) *Psychometrics in Coaching: Using Psychological and Psychometric Tools for Development* (2nd edn). London: Kogan Page.

Public Accounting Report (15 June 2010) *'Women Continue to Advance into Leadership at Largest Firms'*.

Ridler & Co. (2013) *Ridler Report 2013: Trends in the Use of Executive Coaching*. London: Ridler & Co.

van Nieuwerburgh, C. (2014) *An Introduction to Coaching Skills: A Practical Guide*. London: Sage.

von Nordenflycht, A. (2010) 'What is a professional service firm? Toward a theory and taxonomy of knowledge-intensive firms', *Academy of Management Review*, 35(1): 155–74.

7

COACHING IN LOCAL GOVERNMENT

COLIN WILLIAMS AND SAMANTHA DARBY

INTRODUCTION

Improvement, efficiency and value for money were already in focus for local government in England well before the shock waves of the 2008 financial crisis. However, it is widely accepted that councils faced deeper budgetary cuts earlier and harder than the rest of the public sector as the coalition government began to implement its deficit reduction policy following the 2010 election. Yet unlike elsewhere in the economy, there are no signs of any 'green shoots' of recovery. In its preliminary modelling of 2013 (*Funding Outlook for Councils*), the Local Government Association (LGA) concluded that if the anticipated existing pattern of cuts to the public spending is replicated, councils will not be able to deliver the existing service offer by the end of the decade. Furthermore, the way local services are funded and citizen expectations of what councils will provide will need to fundamentally change.

Despite optimistic income and demand forecasts, the LGA modelling identified a likely funding gap of £16.5 billion a year by 2019/20, or a 29% shortfall between revenue and spending pressures. On the assumption that demand in social care and waste are fully funded, statistical projections over the next decade suggest that other services face funding reductions of over 90%, commonly referred to within the sector as the 'graph of doom'. Local government is recognised as one of the most efficient parts of the public sector, but the next round of challenges for those responsible for managing services to communities demands a fundamental rethink as regards the structures of local public services as a whole.

This chapter seeks to explore the changing leadership dynamics required across the sector as demanded by these political, economic and societal factors and identify how coaching has featured as a key element of the response. Whilst the emergence of coaching as a development tool to supplement more traditional leadership development was not an alien concept to the sector at the turn of the century, its increasing deployment predated the financial downturn. Evidence is clear of a rapid growth of the use of coaching across the sector and there are numerous examples of collaborative and cost effective approaches that have seen a marked and substantial shift over the last decade. Perhaps the most interesting characteristic of this growth has been a significant reliance upon self-sufficiency, with the sector largely looking to respond from within and invest in growing its own coaching capacity, rather than deploying external coaches. One may speculate that this may have been driven with costs and external scrutiny in mind, but as is set out throughout this chapter, the evidence suggests that it has released what was a latent capacity to become a valuable internal resource.

In the above context, the current breed of local government managers are being challenged to engage differently with the communities they serve, explore how services can be commissioned more effectively, innovating and thinking more commercially in respect of service delivery, whilst breaking through the traditional 'walls' to deliver greater collaboration across the wider public sector in order to address the complex issues facing citizens and communities. These are new leadership challenges for those working in the sector at a time when investment in their own leadership capacity is subject to the same financial constraint, in addition to sharp public scrutiny over every pound spent. The effective local government manager must have high levels of emotional intelligence, understand their localities, possess the ability to influence and inspire across organisational boundaries, and shape responses from diverse, often competitive and contradictory partners and stakeholders.

THE COACHING CONTEXT

The local government manager of the present must be resilient, self-confident, collaborative, motivational, adaptable to shifting objectives and able to manage a complex range of individual and organisational relationships. As with the private sector, the pursuit of organisational goals remains the central aim and the nature of the demands placed on managers are fundamentally no different. The word 'business' is consciously and increasingly integrated into the language of local government. At the same time, the growth in mixed economy provision of public services challenges the importance of a discrete public sector ethos. However, whilst there are evidently differences between the environments in which managers are operating, the reality is that both are complex, whether managing down costs to grow business and deliver profit, or controlling limited expenditure to protect essential public services and create vibrant economies. Both are about managing resources and relationships to achieve defined goals.

Natalie Holt (2014) offered an external perspective on coaching public sector leaders from her role as a managing consultant at Capita Health and Wellbeing. Holt identifies that in the current economic backdrop the value of coaching has never been more relevant as a means of releasing an individual's full potential and that as the nature of public sector leadership has changed the way those leaders are coached has also had to adapt. She contends that established leadership qualities such as charisma, confidence, impact and decision making, supported by traditional goal-setting models, are no longer sufficient. She highlights resilience, self-belief, emotional regulation and ingenuity as essential when taking unpopular decisions under media and public scrutiny, and questions whether coaches have the psychological perspective required to understand how to develop resilience. To this she adds the prominence of distributed leadership, where consensus or agreement amongst multi-partner settings demands new levels of influencing skills, and that the effective coach will need to nuance their support accordingly.

Holt also argues that the fluidity of circumstances facing senior public sector leaders means they must operate in an 'on demand world where leaders require on demand coaching'. The extent to which this resonates from practical experience of coaching within the local government sector has yet to be clearly evaluated. Three-way contracting (where the organisation is represented to confirm the goals for coaching alongside the client and coachee) remains a common feature in order to ensure a necessary discipline and focus around coaching objectives. The ability to respond to 'on demand' coaching risks losing or changing the focus of the aims agreed at the commencement, and from a practical perspective is much more difficult to resource, especially in a face-to-face setting. Increasing the levels of responsiveness also risks an unintentional shift into mentoring, the borders to which already represent a grey area where this has been introduced as an extension to existing collaborative coaching initiatives.

In a 2010 article in *HR Magazine*, Chris Gulliver, former Director of the European Mentoring and Coaching Council (EMCC), explored some key perceived differences between private and public sector coaching practice. Drawing on the findings of a report from the Institute of Business Consulting (IBC) together with the EMCC, Gulliver questioned whether public sector coaching was falling behind the private sector where increasingly robust processes to monitor outcomes were being developed. The IBC/EMCC study asked participants about the nature and extent of sponsors' involvement at all stages of the cycle and offered feedback from coaches, who routinely saw public sector sponsors as more 'light touch', relying on selection procedures to establish quality assurance and accountability. In contrast, there was evidence of more robust contracting and close sponsor involvement as the 'cornerstones of ROI' in the private sector. The study reported that private sector sponsors strongly express the need for coaches to:

1. Demonstrate their understanding of a sponsor's business sector or organisation, commercial awareness and consulting skills.
2. Understand the brief within the corporate context, clearly stating what would be delivered and how.

It could be argued that there are differences between how private and public sector ROI is identified and quantified, including the extent to which specific and measurable outcomes can reasonably be defined and expressly linked to a positive coaching intervention. Gulliver concluded that public sector coaching is often seen as an asset to support broadly defined change, with the consequential focus being upon individual performance improvement as a contribution to wider corporate goals.

Focusing upon the 'supply fit', the IBC/EMCC survey identified however that terms such as 'affinity' and 'culture fit' were becoming prerequisites for hiring, with evidence of experience and achievement in a business environment becoming mandatory in some private sector organisations. Furthermore, Gulliver reported the experience of professional coaches who were reporting the business-led demand for 'quick wins' rather than a more strategic and longer-term perspective for personal and career development.

Noting the emergence of pooled, reciprocal internal coaching across the public sector and the emergence of employer-led and sponsored coach development, Gulliver identified that 'external' coaches are still preferred at the most senior levels, partly for reasons of confidentiality and partly to bring in the greatest expertise. He also identified that, in both sectors, kudos represents a factor for the most senior of executives. Whilst the evidence of the IBC/EMCC survey may have suggested a divergence of approach, such would appear to represent an overly simplistic analysis. There will surely be differential levels of engagement and an array of objectives set across the personal and organisational spectrum. However, taking account of these variables, experience of coaching in local government would suggest that developing the capacity of the individual is likely to have a greater focus, reflecting an inherent belief in the wider benefits of performance improvement, whilst also acknowledging that the complexities of public sector leadership, as set out earlier, necessitates a shared rather than an individual accountability for the outcomes.

DEPLOYING COACHING IN LOCAL GOVERNMENT

One characteristic of local government is its transparency as a community of practitioners with a willingness to share emerging and best practice. Supported via an injection of central government resources, delivered through 'pump priming' investment in improvement and efficiency during the middle of the last decade, there has been significant growth in collaborative coaching partnerships across local government. The sector has also seen initiatives focusing upon collaborative approaches to Chief Executive coaching and has now developed targeted initiatives upon discrete functional occupational groups (e.g. those working in children's services). Furthermore, there is substantial evidence of the opportunity for coaching becoming integrated within managerial and leadership development programmes. These trends and associated increasing demand raise questions about the resourcing of coaches and the impact upon the quality of the coaching experience.

The 2013 Ridler survey is distinctive in comparison with other coaching surveys because it focuses exclusively on executive coaching (as used in commercial organisations) and articulates the practices and views of users of executive coaching rather than coaches themselves. Accordingly, it provides a useful benchmark for the public sector and local government in particular. The 2013 survey drew evidence from work by the EMCC, and in his Foreword to the report Professor David Megginson notes:

> 'Another big trend is towards the use of internal rather than external coaches. Internal coaching is seen to be growing by 79% of respondents ... with one of the reasons being that internal coaches understand the business better than external coaches. However, the corresponding challenge is that they can be so embedded in their own corporate culture that they cannot help their clients take an objective perspective on it.'

In light of the local government approach centred around mutually beneficial collaborative pool arrangements, it is interesting to note the responses to one item in the Ridler survey, i.e. 'What sponsors value in coaches'. The summary report identifies 'personal chemistry' as the highest rated characteristic, with 'credibility and gravitas' being rated as 'persuasive or very persuasive' by 99% of respondents and traditional listening skills and sincerity following closely (97% and 88% respectively). However, the value attached to organisational and sectoral credibility is increasing, with the 'interest in or appreciation of the sponsor's organisation' at 88% and knowledge of the same at 74%. This suggests that the awareness and understanding of the local government sector available within shared pool arrangements are a definite advantage, and perhaps as important as the levels of professional and personal credibility. Reflecting a trend in local government, the perceived status of coaches (i.e. their professional reputation and proven track record in the sector) was reported as an issue for the most senior clients, although the culture which has developed in local government over the last decade is beginning to challenge that prejudice, with Chief Executives recognising the fundamental and confidential nature of the coaching relationship as equally if not more important.

Amongst its survey data, the Ridler report further explored the question of value for money. The report demonstrated a growth in the number of respondents who identified internal coaching as representing better value for money than external coaching (44%), yet more organisations agreed that internal coaches were more difficult to organise and manage, resulting in the description of such as a 'complex but worthwhile endeavour'. Of the 145 respondents many were multinational and global enterprises, and the definition of what represents an 'internal' coach is therefore anticipated to be broad and therefore may be considered comparable to a multi-public sector partnership arrangement.

Aligned to the current thinking dominant in local government, executive coaching was more highly rated as a form of senior leadership development than business school programmes, with the exception of stimulating new thinking. It was acknowledged as more individualised and likely to result in sustainable behavioural change, with the conclusion that leadership development initiatives supported and followed with coaching interventions are likely to have a maximum combined impact. This reinforces the predominant local government view that coaching interventions are about growing the capacity of the individual and hence the capacity of the sector, rather than supporting the securing of a specific objective to which a financial or competitive advantage can be directly related.

There were a number of early adopters within local government who realised the value of coaching and the opportunity to utilise a collaborative approach. At the forefront was the Kent Coaching and Mentoring Network, established in 2004, which extended its reach from an initial partnership of Kent County Council and the Kent Fire & Rescue Service (KFRS), through to the Police Service, a local NHS Trust and neighbouring councils. A decade later the network remains vibrant, with over 200 members drawn from a wider range of organisations including probation and prison services, charities and higher education institutions. In addition to reciprocal access to a pool of qualified coaches and mentors, the network offers group and peer supervision, an online matching service, and bi-annual conferences focused on continuous learning and development for accredited coaches and promoting a coaching culture. Coral Ingleton, the Learning and Development Manager who led the initiative on behalf of the County Council, emphasised that such networks offered an economical approach to coaching for organisations under pressure to cut costs:

'The main benefit of the network is that a culture of coaching is being implemented in a range of organisations, which can access the services of qualified coaches and mentors at no cost.'

Paul Flaherty, Head of Learning and Organisational Development at KFRS, defined the Coaching Network as 'an integral part of our strategy as it uses managers from outside of the organisation to give a completely fresh and objective perspective on our issues'.

Within the County Council, the coaching network primarily supported the authority's performance management process. Established managers used coaching sessions to reflect on their performance, while younger staff, who are each assigned coaches from the pool, are guided though their progress within the organisation. Radical organisational change was the main motivation for the coaching at KFRS. As a uniformed service, it acknowledged an established command-and-control culture which suited operational demands but was less effective for day-to-day management.

CROSS-SECTOR COACHING

In 2009/10, Suffolk County Council led the development of a cross-sector coaching partnership with the aim of saving money and boosting the perceived value of coaching. The Suffolk Coaching and Mentoring Partnership developed a pool of coaches to be used on a reciprocal basis by private and public sector organisations, seeking to overcome negative views of in-house coaching and raise expectations of the capacity of coaching to boost performance. Reaching beyond the local government family, the partnership engaged a range of local employers, including the Ipswich Building Society, local brewers Adnams, the Havebury Housing Association and the University of Suffolk. Stressing the value of working across a more diverse partnership, Nicola Harrington, Strategic HR Manager for the County Council project, identified the wider benefits of a cross-organisation and cross-sector approach:

'By engaging in cross-organisational coaching, new relationships and networks have already developed which are built around a shared purpose. Going forward, everyone should benefit from the knowledge, insight and experience gained from working across organisational boundaries.'

COACHING SUPPORT FOR TEAMS

The concept of 'team coaching' is now developing traction within local government. For example, North West Employers have positioned team coaching at the heart of their 'Transforming Teams' offer, identifying the intervention as focusing upon:

- clarifying what success looks like for the team and organisation;
- challenging assumptions about what can and cannot be done;
- creating stretching and challenging team and individual goals and the accountability for meeting them;
- developing greater mutual trust, enthusiasm, resilience and engagement;
- having better quality conversations – including those that you may have been avoiding.

The intervention is described as 'More than an away day – you've probably done those already and whilst they may have a lot of short-term benefits they haven't had a sustainable impact on behaviour change and performance'.

This initiative reflects the findings of the Ridler survey referred to earlier, in which respondents anticipated up to 64% growth in the use of team coaching over the next three years, most significantly at teams headed by 'senior managers'. This was seen as complementary to one-to-one coaching, with 'strategy development' and 'behavioural dynamics' representing the initiating factors and the approach being more likely to support high performance teams going through change than to address those that may be dysfunctional.

Note of caution

However, as a word of caution, in the foreword to the 2013 Ridler survey, Megginson comments:

'For sceptics like me, who are not even convinced that such a process differs significantly from action learning, team building or other established interventions, the sharp question raised by the report is "do you want to get on board or will you risk missing the bus?"'

He also questions whether there is yet a common understanding and definition of team coaching, what makes an effective team coach, and what, if any, were the different supervision requirements? Perhaps most significantly, he identifies the 'complex dynamics of managing multiple one-to-one personal relationships, with attendant baggage of prejudices and perceptions embedded through past interaction alongside competing objectives, priorities and styles'.

WHAT CAN WE LEARN?

In 'Creating a coaching culture' (2004), Eldridge and Dembkowski set out ten key success factors which can be used as key success factors for organisations seeking to establish a coaching culture (see Chapter 16: Towards a Coaching Culture, for a further discussion). In broad terms, the local government sector has been working towards the creation of coaching cultures, with, for example, the Welsh Local Government Association (WLGA), producing a 'Coaching Framework for Local Authorities in Wales' (2011). This set out some of the common factors for success identified by authorities with whom the WLGA had worked, offering support on what might be required in the implementation of a successful coaching strategy and programmes, incorporating the following key points:

1. Know why you are introducing coaching or coaching approaches and be able to communicate this to stakeholders.
2. Use coaching to deliver the organisational and people development strategies.
3. Make coaching part of the culture.
4. Secure understanding and a commitment to coaching.
5. Ensure quality control in coaching.
6. Establish the processes for organising coaching.
7. Monitor and promote outcomes.

CONCLUSION

This chapter opened with a summary of the scale of the challenges facing the local government sector which is the perfect storm of increasing demand and reductions in funding. Yet within this challenging context, coaching has flourished across the sector and is now extending across wider public sector boundaries. At a time when resources (human and financial) are scarce, one could argue that the level of investment in coaching is testament to its cost effectiveness and impact.

Skeptics may argue that it is a poor substitute for the provision of high quality development programmes, but the sector would respond that the investment profile and delivery mechanisms for such are also changing with much evidence of coaching becoming integrated as a matter of course. There are also those who would argue that the growth of coaching represents a trend rather than a considered strategic response. This may represent a degree of truth in the stimulating of some of the partnership arrangements that emerged across the country. However, where there is no genuine long-term commitment, weak foundations quickly become exposed. As set out in this chapter, there are many examples where the foundations have proved to be much stronger and are now ready for extension into new coaching dimensions. Others may argue that coaching is often used as an alternative to good management, or as a means of outsourcing dealing with difficult people and relationships. However, positioning three-way contracting at the heart of the process challenges this and deploying quality coaches exposes that inappropriate motivation.

Finally, some might question the extent and effectiveness of evaluation, arguing that employers make a leap of faith as regards coaching delivering outcomes and sustainable improvement for both people and their organisation. This criticism is an area where, in local government, more can be done to get beyond the constraints of measuring impact through self-assessment and sponsor or advocate perceptions, in order to develop longer-term measures upon career trajectories and tangible outcomes for the organisation and its service users. Nevertheless, despite that challenge, the local government perspective on the value of coaching remains widely positive. As an illustration, Jan Britton, Chief Executive of Sandwell MBC, is clear about its value (Britton, 2014).

'We are facing the most challenging of times in local government. Expectations to deliver more with less are commonplace now so I endorse a coaching culture. I feel it is one of the primary tools at a manager's disposal to maximise their employees' potential and improve performance both on an individual and team level.'

Practical suggestions for those working in this sector

- Make sure you promote what is available at an early stage: be prepared to use a variety of different methods to get the message across, and keep promoting.
- Make it easy for staff to access clear information about coaching, with clear and simple access to the service, including where possible 'online matching'.
- Have a clear, robust and consistent coach recruitment process to ensure the right people receive the training and have the capacity to coach once qualified.
- Embed three-way contracting as a discipline to ensure an effective balance between personal development and organisational impact.
- Provide clear exit strategies where the coach/client relationship does not work for either party.
- Invest in structured coach supervision and continuous professional development.

Visit the companion website, https://study.sagepub.com/coachingcontexts, to read the case study that accompanies this chapter:

- Case Study 9: West Midlands Coaching and Mentoring Pool
  Samantha Darby and Colin Williams

REFERENCES

Atkinson-Madhoo, S. (2012) *Coaching Client Survey*. Birmingham: West Midlands Employers.
Boersma, M. (2013) '"We want coaching", say high fliers', *The Financial Times*, 10 October.
Britton, J. (2014) Personal communication.
Carter, A. et al. (2010) *Evaluations of West Midlands Regional Pool*. Brighton: Institute for Employment Studies.

Churchard, C. (2010) 'Suffolk County Council sets up cross-sector coaching pool'. Chartered institute of Personnel and Development. Available at www.cipd.co.uk/pm/peoplemanagement/b/weblog/archive/2013/01/29/suffolk-county-council-sets-up-cross-sector-coaching-pool-2010-07.aspx

Darby, S. (2013) *Perceptions of Coaching*. Birmingham: West Midlands Employers.

Darby, S. (2014) *Coaching – Good for You and Your Organisation*. Birmingham: West Midlands Employers.

Eldridge, F. and Dembkowski, S. (2004) 'Creating a coaching culture', *Coach to Coach*, 4.

Gulliver, C. (2010) 'Public and private-sector opinion diverges on the right conditions for cost-effective coaching', *HR Magazine*. Available at www.hrmagazine.co.uk/hro/opinion/1018704/public-private-sector-opinion-diverges-conditions-cost-effective-coaching#sthash.yUJcK-dUG.dpuf

Holt, N. (2014) 'Coaching public sector leaders', *Coaching at Work*, 9(3): 47.

Local Government Association (2013) 'Funding outlook for councils from 2010/11 to 2019/20'. Available at   www.local.gov.uk/finance/-journal_content/56/10180/4057616/ARTICLE

North, S. (2009) 'Root and branch', *Coaching at Work*, 4(3): 44.

Pickford, K. (2014) *Transforming Teams: North West Employers*. Available at www.nwemployers.org.uk/learning-and-sharing-skills/developing-and-sharing-skills/personal-and-team-support/team-coaching.html

Ridler (2013) *Ridler Report: Trends in the Use of Executive Coaching*. London: Ridler & Co.

Welsh Local Government Association (2011) *Coaching in Local Authorities in Wales*. Cardiff: Welsh LGA.

8

COACHING IN HEALTHCARE SETTINGS
VIVIEN WALTON AND JULIA SINCLAIR

INTRODUCTION

The healthcare settings in which our coaching clients work can vary, not just in terms of size and location, but also in terms of responsibility, so it is helpful to have some understanding of the structure of the NHS (which provides over 90% of the healthcare in the UK) and how private healthcare providers operate within it.

As a publicly funded national body, the structure of the NHS is determined by the government of the day. The different political parties have prompted changes in structure and influenced whether private healthcare will be provided at no cost to patients. The Health and Social Care Act (2012) changed the structure of NHS commissioning and encouraged more provision from private organisations. Since April 2013 the NHS has been divided into commissioners, led in the main by GPs formed into Clinical Commissioning Groups (CCGs) and providers, which come in the form of hospitals (NHS Trusts and some private hospitals and clinics), healthcare in the community (Community Trusts and private providers) and general practices (GPs).

The changes ushered in by the Health and Social Care Act (2012) led to thousands of redundancies, mainly managers and executives, and the calls for career coaching increased significantly. The changes also brought a significant number of clinicians into leadership, commissioning and management roles, calling for skills training and leadership coaching.

This was followed in 2013 by the publication of the Francis Report. Sir Robert Francis, QC, led a public enquiry into failings at Mid-Staffordshire NHS Foundation Trust that resulted in poor care and an unknown number of unexplained deaths. The report contained harrowing detail of the culture and behaviours in the Trust, multiple failures of 'the system' to identify the failings and 290 recommendations for changes, most of which were accepted by the government.

Healthcare professionals typically embark on their career because they want to help people and were horrified at the findings. That was followed by soul searching: could it happen in my organisation? Research published by the Nuffield Trust in 2014 showed that Trusts had taken much of the report on board, paying greater attention to concerns about quality and safety and to numbers and the management of nurses.

COACHING IN HEALTHCARE SETTINGS

This chapter considers the environment in which healthcare professionals operate and how that impacts on coaching relationships. The use of coaching to support career coaching, personal effectiveness, leadership and resilience will be discussed. In particular, we will consider some significant contextual factors that are influencing those who work in health organisations including:

- dealing with patients;
- multi-professional settings;
- increases in demand and in technological innovation;
- the impact of change;
- how coaching is commissioned.

Dealing with patients

The 'customers' for people who work in healthcare settings are often vulnerable or stressed and sometimes afraid. An integral part of doctors' training is the management of the impact of that on their work and wellbeing. Employees without a professional qualification, such as managers and clerical staff, do not have the benefit of such training. The effects are not only found in direct relationships with patients, but also transfer into team relationships and sometimes into coaching sessions as well. A coach may find that it takes some time during the establishment of rapport for the client to express some of the tension, frustration or anxiety before they can start to establish a meaningful coaching relationship.

Multi-professional settings

Tom Kitwood (1999) suggests that 'caring, at its best, springs from the spontaneous actions of people who are very resourceful and aware, able to trust each other and work easily as a team'. He further highlights the 'close parallel' between the way employees are treated and the way in which their clients are treated.

Since the NHS was founded, it has moved from a rigidly hierarchical system, with doctors leading a team of junior doctors who tended to be deferential, and who in turn expected all other clinical professionals to do as they prescribed, to working in multi-disciplinary teams (MDTs) where all clinical professional opinions are valued. The MDT puts the patient at the centre of its discussion and different professional opinions can be resolved by that focus.

However, NHS Trusts are run by Boards of Directors that generally only include one doctor and one nurse. Other directors may have clinical backgrounds, but are more likely not to, and the non-executives come from a variety of backgrounds in other sectors. Tensions can surface between managers and the main body of clinicians when managers are portrayed as having a greater focus on financial issues than patient care.

Increases in demand and in technological innovation

Boards of Directors of NHS Trusts can be seen to have less influence over the amount of money that their organisations have to spend than a Board does in a commercial organisation. The government prescribes a large proportion of the health budget to CCGs and they use that to commission services from the NHS and various private providers. Under the pressure of an ageing population, the impact of modern lifestyle changes, the effects of obesity and long-term conditions, the demands on limited resources are high (NHS England, 2013). Technological improvements that enable the treatment of previously untreatable conditions only exacerbate the difficult financial situation. In addition, the state of the wider economy means that increases in resources have not been forthcoming. This has led to a more stressful working environment for many healthcare professionals.

The impact of change

Research by Sinclair et al. (2008) demonstrated that many people were under significant pressure as a result of changes taking place in the NHS during 2007. Some clients were feeling distressed and demoralised and finding it difficult to cope with the changes. Some of the coaching input, such as preparing for new roles, was directly related to organisational reconfigurations. There were further far-reaching changes during the healthcare reforms of 2012, largely affecting managers, GPs and administrators. While all organisations experience ongoing change, it can be argued that the extent of the change in this public service was out of the control of the local managers and professionals, and the impact of that has been considerably increased levels of stress in the workforce. Research commissioned by the Health, Safety and Well-being Partnership Group suggested that stress may account for over 30% of sickness in the NHS, costing the NHS £300–£400 million per year (NHS Employers, 2013).

How coaching is commissioned

NHS employers have commissioned coaching to support executives and managers in the NHS since the 1990s. Research by Sinclair et al. (2008) found that coaching seemed to be particularly valuable at times of change and suggested that coaching should be available to assist with managing change or transition in the NHS. Clinicians may have coaching at times of personal or organisational transition, but that is less common. However, some organisations see coaching as a 'soft option' that can be ill-afforded at times of financial constraint. The Institute of Employment Studies undertook an evaluation of coaching in the NHS which found that it was delivering benefits to the NHS. It also identified the opportunity for greater benefits if more people could have access to coaching, particularly through internal coaches (Sinclair et al., 2008). In 2010–2011, the NHS National Leadership funded a programme of executive coaching skills training for senior leaders that has created a bank of 'internal' coaches for each region of the NHS. Whilst 'internal' to the NHS, these coaches were available to employees with whom they do not have daily contact through their work. The intention was to emulate the benefits of employing external coaches.

CURRENT PRACTICE

Career coaching

With over 350 different careers in the NHS (www.nhscareers.nhs.uk), there are many opportunities to work within the medical sector. This can make it very difficult to choose a particular pathway. However, careers in this field fall into three broad categories:

- Direct contact with patients in hospitals working as part of a team. Roles would include doctors, nurses, pharmacists, scientists, dentists, therapists and other allied healthcare roles.
- Community-based roles often working on a one-to-one basis with patients. This may include working in clinics, GP surgeries or patients' own homes.
- Non-clinical roles which help to support the infrastructure of the NHS. Roles may include administrative personnel, human resources, IT and facilities staff.

Science-based careers

Many individuals choosing a medical-based career express a passion and an aptitude for the sciences. Those applying for a medical or dentistry degree face tough competition for university entry, and only those who achieve the highest grades in their science-based A-levels and pass an interview will be accepted onto most UK university courses. This can be helpful knowledge for those coaches who work in career guidance at schools as they can support students to identify whether an individual's academic achievements are sufficient to pursue highly competitive selection processes. However, only around 50% of the NHS workforce possesses a professional qualification, so there is much scope and variation in educational requirements for a number of roles in the wider healthcare system.

A CAREER-PLANNING PROCESS

One of the most complex of the medical careers is that of doctor, as it includes approximately 60 specialist areas, therefore requiring that decisions about specialty must be made quite early on in a person's career. Viney et al. (2012) identified that choosing a specialty, getting onto a specialist register and career hurdles such as examinations and interviews could be a significant challenge for trainees, whilst more experienced doctors spoke of being at career crossroads. Many established doctors reported feeling disillusioned with the lack of autonomy, unprecedented monitoring and the financial pressures placed on them, resulting in their having to cope with limited resources within an overburdened NHS system. Some older doctors have viewed early retirement as a more favourable 'way out' of the profession. Reid (2012) identified that the challenges which arose from understanding the medical career pathway were important for coaches who worked with doctors as these developed and changed over time. However, her research with doctors showed that they valued an outsider's help as opposed to a mentor in the field as they were able to remain non-judgmental in the development of an individual's career.

Through her research with doctors and coaches, Reid proposed a four-stage career planning process:

1. Self-assessment

This process of 'understanding oneself' is widely used by coaches as a starting point for helping coachees to identify their values, skills, interests, work environment and personality types. These can be assessed through questionnaires and psychometric testing (for further discussion about the use of psychometrics, see Passmore, 2012). This insight and increase in self-awareness should form the discussion for an early session in preparation for the next stage of career exploration.

2. Career exploration

This stage should explore the nature of the work, the team environment, the training required, and any wider NHS issues affecting a particular healthcare sector (eg. some hospital-based services becoming more community focused). A coach should help to explore the numerous ways in which an individual can seek information which may include online searches, contacting the medical colleges, medical careers fairs, or observing an experienced professional in their particular environment.

3. Decision making

Three influential decision-making theories should be considered at this stage. Firstly, Holland's (1959) trait and factor matching approach may suit the logical, analytical mind-set of many medical professionals. Secondly, Reid (2012) identified that doctors may find career decisions difficult because of the pressure from wider social influences, therefore identifying how relationships have impacted on a client's career choices may be helpful (Schultheiss, 2003). Thirdly, a post-rational approach may be of benefit for mid-career changers in supporting them to build a new professional identity (Schein, 1978). A number of practical tools can support these decision-making theories. For example, coaches could employ a life-line exercise, support coachees to draft a 'pros and cons' list or decision-balance weighting, sketch a decision matrix (based on the top three choices) or lead some visualisation exercises of a future self in different roles (see the box below).

Lifeline exercise

Take a large sheet of paper and draw a horizontal line across the middle. Mark the significant events in your life, both good and bad, by drawing your curve above (positive experience) or below the line (negative experience). Identify a couple of decisions that worked out well and not so well, and think about how you approached each of these (e.g. getting advice from others close to you, applying a structured, rational approach, or going with your gut feeling). Try to correlate this analysis of decision making to give you insight into how you could approach future career choices.

Pros and cons list

Make a table with two columns: pros and cons. Write down as many effects and implications of your top few specialty choices. Add a weighting to each (1 for minor significance and 5 for major significance). Compare the total score between the columns for your results. This process can support or challenge your initial thoughts.

Decision matrix

Insert up to three specialties you are considering. In the left-hand column list the five most important factors (e.g. a good work–life balance). Create a column entitled 'importance' and rate how important the factors are on a scale of 1–5. Then create another column entitled 'probability' and rate the likelihood of each option on a scale of 1–5. Multiply the importance number by the probability number and enter the result in a sub-total box. Add the sub-totals for each option and write the totals in the spaces at the bottom. Compare the totals. This activity is outlined on the following website: www.medicalcareers.nhs.uk

---

> ### Visualisation
>
> Ask the client to consider a world where anything is possible. They should imagine arriving at work and walking through the doors (i.e. entering a specific department). Ask them to think about how they feel in this environment, what they are wearing, how people look around them, and what those people are doing. They should also imagine the tasks they would do and how they feel while completing these tasks.

Implementation

During the final stage, a coach would support an individual with their job search strategies, including writing application forms, CVs and preparing for the interview process. Person Specifications should be used to tailor a response to suit the requirements of the job. The coach can support the coachee by roleplaying a member of the interview panel.

SKILLS COACHING

The structure of the NHS has traditionally 'funnelled' staff into professional hierarchies and their training has tended to focus on developing their professional expertise rather than their people management or leadership skills. In recent years, there has been a move towards clinical leadership. The career structure of nurses and professionals allied to medicine means that they take on aspects of management as they progress through their careers, but doctors become consultants at the end of their clinical training having had little exposure to the demands of management. Organisations may call upon coaching, either with a specified internal coach or an external coach, to help a client develop their management skills.

Coaching for doctors whose clinical skills need to be addressed is generally provided through the academic route (the regional Deanery) or the performance route (mentoring by a clinical professional). Some typical coaching requirements for the development of professionals' non-clinical skills are outlined below.

Interpersonal or communication skills

Typically this will arise from the tensions between those with different backgrounds whether these be professional or ethical, perceived or real differences in the 'power' relationship, and from the tensions that arise from day-to-day pressures.

Performance management or managing conflict

Dealing with the 'difficult' issues that arise when supervising or managing others can be one of the most challenging aspects of work for anyone, in any context, but particularly for those who have worked independently throughout their career as many clinical professionals do. Working with a coach can help them take a structured approach, to balance their often natural empathy for those they manage with the needs of the organisation and to 'rehearse' particular discussions.

Personally coping with change

Change is continuous in healthcare settings, but in the NHS it can often feel out of an individual's control. The requirement for a period of consultation prolongs the uncertainty and the coach can help the individual to build their resilience, understand the 'phases of change' and work through them.

Time management and chairing meeting or facilitating groups

These skills are better developed using a mentoring approach. However, coaching conversations can highlight the need for particular areas for development. The coaching might be commissioned by the individual or by the organisation as part of that person's personal development plan, or to address specific performance issues. It is important to have a clear three-way contract between the client, the commissioner and the coach so that all parties are comfortable with the topic and the reporting requirements of the commissioner (Tulpa, 2006). In terms of development, NHS East Midlands reported that 'where sponsors were involved in the tri-partite contracting process this was highly valued and often provided additional insights, confirming the benefits of internal sponsorship'. All parties need to be aware that the coach will provide a framework within which the coachee works to develop their own skills and motivation.

Leadership coaching

Recognising the importance of both formal and informal leaders to a high performing organisation, this section focuses on those who are in leadership positions. It is when coaching leaders in NHS organisations that coaches may be most aware of the context in which they are working. Leaders lead their teams and their organisations in their own style and can work with other local stakeholders to set strategy and priorities, but will do so within a national framework in order to achieve national targets. This may call for skills in managing 'upwards', particularly in the 'home countries' of Wales, Scotland and Northern Ireland where there are two levels of politicians to consider. Although some leaders may have been prepared for their roles by a range of leadership courses available to current and future leaders in the NHS and larger private healthcare organisations, some will find themselves in that position through promotion or reorganisation.

Some GPs also found themselves unprepared for the roles that they took on in April 2013 when a change of policy gave them the opportunity to determine the shape of local services through CCGs whose governing bodies are made up largely of GPs. Although in many ways the challenges that some GPs found in their transition into leadership roles typify those seen by many moving into such positions, the situation was made more challenging because of the lack of role models. Some of the issues that they faced are set out below.

Forming a new organisation with new leadership

GPs had traditionally worked independently and so those who were interested in taking the opportunity to lead had to form themselves into formal bodies that would work well together. A key individual at this stage in the development of the governing body was the chair who was typically a GP, often with a full list of patients. Some chairs used coaching to help them think through what being a good leader would mean for them personally, to consider the agenda in terms of building the organisation, leading the development of strategy and forming positive networks with local bodies and individuals to help shape the future services for the local population.

NHS England provided guidance about the expectations of governing body roles. Coaching enabled a better understanding of individuals' strengths and preferences in terms of communication and decision making. It supported them to develop the vision, values and underpinning behaviours upon which the organisation would be formed. An understanding of individual preferences would help members of the governing body to make good decisions together, challenging each other without causing offence.

Shaping the services for the future

Arguably, GPs found themselves for the first time not only able to influence the shape of services for the future, but also expected to do so. Coaching has helped leaders think through their strategic aims and then reconcile their ambitious objectives to address the health needs of their local community within stringent financial constraints.

Stakeholder engagement

The extent of interest in local health issues was underestimated by some CCGs. Formal and informal interest groups included the community, patients and their carers, other NHS bodies, local authorities and other public sector organisations, charities, advocates to local businesses, Members of Parliament and the media. Coaching is able to give CCG chairs the time, space and challenge to 'map' the various interests and think through how to work with the different stakeholders to further the strategic aims of the organisation, before taking the discussion to the full governing body.

When working with leaders it is helpful to have a range of techniques to hand. Some clients may wish to explore a specific model of leadership (for a detailed account of the use of leadership models in coaching conversations, see Passmore, 2010). Fundamentally, many leaders want to be challenged robustly in a coaching situation, so that their ideas and strategies are thoroughly tested in a 'safe' environment and they have confidence to articulate these to the people they lead. This does not mean that the coach has to necessarily have a detailed understanding of the leader's context or to have been a leader themselves, although this may enhance their professional credibility.

Resilience through organisational change

Coaching is seen as a means of supporting individuals through change, particularly when that might impact on their future employment. The complexity of the NHS and the requirement for periods of formal consultation regarding changes mean that individuals (and organisations) can live with uncertainty for long periods of time. For example, the recent changes were agreed publically by the coalition government upon its election in 2010, followed by the publication of a White Paper, *Equity and Excellence: Liberating the NHS*, in July that year, and of the Health and Social Care Bill in January 2011. This was followed by a 'pause' for a 'Listening Exercise' in July 2011 before the publication of the Health and Social Care Act in March 2012. The changes finally came into effect from April 2013. Throughout that time, some staff had the opportunity to receive coaching to bolster their resilience and consider their individual futures. An example of how one team of coaches supported people through change is given in Case Study 11.

Lack of confidence in an unfamiliar forum

Coaching to increase confidence and resilience often comes at a time of change for an individual in terms of a career move or a personal crisis of confidence. Examples of this are a consultant taking up their first appointment and finding their feet in multi-disciplinary team meetings; a clinician moving into a management role at a senior level when taking up their first post as a Board Director; healthcare staff having to influence outside their immediate environments, possibly in a public forum; or more specific difficulties such as presenting to large audiences.

Dealing with criticism of professional competence

Healthcare settings are challenging environments in which to work, for all the reasons set out earlier in the chapter. The challenges of the 'day job' include a lack of confidence when amongst peers, whether in formal settings such as multi-disciplinary meetings, management meetings or Board meetings, or concerning the self-doubt and criticism of professional competence. The frequent restructuring of the NHS adds an extra source of stress for those in senior management posts. The British press tend to focus on shortcomings in the NHS, which some find demoralising. Most people who embark on clinical training do so for altruistic reasons, with empathy and caring high on their list of personality traits (Wicks et al., 2011). Having one's professional competence challenged may be uncomfortable even to a seasoned professional.

Coaches will recognise that the best tools and techniques to use for coaching for resilience will be determined by the individual client, and their personality and preferences, rather than the environment in which they work. The basic coaching skills of listening, asking questions, paraphrasing, summarising and giving feedback (van Nieuwerburgh, 2014) are all important. Sometimes developing self-awareness and helping clients to understand their preferred way of looking at things can be a good starting point. Psychometric instruments such as the Myers Briggs Type Indicator (MBTI), the Hogan Assessments, the Emotions and Behaviour at Work (EBW) questionnaire or the Mental Toughness Questionnaire (MTQ48) (for more information on these, see Passmore, 2012) can highlight particular areas to work on, and give some insight into how a client responds to stressors, pressure and challenges.

CONCLUSION

Research has shown that coaching in healthcare settings brings benefits both for managers and medics (Sinclair et al., 2008). Many individuals feel under constant pressure from working in a health service that is ever changing and evolving (NHS Employers, 2013). Therefore having the skills to cope with this difficulty becomes essential in such an environment.

As we have discussed, coaching can be used to help shape the future of a medical career, increase resilience, improve leadership and management skills and increase personal effectiveness. The benefits to the individual may include increased enthusiasm and motivation, improved self-awareness and direction, better team management and increased confidence (North West Academy, 2012). Ultimately, a more committed and productive employee will benefit the organisation in achieving its goals from improved patient outcomes, meeting targets and creating efficiencies through improved management.

The days of a coaching service only offered to those most senior executives or for remedial purposes are behind us. As the coaching industry gains increasing recognition, many

Trusts are now setting up their own in-house coaching and mentoring services offering accredited training in coaching skills for NHS staff. Whilst the NHS also maintains an external register of qualified coaches, these are selected via a rigorous process and expected to be highly experienced. Finally, although we have discussed the complexity and challenges of coaching in the healthcare sector, it can be highly rewarding to be working with individuals who want to make a difference to society by delivering the best possible service and patient care.

Practical suggestions for those working in this sector

- The NHS and the professional bodies (including the Royal Colleges that supervise doctors' training), and the relationships between them, are complex. Do as much research as you can before meeting a client for the first time to maximise credibility. Websites such as the Department of Health website, NHS Choices and NHS Careers listed at the end of the chapter are useful resources.
- We hope that this chapter has given you the flavour of the political and media focus on the NHS. It is important not only to keep up to date, but also to keep an open mind.
- The NHS is awash with acronyms. Ask clients to explain any that impede your understanding of their situation.
- Many healthcare staff are used to being 'on call' all the time. It is important to manage this sensitively as it may not be possible for the coachee to switch off their mobile phone or pager.
- Emphasise the confidentiality and objectivity that your external perspective brings to the coaching relationship. This is often appreciated.

Visit the companion website, https://study.sagepub.com/coachingcontexts, to read the case studies that accompany this chapter:

- Case Study 10: Career coaching for a doctor
  Julia Sinclair

- Case Study 11: Coaching assistant directors within the NHS
  Vivien Walton

- Case Study 12: Coaching general practitioners
  Jane Cryer

REFERENCES

Allen, P. (2008) 'Coaching and the future', *'In View': NHS Institute for Innovation and Improvement.*

Brock Associates (1986, revised 1992) Phases of change based on and adapted from C. Scott and D. Jeffe (1989), *Managing Organizational Change and Managing Personal Change.* Los Altos, CA: Crisp Publications.

Champion, C. (2011) 'Coaching for success in the East Midlands', *HSJ.* Available at www.hsj.co.uk (last accessed 15 May 2014).

Dayan, M., Smith, J., Thorlby, R. and Williams, S. (2014) *The Francis Report: One Year On.* London: The Nuffield Trust.

Douglas, J., Komaromy, C. and Robb, M. (2007) *Diversity and Difference in Communication in Analysing Aspects of Communication.* Milton Keynes: Open University Press.

Francis, R. (2013) *Report of the Mid-Staffordshire NHS Foundation Trust Public Inquiry.* London: HMSO.

Holland, J. (1959) 'A theory of vocational choice', *Journal of Counseling Psychology,* 6: 35–45.

Keogh, B. (2013) *Review into the Quality of Care and Treatment Provided by 14 Hospital Trusts in England: Overview Report.* Redditch: NHS England.

Kitwood, T. (1999) *Dementia Reconsidered: The Person Comes First* (4th edn). Buckingham: Open University Press.

Kitwood, T. (2004) 'The caring organisation'. In M. Robb, S. Barrett, C. Komaromy, and A. Rogers (eds), *Communication, Relationships and Care: A Reader.* London: Routledge.

National Advisory Group on the Safety of Patients in England (2013) *A Promise to Learn – A Commitment to Act: Improving the safety of patients in England.* London: HMSO.

National Health Action Party www.nhap.org (last accessed 31 August 2014).

NHS Employers HSWPG (2013) *Health and Wellbeing in Healthcare Settings Research* Available at www.nhsemployers.org (last accessed 22 August 2014).

NHS England (2013) *The NHS Belongs to the People: A Call to Action.* Available at www.england.nhs.uk/2013/07/11/call-to-action (last accessed 22 August 2014).

North West Academy (2012) 'Benefits of coaching'. Available at www.nwacademy.nhs.uk (last accessed 23 May 2015).

Passmore, J. (ed.) (2010) *Leadership Coaching.* London: Kogan Page.

Passmore, J. (ed.) (2012) *Psychometrics in Coaching* (2nd edn). London: Kogan Page.

Reid, J. (2012) 'Medical careers and coaching: An exploratory study', *International Journal of Evidence Based Coaching and Mentoring* (Special Issue No.6): 146–65.

Schein, E.H. (1978) *Career Dynamics, Matching Individual and Organizational Needs.* Reading, MA: Addison-Wesley.

Schultheiss, D.E.P. (2003) 'A relational approach to career counselling: Theoretical integration and practical application', *Journal of Counseling and Development,* 81: 301–10.

Sinclair, A., Fairhurst, P., Carter, A. and Miller, L. (2008) 'Evaluation of coaching in the NHS'. Brighton: Institute for Employment Studies.

Tulpa, K. (2006) 'Coaching within organizations'. In J. Passmore (ed.), *Excellence in Coaching*. London: Kogan Page. pp. 26–43.

van Nieuwerburgh, C. (2014) *An Introduction to Coaching Skills: A Practical Guide*. London: Sage.

Viney, R., Sensky, T. and Paice, E. (2012) 'Why do doctors want a mentor? A study of applications to a UK mentoring service', *International Journal of Coaching and Mentoring*, *10* (2): 40–55.

Whitmore, J. (2002) *Coaching for Performance* (3rd edn). London: Nicholas Brealey.

Wicks, L., Noor, S. and Rajaratnam, V. (2011) 'Altruism and medicine', *BMJ Careers*. Available at www.careers.bmj.com

USEFUL WEBSITES

www.gov.uk/government/organisations/department-of-health
www.dhsspsni.gov.uk/index/hs
www.england.nhs.uk
NHS Choices: www.nhs.uk
www.nhsemployers.org
www.nhsgraduates.co.uk
www.hsj.co.uk
www.medicalcareers.nhs.uk
www.nhscareers.nhs.uk
www.leadershipacademy.co.uk
www.support4doctors.org
www.scotland.gov.uk
www.wales.gov.uk

9

COACHING PATIENTS

RACHEL HAWLEY

INTRODUCTION

This chapter will encourage readers to reflect on their own experiences of health and healthcare and engage in a critical dialogue with the dominant discourses of coaching theory and practice. The idea of 'making every conversation count' (Hawley, 2012) is a philosophy that underpins this chapter. We are committed to the view that through open and creative dialogue, coaching patients can open new opportunities for achieving improved health and wellbeing.

The conversation between patient and clinician is one of the fundamental building blocks of the National Health Service (NHS) in the UK. But these interactions are too often characterised by an imbalance of power, control and information. Fischer and Ereaut (2012) argue that if we want a different health system we need a different kind of relationship. Thus new approaches are required for engaging with patients to address the complex challenges associated with improving health outcomes: improving patient experience, engagement in decision making and reducing care costs. A raft of policy in the UK has increasingly painted a picture of inclusivity over the last decade. More equal partnerships between professionals, patients and the public are now considered crucial to improving public services, together with a growing evidence base that helps us to aspire towards the principle of 'co-production' (Boyle et al., 2009, 2010; Wallace et al., 2012).

However, although the involvement of patients and the public has gained appeal as a way of enhancing the quality and efficiency of healthcare services, the overall responsiveness of the systems and defining what is needed remain a challenge (Coulter, 2012a, 2012b; Fischer and Ereaut, 2011; Pederson et al., 2013). A more sophisticated understanding of the nature of 'relationship' is needed. Research shows that the relationship between health professional and patient is affected by the context in which conversations take place (Bates, 2014). In a collection of essays on perspectives of context, Bates (2014) creates a compelling case that 'context is everything'. How we think about the concepts of 'patients' and 'coaching' will each determine how we might apply coaching principles in practice.

Coaching patients offers the potential to address the complexities and ambiguities of contemporary engagement, leadership and healthcare practice in a number of ways. This can have an effect on the single conversations that support patient recovery, self-management of long-term conditions, lifestyle and behaviour change to improve public health and wellbeing and support wider public engagement in shaping our future health services. We want to explore the concept of coaching patients by beginning with the notion that 'we are *all* patients'. Whether past, present or future, we all share experience of using healthcare services. Throughout this chapter we embark on a metaphorical journey of exploration to consider the process of coaching patients through a lens of co-production. This is a shared endeavour. We all have a role to play.

Definition of key terms

Co-production: The principle of co-production is increasingly being applied to the delivery of health services in the UK. There is no single definition. In the context of health, 'co-production' is a term that refers to a way of working when decision makers (staff, patients and carers) work together to create a decision about care, quality and service improvements. The term 'co-production' represents a set of values and principles that have emerged over a period of time with elements of engagement, participation, choice and control, and involvement (Department of Health, 2010). Working together in this way is built on the principle that those who are affected by a service are best placed to help design it. Therefore co-production is a way of working and thinking.

Patients: Many terms are used to describe someone who uses health or social care services: patients, service users, carers, consumers and citizens. We are all either actual or potential users of health services. At some time, health will impact on our future. Whether we experience an acute illness or chronic condition, we are all patients.

WHAT IS UNIQUE ABOUT COACHING IN THIS CONTEXT?

The terms 'coaching' and 'patients' are viewed as complex and multi-faceted phenomena. Each is bound with the interactions between language and meaning, experience and context. Research shows that what often gets in the way of people taking a more active role in their own healthcare are the beliefs that each party holds about themselves, and each other, and how these beliefs become reflected in behaviour, whether as a patient, clinician, educator or leader

(Fischer and Ereaut, 2012). It is necessary to stand back and consider which philosophies, theoretical and practical models are most helpful for exploring and addressing these issues.

This section shows how coaching patients offers a unique alternative to current dominant approaches to healthcare by reframing the patient relationship within a coaching context. We would encourage you to reflect on the following question: 'Is this about a single coaching conversation, a system, or a process?' With this in mind, Fischer and Ereaut (2012) point to the importance of thinking about individual patient and clinician conversations as part of a much larger conversation, i.e. that between patients and the system as a whole. Coaching patients is an innovative approach that supports patients to become more active participants in their own health. Coaching conversations start from where a patient is.

Meaning and language: The challenge of definition

The NHS possesses myriad words to describe varieties of care, coaching and learning, 'just as Eskimos describe snow' (Rosinski, 2003). Most of us do not master that language and therefore are unable to master the subtleties of issues around coaching patients. Terms are used interchangeably, sometimes with little, or no agreement. For example, consider the terms 'health coaching', 'wellness coaching', 'self-management coaching', 'motivational interviewing', or simply 'conversation'. These can be both confused and confusing. One widely cited definition states that coaching patients is an approach for 'helping people gain the knowledge, skills, tools and confidence to become active participants in their own care so that they can reach their self-identified health goals' (Bennett et al., 2010.) An alternative definition shows the importance of context. The following definition, for example, shifts the emphasis away from 'illness' to 'wellness'. Wellness coaching 'facilitates a partnership and change process that enables clients to change their mind-sets, and develop and sustain behaviours proven to improve health and wellbeing, going beyond what they have been able to do alone, moving from where they are to where they want to be' (Moore, 2013). Beyond this, Garvey (2004) shows that focusing on a definition and all things rational in relation to coaching and mentoring is to misunderstand the nature and reduce it to a simple management technique, which commits us to the mistakes of the past.

Experience and context: Creating a paradigm shift

The need to reconceptualise the relationship between patient and clinician or any member of staff in a healthcare setting is key. The landscape of the NHS is changing. No longer is it adequate to rely on hierarchical models of healthcare and leadership. The increasing pace of change and complexity in health and healthcare requires a shift for clinical and non-clinical leaders from 'expert' to 'enabler'.

Coaching patients changes the nature of the relationship between patients and staff. Coaching is congruent with the paradigm shift that has evolved in the context of health. We are moving away from traditional approaches of 'doing to' patients towards more collaborative approaches of 'doing with' patients. The increasing call for collaboration across health and social care resonates with the core principles of coaching. To harness the potential for coaching patients we are drawn to the idea that healthcare leadership and its development can, and must, be shared if we are to achieve sustainable health and social care systems. This requires a fundamental shift away from traditional dominant approaches, towards open and collaborative systems that can engage staff, learners, patients and the wider public in health and social care practice and learning. There is a raft of literature in which authors advocate a particular approach to healthcare leadership as if there were only one 'right' way of doing it: transformational, transactional, collaborative, shared, consultative, distributed and collective. Note that these terms are often used interchangeably. The language, together with traditional hierarchies and assumptions, often get in the way of creating a shared understanding of how co-produced services might look and how these might be led. The weight of meaning on the words 'coaching' and 'leadership' chimes. It highlights the many views, perceptions and pressures that sit on a single word. It is the description of the experience that seems more important than the language we use to define it.

An emerging philosophy: Making every conversation count

Simply put, coaching patients can happen anywhere. By anywhere, we mean that the core principles of coaching can be used in any interaction between patients and staff. We begin from the premise that every contact, however brief, is an opportunity to harness the principles of coaching in healthcare practice. 'Making every conversation count' (Hawley, 2012) then is the philosophy that underpins how coaching can, and could, be used in this context. The model of coaching described is necessarily emergent and pragmatic. Referencing both behavioural and cognitive science, it is essentially a constructionist approach. We believe that as coaches we should each adopt a pragmatic approach to our work with patients. Traditional thinking regarding coaching in a health context has led organisations to favour systematic approaches over systemic; qualifications over lived experience; formal approaches over informal. Coaching patients tips the traditional hierarchies of patient care on their head.

HOW CAN COACHING BE USED IN THIS CONTEXT?

In this section, we explore coaching for patients across a range of diverse boundaries to show a model for coaching patients that forms a conversational architecture. Illustrative examples are used to illuminate the nature of coaching conversations between patients and staff. Beyond this we explore the potential for patient conversations with the wider healthcare system.

Coaching patients is not new. The roots of health coaching can be found with psychologists treating persons addicted to alcohol (Ossman, 2004). In the USA 'health and wellness' coaching is used increasingly with patients, where it is delivered by a range of providers who offer coaching to private individuals and as part of health programmes and systems to increase patient and client engagement and the uptake of interventions, improve wellness, and reduce risk (Moore, 2013). In the UK, earlier research findings (Hawley, 2012) and many conversations with staff, patients and coaches show a number of core features that determine the ways in which coaching patients can be used.

Current situation

- Much coaching research fails to look at the whole workforce or take a wider citizen view.
- Health policy and the structures that support education and learning in the NHS have tended to concentrate on linear approaches, thereby making discussion about learning for patients and staff problematic in practice.
- Individual and organisational benefits of coaching are evident but evaluations tend to focus on a more formal and schematic design.
- Although a systematic approach is the most widely adopted approach in the NHS, organisations that want to embed a coaching and mentoring culture perhaps need to employ a more systemic approach.

Perspectives of coaching patients in context

It is clear that coaching patients sits on a spectrum that spans formal and informal approaches (see Figure 9.1). Whether we consciously choose to encourage informal coaching or not, it is likely that this exists in some form within most public sector organisations. However, informal coaching often goes unrecognised and thus risks being an underutilised resource. Much is written about informal versus formal coaching schemes and suggests that perhaps 'rather than thinking we should choose either informal structures or formal structures, we should consider that they may be complementary and related to the level of development within an organization' (Foster-Turner, 2006: 97). Reflecting on the continuum that spans formal and informal coaching seems to carry an assumption that people enter into these kind relationships with a degree of awareness and understanding of these constructs. This is particularly significant for the wider workforce in healthcare who traditionally have fewer opportunities to engage in formal coaching or learning. For example, staff in support roles such as porters and healthcare assistants do not always recognise the nature of this kind of enabling conversation, raising issues around the drive to 'professionalise' the coaching profession together with the need to value 'lived experience', showing the necessity of having to 'nurture those skills rather than worrying so much about the label that's ascribed to them' (Hawley, 2012).

The consultation

Research indicates that half of patients leave primary care visits not understanding what the doctor has told them (Bodenheimer, 2007). Indeed, only 9% of patients have been found to participate in decisions despite shared decision making being associated with improved outcomes (Braddock et al., 1999). Average adherence rates for prescribed medications stand at around 50% and average adherence rates for lifestyle changes are below 10% (Haynes et al., 2002). In the face of these discouraging statistics, primary care must take on a new task: working with patients to ensure that they understand, agree with, and participate in the management of their chronic conditions. According to Bennett et al. (2010) health coaching is one way to accomplish this function.

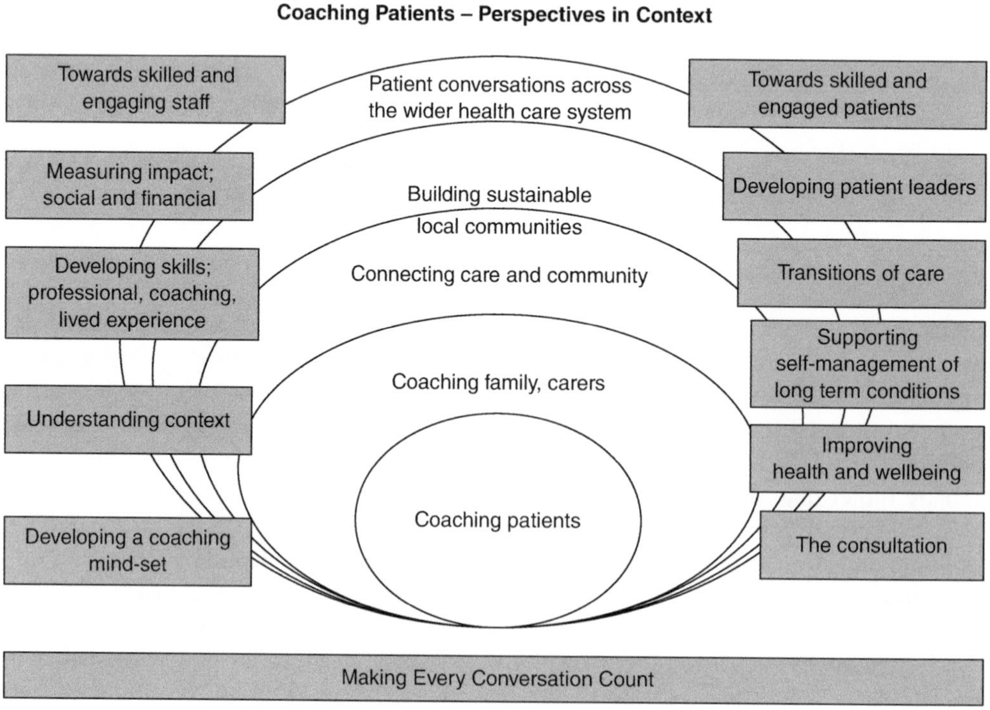

Coaching Patients – Perspectives in Context

- Towards skilled and engaging staff
- Patient conversations across the wider health care system
- Towards skilled and engaged patients
- Measuring impact; social and financial
- Building sustainable local communities
- Developing patient leaders
- Developing skills; professional, coaching, lived experience
- Connecting care and community
- Transitions of care
- Understanding context
- Coaching family, carers
- Supporting self-management of long term conditions
- Improving health and wellbeing
- Developing a coaching mind-set
- Coaching patients
- The consultation
- Making Every Conversation Count

Figure 9.1

Improving public health and wellbeing

As choice and control are passed to local communities, there is a shift away from intrusive, directive approaches. Supporting individuals to change their behaviour as described in MINDSPACE (Dolan et al., 2010), and influencing behaviour through public policy, are both key drivers and challenges for the wider public health workforce. In this shift towards more personalised care and planning, clinicians and patients need to work together using collaborative processes of shared decision making to agree goals, identify support needs, develop and implement action plans, and monitor progress. At the heart of the House of Care Model (Coulter et al., 2013) recently adopted by the NHS is a collaborative process designed to bring together the perspectives and expertise of both the individual and the professionals involved in providing care, offering tailored personal support to develop the capability, competence and confidence needed for effective self-management. This model has great congruence with coaching approaches. Implementing the model requires healthcare professionals to set aside traditional ways of thinking, where they see themselves as the primary decision makers.

Supporting the self-management of long-term conditions

Long-term conditions remain a global challenge. It is predicted that three quarters of all deaths in England by 2020 will be from chronic disease. The number of people with three or more long-term conditions is also predicted to rise from 1.9 million in 2008 to 2.9 million in 2018, and there will be growing demand for the prevention and management of multi-morbidity rather than of single diseases. The UK Department of Health compendium of information on long-term conditions (Department of Health, 2012) suggests that people with such conditions account for 50% of all GP appointments, 70% of all inpatient bed days and 70% of overall NHS spend, highlighting the need to respond to this challenge.

From principles to practice: My Health, My Way

My Health, My Way Dorset is a non-clinical self-management support service provided by My Health Dorset. It shows the potential of creating value through coaching patients by working across traditional boundaries. This approach to coaching patients ('self-management coaching') is supported by a collaborative of organisations that include Help & Care (a local third sector group), the three local acute NHS Trusts, the community and mental health NHS Trust, a chain of chemists, Know Your Own Health and BH Live.

(See www.myhealthdorset.org.uk)

Connecting communities

Perhaps one of the reasons that our current health services struggle to respond is because they have largely overlooked the underlying operating system that high quality patient care and experience depend on, i.e. the social economy of family and neighbourhood. It is no longer advisable to rely on continuing economic growth to finance our public services, or on pseudo-market mechanisms to make sure they are efficient. We have seen that the financial system is unreliable, that markets cannot tackle inequalities, and that unchecked growth puts the planet at risk (Boyle and Harris, 2009). If we are to avoid a massive decline in our services, we need new ideas to reshape these to harness potential for organisations and the communities that they serve. There is growing interest in the idea of developing coaching for social inclusion that uses 'expert' public knowledge and experience to enhance the quality of health and wellbeing.

From principles to practice: Connecting Communities

The Connecting Communities programme, founded by Hazel Stutley, illustrates the wider potential for coaching patients to reach and connect with families and communities. To quote a resident leader, 'We thought we were doing up houses but we were doing up lives'. The starting point for this dramatic change was the firm belief by local health workers that residents 'were the solution and not the problem'.

(See www.healthcomplexity.net)

Developing patient leaders

It is as important to invest in patient, community, citizen and frontline leaders through coaching approaches. Too often, in the context of health, an emphasis is placed on the development of new processes rather than on people. We are not struggling for want of aspirations or solutions. Rather, what we have lacked is a model to sustain people as they engage with the challenges of reform in diverse local contexts. The health sector is in an era of fragmented engagement and without the right kind of leadership this fragmentation will only increase. The design of healthcare services and education must be one of partnership between patients, communities and providers, each with a role to play. However, citizens and professionals do not engage unless and until they have a *reason* (clear purpose) and the *confidence* (self-learned and peer supported) to change, together. The ability to learn quickly, and in transition, without an over-programmed established framework, is increasingly important. Coaching patients is an essential ingredient to help them find their voice, and thus harness the potential for staff, learners and the public to influence future services through everyday conversations.

| Myth: | Patients need to be coached by clinical staff. |
| Myth buster: | Coaching patients needs to involve everyone (e.g. patients as peer coaches, clinicians, leaders and managers, educators, support staff etc.). |

Coaching patients for conversations with the wider health care system

Although there is a plethora of literature on the involvement of patients and the wider public in healthcare practice and learning, the research evidence is patchy and often contradictory. Traditionally, attention has largely been paid to the 'process' rather than 'relationships' (Pederson et al., 2013). This highlights the need for a stronger underlying theory of how a range of interventions for supporting patients (such as coaching) impacts on relationships, and as a consequence healthcare outcomes. There is no shortage of examples of staff working to develop new initiatives to support involvement in health and social care. However, these examples hardly scratch the surface of the organisational and cultural change that is needed if the NHS is to become truly patient-centered (Coulter, 2012a). In the wider context of coaching patients, 'involvement' refers to the appropriate and active participation of staff, learners and the public as equal partners in decision making. Thus it is important that we consider the role of coaching as part of a larger conversation between patients and the healthcare system as a whole to achieve high quality and sustainable health services.

A conversational architecture: Making every conversation count

Just as coaching in the context of healthcare is not new, there are many types of engagement in health. It is important to develop clarity for coaching patients according to the context and nature of the organisation. Done well, the very process of engagement enables people (patients, staff and learners) to share their stories, experiences and perceptions about how coaching patients is and could be used. Mintzberg et al.'s book *Strategy Safari* (2008) reminds us of the importance of ensuring that multiple perspectives are interwoven into healthcare. The real point is that no individual perspective is wrong. We need to stand back and see the whole. It is the synthesis of views that brings the best results in the context of health. That is what we can get from coaching patients: staff and patients working together in a more equal partnership. In the context of coaching patients, it is not simply a certain set of skills (competences) but rather a set of attributes, which emerge from character, commitment, personal integrity and authenticity.

Table 9.1 Key coaching competences

	Key coaching competencies
Core Coaching Skills	e.g. listening, questioning, challenging, support, giving and receiving feedback
Human Qualities	e.g. self-awareness, commitment, authenticity, trust, integrity, 'way of being'
Behaviour Change Techniques	e.g. motivational interviewing, cognitive behaviour therapy (CBT), adult learning theories
Professional Skills and Competence	e.g. nursing, medicine, allied health professions (e.g. physiotherapists, pharmacists, dieticians, radiographers and chiropodists, to name just a few, as well as wider public services including for example fire, police, prison services etc.)

A closer look at the literature reveals key clusters of competences (knowledge, skills and behaviours) relevant to coaching patients (EMCC, 2009; Garrett-Harris and Garvey, 2005; van Nieuwerburgh, 2014) (see also Table 9.1).

Coaching patients requires engagement by the entire workforce, building capacity, capability and confidence for all staff and patients to have effective conversations. To harness the potential for coaching in the NHS is to move beyond the range of skills and capabilities to acknowledge the significance of the contextual nature of coaching patients, valuing the lived experience as much as the qualification. Coaching patients begins with a developing a readiness for engaging in these kinds of conversations in formal and informal settings. In this way we can move towards making every conversation count, from individual conversations between patients and staff, to patient conversations across the wider system (see Table 9.2).

Table 9.2 A process for introducing coaching

Level	Process
Level 1 Readiness	Readiness for engaging in these kinds of conversations
Level 2 Getting Started	All staff (clinical and non-clinical) are able to recognise opportunities for making every conversation count by using basic coaching skills in every interaction with patients
Level 3 Getting Going	Staff are able to select and use a range of professional, behavioural change and coaching techniques (e.g. GROW) to provide support to individual patients
Level 4 Making Every Conversation Count	Staff are able to harness the potential for coaching patients from the individual conversations to the wider conversations across the health system as a whole

Impact of coaching patients

Success for coaching patients depends on sharing best practice and comparing processes and outcomes across traditional boundaries. Listening to people's stories shows that the key human characteristics which they describe in relation to coaching are not 'predominantly technical skills of an esoteric sort that have to be acquired from new' (Garvey and Williamson, 2002: 147), rather they are capabilities that all of us use in our everyday lives.

Much has been written already on the benefits of coaching patients (Bennett et al., 2010; Cox et al., 2014). Wolever et al. (2013) published a systematic review of health and wellness literature to show 284 articles that operationalised health and wellness coaching for patients. Cox et al. (2014) noted that despite there being some limitations, the research literature was beginning to show that a range of coaching interventions were improving health outcomes for patients with long-term conditions. Beyond the specific impact on patient outcomes, wider benefits are emerging for staff who are engaging in coaching patients (Butterworth, 2006; Cox et al., 2014; Frates and Moore, 2013). So the coaching of patients is already starting to have an impact, both on patients and the staff who work with them.

Towards a model for coaching patients

The stories, the myths, our values and perceptions are the threads that bind us together. These kinds of conversations show the need to reconceptualise this kind of learning and this is reflected in the model below for coaching patients (see Figure 9.2).

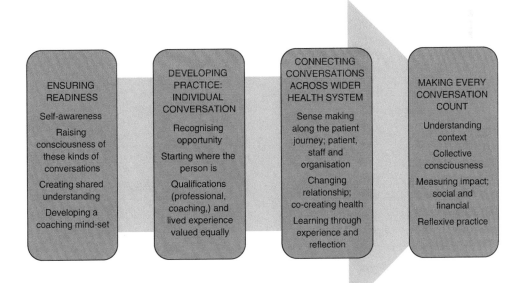

Figure 9.2

The concept of 'making every conversation count' (Hawley, 2012) in the context of coaching patients shows:

- It is important to recognise that informal coaching conversations can happen anywhere.
- Those involved should be aware that formality and the processes that support coaching patients can sometimes get in the way.
- The value of these conversations needs to be championed and communicated as widely as possible.

CONCLUSION

Over the last decade, changes in health policy in the UK have increasingly reinforced the message that people (patients, learners and staff) are to be at the centre of health service delivery and reform. This marks a paradigm shift away from traditional approaches of 'doing to' patients towards more collaborative approaches of 'doing with' patients. Greater collaboration in health and healthcare resonates with the core principles of coaching. Coaching patients is an idea whose time has come.

Practical suggestions for those working in this sector

- A shared understanding of coaching patients – Ensure a shared understanding of coaching for patients by working in partnership to take a whole system approach.
- Formal versus informal approaches to coaching patients – Informal approaches to coaching patients need to be equally balanced with more formal approaches. There needs to be a structure but this should not add unnecessary complexity.
- A coaching mind-set – Develop the coaching relationship by seeking a mind-set that begins by seeing the patient as 'holding the solution, rather than holding the problem'.
- Systematic approaches versus systemic approaches – Embrace a systemic approach by utilising existing frameworks such as 'The House of Care'.
- Creating value by working across boundaries – Work with a coaching approach across boundaries (multi-professional and multi-site); benefits patients, staff and organisations.
- High quality training and development – Build an academic home for health coaching by establishing a cohesive framework for the training and development of health coaches that is competence based and values lived experience.
- Developing the evidence base for coaching patients – Create a collaborative, multi-site strategy for coaching patients and undertake research into the outcomes, building a robust evidence base from multiple perspectives.
- The ethical practitioner – Create shared standards and competences for health coaching, valuing the qualification and lived experience in equal measure.
- Impact and evaluation – Develop an outcomes-based evaluation to demonstrate the financial and social return on investment.

Visit the companion website, https://study.sagepub.com/coachingcontexts, to read the case studies that accompany this chapter:

- Case Study 13: Coaching conversations, care and confidence
  Anya de Iongh

- Case Study 14: Better conversations, better care
  Penny Newman

REFERENCES

Bates, P. (2014) 'Context is everything'. In *Perspectives on Context: A Selection of Essays Considering the Role of Context in Successful Quality Improvement*. London: The Health Foundation.

Bennett, H., Coleman, E. and Parry, C. (2010) 'Health coaching for patients with chronic illness. Does your practice "give patients a fish" or "teach patients to fish"?', *Family Practice Management*, 17(5): 24–9.

Bodenheimer, T. (2007) 'A 63-year-old man with multiple cardiovascular risk factors and poor adherence to treatment plans', *JAMA*, 298: 2048–55.

Boyle, D. and Harris, M. (2009) *The Challenge of Co-production: How Equal Partnerships between Professionals and the Public are Crucial to Improving Public Sector Services*. London: NESTA.

Boyle, D., Slay, L. and Stephens, L. (2010) *Public Services Inside Out: Putting Co-Production into Practice*. London: NESTA.

Braddock, C.H., Edwards, K.A., Hasenberg, N.M., Laidley, T.L. and Levison, W. (1999) 'Informed decision making in outpatient practice', *JAMA*, 282: 2313–20.

Butterworth, S. (2006) 'Effect of motivational interviewing-based health coaching on employee's physical and mental health status', *Journal of Occupational Health Psychology*, 11(4): 358–65.

Coulter, A. (2012a) *Leadership for Patient Engagement*. London: The King's Fund. Available at www.kingsfund.org.uk/sites/files/kf/leadership-patient-engagement-angela-coulter-leadership-review2012-paper.pdf

Coulter, A. (2012b) 'Patient engagement: What works?', *Journal of Ambulatory Care Management*, 35(2): 80–9.

Coulter, A., Roberts, S. and Dixon, A. (2013) *Delivering Better Services for People with Long-term Conditions: Building the House of Care*. London: The King's Fund.

Cox, E., Bachkirova, T. and Clutterbuck, D. (2014) *The Complete Handbook of Coaching*, 2nd edn. London: Sage.

Department of Health (2010) *Practical Approaches to Co-production: Building Effective Partnerships with People Using Services, Carers, Families and Citizens*. London: DoH.

Department of Health (2012) *Long Term Conditions Compendium of Information*, 3rd edn. London: DoH. Available at www.dh.gov.uk/prod_consum_dh/groups/dh_digitalassets/@dh/@en/documents/digitalasset/dh_134486.pdf

Department of Health (2013) 'The NHS constitution: The NHS belongs to us all'. London: DoH.

Dolan, P., Hallsworth, M. and Halpern, D. (2010) *MINDSPACE: Influencing Behaviour through Public Policy*. London: Institute for Government.

European Mentoring and Coaching Council (EMCC) (2009) *Competence Framework*. Marlborough: EMCC.

Fischer, M. and Ereaut, G. (2011) *Can Changing Clinician-Patient Interactions Improve Healthcare Quality? A scoping report for the Health Foundation*.' London: The Health Foundation.

Fischer, M. and Ereaut, G. (2012) *When Doctors and Patients Talk: Making Sense of the Consultation*. London: The Health Foundation.

Foster-Turner, J. (2006) *Coaching and Mentoring in Health and Social Care*. Oxford: Radcliffe.

Frates, B. and Moore, M. (2013) 'Health and wellness coaching: Skills for lasting change'. In J. Rippe (ed.), *Lifestyle Medicine*, 2nd edn. New York: CRC Press. pp. 343–62.

Garrett-Harris, R. and Garvey, B. (2005) *Towards a Mentoring Framework for the NHS* (Evaluation Report on behalf of NHSU prepared by Mentoring and Coaching Research Unit, Sheffield Hallam University).

Garvey, B. (2004) 'The mentoring/coaching/counselling debate: Call a rose by any other name and perhaps it's a bramble?', *Development and Learning in Organisations*, 18(2): 6–8.

Garvey, B. and Williamson, B. (2002) *Beyond Knowledge Management: Dialogue, Creativity and the Corporate Curriculum*. Hemel Hempsted: Prentice-Hall.

Hawley, R. (2012) 'Making every conversation count: The role of informal coaching and mentoring in the NHS'. In P. Lindall and D. Megginson (eds), *Developing Mentoring and Coaching Practice: Papers from the 2nd EMCC Research Conference*. Marlborough: EMCC.

Haynes, R.B., McDonald, H.P and Garg, A.X. (2002) 'Helping patients follow prescribed treatment: Clinical applications', *JAMA*, 288: 2880–3.

Mintzberg, H., Ahlstrand, B. and Lampel, J. (2008) *Strategy Safari: The Complete Guide through the Wilds of Strategic Management*, 2nd edn. Hemel Hempsted: Prentice-Hall.

Moore, M. (2013) *Health Coaching Summit*. NHS Institute (video recording). Available at www.eoeleadership.nhs.uk/page.php?page_id=519 (last accessed 14 July 2014).

Newman, P. et al. (2014) *Health Coaching for Behaviour Change: Better Conversations, Better Care*. Colchester: Health Education East of England.

Ossman, S.S. (2004) 'Motivational interviewing: A process to encourage behavioral change', *Nephrology Nursing Journal*, 31(3): 346–7.

Pederson, J., Brereton, L., Newbould, J. and Nolte, E. (2013) *The Puzzle of Changing Relationships: Does Changing Relationships between Healthcare Service Users and Providers Improve the Quality of Care?* London: The Health Foundation.

Rosinski, P. (2003) *Coaching Across Cultures: New Tools for Leveraging National, Corporate and Professional Differences*. London: Nicholas Brealey.

van Nieuwerburgh, C. (2014) *An Introduction to Coaching Skills: A Practical Guide*. London: Sage.

Wallace, L.M., Turner, A., Kosmala-Anderson, J., Sharma, S., Jesuthasan, J., Bourne, C. and Realpe, A. (2012) *Co-creating Health: An Evaluation of the First Phase: An independent evaluation of the Health Foundation's Co-creating Health improvement programme*. London: The Health Foundation.

Wolever, R. et al. (2013) 'A systematic review of the literature of health and wellness coaching: Defining a key behavioural intervention in healthcare', *Global Advances in Health and Medicine*, 2(4): 35–53.

10

COACHING IN SCHOOLS

JOHN CAMPBELL

INTRODUCTION

In response to burgeoning interest and research on the potential impact of coaching on students and educators, this chapter provides a broad overview of how coaching is being used in schools in the UK, the USA and Australia. It considers the use of coaching with school leaders, educators and students.

In recent years coaching has emerged as a significant development intervention in schools across Australia, the United Kingdom and the USA (Knight, 2007; Lee et al., 2010; Reiss, 2007). Coaching is now widely used as a school improvement initiative to help develop, among other things, headteachers, principals and other school leaders, classroom teachers and their teaching practice, as well as students in regard to study skills and career planning (van Nieuwerburgh, 2012).

Some commentators argue that organisations are networks of people relating to each other, through conversations, to achieve common purposes and goals (Cross and Parker, 2004; Jackson and McKergow, 2007). Such a view of organisations highlights the importance of conversational quality. Others have made similar arguments for the importance of conversational quality as a factor profoundly impacting on organisational effectiveness (Amabile and Kramer, 2011; Groysberg and Slind, 2012; Stacey, 2007). If we accept the fundamental role of the conversation as a unit of influence in organisations in general (Jackson and Waldman, 2011), it would seem to be the case that conversations are particularly important in schools. Not only are the leadership and organisation of a school progressed through various conversations – between heads and teachers; school leaders and government bodies; school leaders and central authorities; school leaders and academic institutions; principals and parents; teachers and teachers; teachers and students; students and students – but conversations are also *central* to the work of that school. Learning and teaching occur through various forms of conversation (real and virtual) taking place in classrooms and playgrounds across the globe every day. Consequently coaching resonates strongly with many educators. At its essence coaching is a conversation, and conversations are at the heart of learning, school life and work.

When viewed in this context it is not surprising that coaching has emerged as a significant methodology for development in schools. While coaching is viewed primarily as an executive or leadership development approach in many corporate contexts, in schools it is now applied in a range of different conversational contexts. Indeed the concept of 'a coaching culture', where coaching infuses a wide range of practices in an organisation, is now being explored (Gormley and van Nieuwerburgh, 2014; Hawkins, 2012; van Nieuwerburgh and Passmore, 2012) (see Chapter 16: Towards a Coaching Culture, for a more detailed consideration of this concept). Various entry points to a 'coaching culture' are being identified and developed in order to move towards the broad application of coaching and coaching approaches as a fundamental way of working, relating and talking together across the school community. These entry points or 'portals' are incorporated within the Global Framework for Coaching in Education (van Nieuwerburgh and Campbell, 2015) outlined later in this chapter.

In discussing the topic of coaching in schools it is helpful to define what is meant by 'coaching' since there is still some confusion about how this is similar to and different from other 'helping by talking' activities (Burley and Pomphrey, 2011). One of the clearest definitions of coaching is also one of the simplest. John Whitmore, one of the pioneers of coaching in the workplace, defines coaching as 'unlocking a person's potential to maximise their own performance' (2009: 8). Many educators identify with this definition since it highlights aspects of the whole teaching–learning process with which they are familiar.

Of the various other 'helping by talking' activities, coaching is most often linked with mentoring. Typically, mentoring has involved a more experienced practitioner sharing this experience and knowledge with a less experienced person in order to assist in their professional learning and career development (Bloom et al., 2005: 9). Central to this relationship is the expectation that the mentor has expert knowledge in the particular field and will share that in the course of the mentoring relationship. Following Downey (2003), van Nieuwerburgh has argued that the relationship between coaching and mentoring in educational settings can best be viewed along a spectrum (2012: 16). At one end, the more *directive* end, is mentoring with the expectation that the mentor will play a more directive role in the shape and content of the interaction. At the *non-directive* end, coaching is positioned with an emphasis on the self-direction of the coachee. This requires the coach to focus on listening and questioning to help the coachee gain greater clarity, awareness and commitment to action. It can be argued that effective mentors use coaching approaches in their interactions and that good coaches will at times operate more towards the directive end of the spectrum, sharing insights and experiences in ways that will seek to preserve the coachee's autonomy.

A helpful definition of *coaching in education* is that proposed by van Nieuwerburgh: ' ... a one-to-one conversation that focuses on the enhancement of learning and development through increasing self-awareness and a sense of personal responsibility, where the coach facilitates the self-directed learning of the coachee through questioning, active listening, and appropriate challenge in a supportive and encouraging climate' (2012: 17).

THE GLOBAL FRAMEWORK FOR COACHING IN EDUCATION

Many corporate and government organisations employ coaches to support the development of their leaders and executives. In addition to this widely used leadership application of coaching, in schools coaching is taking place in a broad range of contexts. It is positioned as a way for teachers to reflect on and improve teaching practice (Kise, 2006; Knight, 2007). Coaching is taking place between teachers and students beyond the traditional sporting context (Passmore and Brown, 2009). Some schools are even training students in coaching skills in order to coach other students (Madden et al., 2011; van Nieuwerburgh and Tong, 2013). In others, coaching approaches are being introduced to parents (Bamford et al., 2012; Sterling, 2008). All of these coaching contexts constitute the various components of what has been proposed as a Global Framework for Coaching in Education (van Nieuwerburgh and Campbell, 2015). It is argued that such a framework provides a comprehensive and coherent way of describing the various conversational contexts where coaching (and coaching approaches) can be explored within schools. Each of these conversational contexts or 'portals' provides an opening for coaching to be applied more broadly in schools.

The concept of 'portals' is a helpful one in discussing coaching applications in schools. A portal is a gateway or entry point and in this sense there are several 'portals' into coaching in schools. Many schools start the journey into coaching by opening the leadership portal, since coaching in many organisations has often been introduced at the leadership or executive level. Others have commenced by opening the student coaching portal through various goal-setting initiatives. When one portal is opened, it is not uncommon for school leaders and teachers to begin exploring the various other interconnected conversational contexts where coaching approaches can add value. This has enabled a broader way of thinking about coaching in schools so that coaching can be viewed as a broad-based school improvement approach. It is the implementation of coaching in several of these portals that leads schools towards the establishment of what has been termed a 'coaching culture for learning' (van Nieuwerburgh and Passmore, 2012) or coaching ethos where coaching approaches permeate conversations across the school community.

The global framework portals

Leadership coaching

A good deal of emphasis by education systems, both government and independent, is placed on developing the leadership capabilities of current and aspiring school leaders. Increasingly, coaching has been used as a supplementary component of school leader development programmes, or in some cases, as an alternative to traditional workshop-based programmes. This is driven by the same kinds of reasons that have contributed to the popularity of coaching in other organisational contexts – it is professional development that is customised, contextualised and confidential. It also provides continuity and accountability, dimensions that are often lacking in traditional workshops, and which by their absence, hinder the sustained application of learning back on the job (Joyce and Showers, 2002; Knight, 2007). Some school systems have invested considerably in the provision of external coaches to support the development of current and aspiring leaders in this way (Department of Education and Early Childhood Development, 2013).

Not only is coaching being made available to support the leadership development of current and future school leaders, a great deal of work is now being undertaken to develop coaching skills and coaching approaches in school leaders themselves (Creasy and Paterson, 2005). Senior school leaders are increasingly being trained in coaching methodologies and skills so that they can work as coaches supporting newly appointed or aspiring principals in other schools. These leaders are then able to bring a more skilled coaching approach to educational leadership roles in their own schools. Many school leaders who may have experienced the value of coaching support at various stages of their careers are keen to build the key aspects of coaching into the way they lead their staff teams. Consequently school leaders are participating in various kinds of 'Leader as Coach' programmes in order to develop their coaching skills to higher levels. Some school leaders approaching the end of their formal careers are seeing coaching as a way to not only enhance their effectiveness as leaders but also to continue their contribution to education beyond retirement (Marks, 2012).

Coaching to enhance professional practice

Increasing recognition that 'teacher quality' is one of the most significant influences on student learning outcomes (Hattie, 2003, 2012) has led to greater focus on the professional performance and development of teachers, including observation of teaching practice coupled with feedback and goal setting (Knight, 2007). In this context, coaching has emerged as an important methodology which provides a coherent, constructive approach that brings all of these dimensions together. The 'coaching to enhance professional practice' portal can operate in a number of ways.

Headteacher-based approaches

Many schools and systems have renewed their focus on the role of the headteacher as a leader of teaching practice, arguing that the headteacher is the key person in developing teaching and learning expertise within their school. As such, the headteacher is required to lead initiatives related to improving teaching practice through more frequent and intentional classroom visits (Fink and Markholt, 2011). Sometimes the 'leader of teaching practice' role is described as a coaching role (Barkley and Bianco, 2010; Cheliotes and Reilly, 2010) but at other times it is positioned as more supervisory (Fink and Markholt, 2011). This approach is not without its challenges though, as in schools the time demands on headteachers are substantial. It also raises questions about the relationship between coaching and managerial supervision (see Chapter 3: Manager as Coach, for a more detailed consideration of this topic).

Specialist-based approaches

Others would argue that specialist 'instructional coaches' should be established in each school (or in a cluster of schools) (Annenburg Institute for School Reform, 2004; Cornett and Knight, 2008; Knight, 2007; Shidler, 2008). In some contexts, these 'instructional coaches' have a focus on particular areas such as literacy and numeracy. In other contexts, they work with a variety of teachers from a range of subject areas helping to enhance teaching practice. They typically observe teachers in their classrooms and work in partnership with them to help develop each teacher's pedagogical effectiveness through feedback and goal setting. In this type of interaction, the instructional coach is often expected to bring and share subject-specific and general pedagogical knowledge to their interactions with teachers. A pioneer in the field of instructional coaching, Dr Jim Knight, defines what instructional coaches do in the following way:

> 'Instructional coaches partner with teachers to help them incorporate research-based instructional practices into their teaching. They are skilled communicators or relationship builders, with a repertoire of communication skills that enable them to empathize, listen and build trusting relationships. Instructional coaches also encourage and support teachers' reflection about their classroom practices.' (Knight, 2007: 12–13)

This approach has been used with growing success in many parts of the USA. Knight argues strongly that several important Partnership Principles should underpin this approach. For example, among several core Partnership Principles are the following:

> 'Equality: Instructional coaches and teachers are equal partners; Choice: Teachers should have choice regarding what and how they learn; Voice: Professional learning should empower and respect the voice of teachers.' (Knight, 2007: 40–50)

It is clear that these principles give a strong and overt emphasis to partnership and equality in the relationship, but inherent in the structure of the instructional coaching relationship is the coach as 'expert'.

Peer-based approaches

Others have developed approaches designed to equip teachers to work in collaborative ways with fellow teachers as coaches. Various kinds of peer-based approaches, including Lesson Study (Fernandez, 2002), have been in use for some time (Showers and Joyce, 1996). These initiatives have usually involved some classroom observation followed by exploration of the emerging data and subsequent coaching conversations that lead to goal setting and action planning. Follow-up sessions allow for ongoing mutually agreed accountability without any supervisory element. These approaches have become popular again recently since they help to broaden the coaching skill base in the school, and when properly implemented they offer a cost-effective way to provide skilled coaching to large numbers of classroom teachers in a way that respects their professionalism.

Coaching for student success and wellbeing

Since student success and wellbeing are central to what schools are about, this area is often the starting point for exploring how coaching might work in school contexts. Often, explicit interest in student wellbeing has been sparked by emerging research from the field of positive psychology. Since coaching shares similar aims with positive psychology – optimising performance and wellbeing – various kinds of student-coaching initiatives have been included in 'positive education' programmes. Some of these have been the subject of research studies (e.g. Green et al., 2007) indicating that coaching has a positive impact in relation to goal striving and resilience for both students and teachers. (For more on this topic, see Chapter 12: Integrating Coaching and Positive Psychology in Education.) When coaching has been explicitly embraced in relation to student success and wellbeing it has often involved teachers coaching students, and less frequently it has also involved students coaching other students.

Coaching students

Educators experiencing the value of coaching approaches themselves have been exploring how the structured conversation that coaching offers can make a contribution to students' academic achievement and general wellbeing. These conversations can take place in formal settings (in pastoral care lessons) and informal settings (in the playground, at school events). Some schools and school systems have introduced customised coach training for those staff with specific pastoral care responsibilities. Careers advisors and other specialised non-clinical roles (e.g. pastoral care teachers, heads of house) have also benefited from coach-related training. Some schools have also offered professional learning programmes to all staff.

Students coaching students

More recently, some initiatives have been undertaken that have sought to involve students in learning specific coaching skills and deploying these in coaching conversations with peers. One published study (Madden et al., 2011) involved training Year 5 boys in coaching skills, and other recent studies have highlighted the benefits to *both* coachees and coaches from these programmes (Briggs and van Nieuwerburgh, 2011; van Nieuwerburgh and Tong, 2013).

Coaching the wider school community

A new and less widely-used portal is the application of coaching approaches to parents and other community members (Bamford et al., 2012; Golawski et al., 2013). School leaders exposed to some coach training will often use various coaching approaches in their conversations with parents, helping them to explore what is really wanted and which options might be undertaken to achieve the identified outcomes. Some schools have also found it useful to offer formal programmes (Sterling, 2008) to help parents (as well as other adults involved in their students' lives) develop coaching skills, thus enabling them to learn about constructive conversational approaches that might be used with children. This approach draws on a recognition that students live and learn in a broader social system, and that family and community are clearly a major component of each student's learning system. If this component can be operating in a way that is aware of and supports approaches and practices in other parts of the student's learning system, then it is likely that the alignment of approaches will have a greater impact.

Positive Education and coaching

The last decade has seen considerable growth in the field of positive psychology, the area of psychology focused on the study of human flourishing. Popularised by Martin Seligman in *Authentic Happiness* (2002), positive psychology has been prominent in educational contexts (Green et al., 2012; Norrish et al., 2013; Norrish, 2015). In Australia, major positive psychology initiatives have been undertaken and these have helped shape the field of Positive Education. Positive Education refers to a range of positive psychology and coaching interventions, including comprehensive curricular and extra-curricular programmes as well as various one-off activities, designed to facilitate student, staff and whole school wellbeing (Green et al., 2012).

Consequently, Positive Education has been an intervention that has often sparked an interest in coaching, particularly for students. It has also been the case that when student coaching has been embraced by a school, Positive Education programmes are also considered. Given the clear links between positive psychology and coaching, it likely that initiatives in both these areas could be further developed in mutually reinforcing ways.

Issues and challenges

Culture of open classrooms

One of the challenges faced in relation to coaching and teaching practice is the 'closed door' culture that exists in some school systems. Quite often teachers have been somewhat defensive about what happens in their classrooms. As a consequence, some educators have not

(Continued)

(Continued)

welcomed others entering their teaching spaces to observe and provide feedback. Overcoming this reticence will be an important part in opening up classrooms for observation as a way to facilitate the continued growth and development of educators.

Relief time

As the application of coaching broadens its scope to include all educators, schools face the particular logistical and financial challenges of providing relief or cover for staff to enable professional learning activities. This has been an ongoing issue for all professional learning provided in schools. It has particular significance for coaching-related professional learning given the time demands required to develop high-level coaching skills and implement the initiatives that flow from such training. It will be increasingly the case that professional learning skill development, for teachers in particular, will be offered as part of blended online learning that includes 'in person' workshops which can focus on those aspects of coach skill development that will most clearly benefit from face-to-face interaction.

Continuing confusion around coaching and mentoring

Coaching and mentoring are often used as closely linked terms, and while there is significant overlap between these 'helping by talking' interventions there are some key differences as well. Mentoring has long been practised in educational contexts while in the past coaching has often been associated with sports coaching or with individual tutoring. Consequently, as indicated earlier in this chapter, it seems that a lack of definitional clarity has hindered the progress of coaching in schools. Greater definitional clarity would be of benefit to all who work in this field.

Ethical challenges

Evaluation and coaching

The 'Leader as Coach' question, as in other organisations, is one that arises frequently in this context. Is it possible for a headteacher to *really* be a coach for someone on their staff? Are elements of the power relationship too significant to allow for the levels of trust that lead to new insights and discoveries that make coaching impactful? These questions are often partially resolved by references that highlight distinctions between 'coaching' and the use of 'a coaching approach'. All leaders may use a coaching approach in informal conversations with staff though not all may be coaches. A 'coaching approach' is one in which the elements of effective coaching can be observed in an interaction between people where a coach-coachee relationship has not been formally established. These elements would include:

- an intention to define a preferred outcome in relation to the topic being explored;
- the exploration of the topic to clarify the current situation and create greater awareness, particularly in relation to strengths and resources that might assist in achieving the outcome;
- clear and agreed next steps that create movement towards the preferred outcome.

If such an interaction is conducted deploying the various skills of coaching – active listening, well-structured questions, presence, demonstrating empathy – such a conversation could be said to be using a 'coaching approach'.

Coaching, counselling and duty of care

The relationship between coaching and therapy or counselling is well canvassed in most coach skill training programmes. Coaches are encouraged through various ethical frameworks (e.g. the Association for Coaching, the European Mentoring and Coaching Council, the International Coach Federation) to ensure that coachees are referred to qualified specialists if issues of a clinical nature begin to emerge. These guidelines are adequate in most cases. Such matters take on additional significance in a school environment whenever students are involved in coaching interactions. Given the maturity levels of students, careful thought needs to be given to the development of 'coaching in education' specific guidelines that can ensure that these coaching arrangements guarantee the safety and wellbeing of all involved.

Recommendations

Research

Recently more and more studies are beginning to appear exploring various aspects of 'coaching in education'. This is an encouraging development and one that will continue in coming years. Various research questions related to how coaching initiatives introduced through the 'coaching to enhance professional practice' portal require further research to deepen our understanding of what works.

(Continued)

(Continued)

Coaching skill development

In defining coaching as a form of 'conversation' it can be easy to trivialise and underplay the critical importance of effective coach skill development training. Coaching *is* a specific kind of conversation, full of intention; subtle and not so subtle shifts in perspective; carefully nuanced language; and acutely refined listening among other things. While less fluent coaching, based on sound fundamentals can be helpful, to become an effective coach requires considerable training, practice and intentional reflection over an extended period of time. If coaching is to continue as an established development initiative for school leaders, classroom teachers, support staff, students and parents, then the skill level of those practising as coaches and those using coaching approaches needs to be raised beyond that provided by short introductory workshops. University-level postgraduate programmes are now emerging, some with a particular focus on education, and it is hoped that this trend will continue.

Positive psychology and coaching in education

As indicated earlier in this chapter there is much overlap between positive psychology, positive education and coaching. It would seem that there is much to be gained from exploring how these two fields of study, both committed to human flourishing, can be integrated in ways that benefit the wellbeing and achievement of both students and educators (see Chapter 12: Integrating Coaching and Positive Psychology in Education).

Coaching culture in schools

As indicated earlier, the concept of coaching culture has emerged recently to describe the broad implementation of coaching across an organisation. In this discussion there is an implicit assumption that this is a positive development. It seems however that there is lack of clarity around just what constitutes a coaching culture, especially in school contexts. Further research in this area would be of considerable benefit to educators as they develop plans to take coaching beyond the initial successful steps that many have begun to experience.

Online professional development for educators

In light of the time constraints facing classroom teachers, schools and colleges, the creation of online and blended learning opportunities for professionals to learn about the application of coaching in schools would be helpful. Organisations such as Growth Coaching Online are already offering an online Foundation Certificate for Coaching in Education. It is hoped that more online and blended learning content is developed to support educators in their efforts to leverage the benefits of coaching within their schools.

Visit the companion website, https://study.sagepub.com/coachingcontexts, to read the case studies that accompany this chapter:

- Case Study 15: Opening the coaching portals
  James Hayres and Nancy McNally

- Case Study 16: Empowering our greatest resource
  Peter Webster and Nicole Morton

REFERENCES

Amabile, T. and Kramer, S. (2011) *The Progress Principle: Using Small Wins to Ignite Joy, Engagement and Creativity at Work*. Boston, MA: Harvard Business Review Press.

Annenburg Institute for School Reform (2004) *Instructional Coaching: Professional Development Strategies that Improve Instruction*. Providence, RI: Brown University.

Bamford, A., Mackew, N. and Golawsksi, A. (2012) 'Coaching for parents: Empowering parents to create positive relationships with their children'. In C. van Nieuwerburgh (ed.), *Coaching in Education: Getting Better Results for Students, Educators and Parents*. London: Karnac. pp. 133–52.

Barkley, S. and Bianco, T. (2010) *Quality Teaching in a Culture of Coaching*. Lanham, MD: Rowman and Littlefield.

Bloom, G., Castagna, C., Moir, E. and Warren, B. (2005) *Blended Coaching: Skills and Strategies to Support Principal Development*. Thousand Oaks, CA: Corwin.

Briggs, M. and van Nieuwerburgh, C. (2011) 'Ways of working', *Coaching: An International Journal of Theory, Research and Practice*, 4(2) 163–7.

Burley, S. and Pomphrey, C. (2011) *Mentoring and Coaching in Schools: Professional Learning through Collaborative Inquiry*. Abingdon: Routledge.

Cheliotes, L.C. and Reilly, M.C. (2010) *Coaching Conversations: Transforming your School One Conversation at a Time*. Thousand Oaks, CA: Corwin.

Cornett, J. and Knight, J. (2008) 'Research on coaching'. In J. Knight (ed.), *Coaching: Approaches and Perspectives*. Thousand Oaks, CA: Corwin Press. pp. 192–216.

Creasy, J. and Paterson, F. (2005) 'Leading coaching in schools'. Nottingham: National College for School Leadership.

Cross, R. and Parker, A. (2004) 'The Hidden Power of Social Networks: How Work Really Gets Done in Organisations'. Boston, MA: HBR.

Department of Education and Early Childhood Development (2013) *From New Directions to Action: World Class Teaching and School Leadership*. Melbourne, Victoria: DEECD.

Downey, M. (2003) *Effective Coaching: Lessons from the Coach's Coach*, 2nd ed. London: Texere.

Evidence Base UWS (2014) 'A three year longitudinal study conducted confirmed the Peer Support Programme has a positive effect on young people and their school communities'. Available at http://peersupport.edu.au/docs/Evidence_Base_UWS_Colour.pdf (last accessed 2 December 2014).

Fernandez, C. (2002) 'Learning from Japanese approaches to professional development: The case of lesson study', *Journal of Teacher Education*, 53(5): 393–405.

Fink, S.L. and Markholt, A. (2011) *LEADING for Instructional Improvement: How Successful Leaders Develop Teaching and Learning Expertise*. San Francisco, CA: Jossey-Bass.

Golawski, A., Bamford, A. and Gersch, I. (2013) *Swings and Roundabouts: A Self-coaching Workbook for Parents and Those Considering Becoming Parents*. London: Karnac.

Gormley, H. and van Nieuwerburgh, C. (2014) 'Developing coaching cultures: A review of the literature', *Coaching: An International Journal of Theory, Research and Practice*, 7(2): 90–101.

Green, L.S., Grant, A.M. and Rynsaardt, J. (2007) 'Evidence-based coaching for senior high school students: Building hardiness and hope', *International Coaching Psychology Review*, 2(1): 24–31.

Green, L.S., Oades, L.S. and Robinson, P.L. (2012) 'Positive education programmes: Integrating coaching and positive psychology in schools'. In C. van Nieuwerburgh (ed.), *Coaching in Education: Getting Better Results for Students, Educators and Parents*. London: Karnac. pp. 115–32.

Groysberg, B. and Slind, M. (2012) *Talk Inc: How Trusted Leaders use Conversation to Power their Organisations*. Boston, MA: Harvard Business Review Press.

Hattie, J. (2003) 'Teachers make a difference: What is the research evidence?' Paper presented at ACER Research Conference, October 19–21, Melbourne.

Hattie, J. (2012) *Visible Learning for Teachers: Maximising Impact on Learning*. Abingdon: Routledge.

Hawkins, P. (2012) *Creating a Coaching Culture: Developing a Coaching Strategy for Your Organisation*. Maidenhead: McGraw-Hill.

Jackson, P. and McKergow, M. (2007) *The Solutions Focus: Making Change SIMPLE*, 2nd edn. London: Nicholas Brealey.

Jackson, P. and Waldman, J. (2011) *Positively Speaking: The Art of Constructive Conversations with a Solutions Focus*. St Albans: Solutions Books.

Joyce, B. and Showers, B. (2002) *Student Achievement through Staff Development*, 3rd edn. Alexandria, VA: Association for Supervision and Curriculum Development.

Kise, J. (2006) *Differentiated Coaching: A Framework for Helping Teachers Change*. Thousand Oaks, CA: Corwin.

Knight, J. (2007) *Instructional Coaching: A Partnership Approach to Improving Instruction*. Thousand Oaks, CA: Corwin.

Lee, K. et al. (2010) *Results Coaching: The New Essentials for School Leaders*. Thousand Oaks, CA: Corwin.

Madden, W., Green, L.S. and Grant, A.M. (2011) 'A pilot study evaluating strengths-based coaching for primary school students: Enhancing engagement and hope', *International Coaching Psychology Review*, 7(1): 71–83.

Marks, W. (2012) 'The late-career and transition to retirement phases for school leaders in the 21st Century: The aspirations, expectations, experiences and reflections of late-career and recently-retired principals in New South Wales (2008–2012)'. Doctoral thesis, Macquarie University, Sydney, Australia.

Norrish, J.M. (2015) *Positive Education: The Geelong Grammar School Journey*. Oxford: Oxford University Press.

Norrish, J.M., Williams, P., O'Connor, M. and Robinson, J. (2013) 'An applied framework for positive education', *International Journal of Wellbeing*, 3(2): 147–61.

Passmore, J. and Brown, A. (2009) 'Coaching non-adult students for enhanced examination performance: A longitudinal study', *Coaching: An International Journal of Theory, Practice and Research*, 2(1): 54–64.

Reiss, K. (2007) *Leadership Coaching for Educators: Bringing Out the Best in School Administrators*. Thousand Oaks, CA: Corwin.

Seligman, M. (2002) *Authentic Happiness: Using the New Positive Psychology to Realize Your Potential for Lasting Fulfilment*. New York: Free Press.

Shidler, L. (2008) 'The impact of time spent coaching for teacher efficacy on student achievement', *Early Childhood Educational Journal*, 36(5): 453–60.

Showers, B. and Joyce, B. (1982) 'The coaching of teaching', *Educational Leadership*, 40(1): 4–8.

Showers, B. and Joyce, B. (1996) 'The evolution of peer coaching', *Educational Leadership*, 53(6): 12–16.

Stacey, R. (2007) *Strategic Management and Organisational Dynamics: The Challenge of Complexity*, 5th edn. London: Prentice-Hall.

Sterling, D. (2008) *The Parent as Coach Approach*. Rio Rancho, NM: White Oak.

van Nieuwerburgh, C. (ed.) (2012) *Coaching in Education: Getting Better Results for Students, Educators and Parents*. London: Karnac.

van Nieuwerburgh, C. and Campbell, J. (2015) 'A global framework for coaching in education', *CoachEd: The Teaching Leaders Coaching Journal*, (1): 2–5.

van Nieuwerburgh, C. and Passmore, J. (2012) 'Creating coaching cultures for learning'. In C. van Nieuwerburgh (ed.), *Coaching in Education: Getting Better Results for Students, Educators and Parents*. London: Karnac. pp. 153–72.

van Nieuwerburgh, C. and Tong, C. (2013) 'Exploring the benefits of being a student coach in educational settings: A mixed-method study', *Coaching: An International Journal of Theory, Practice and Research*, 6(1): 5–24.

Whitmore, J. (2009) *Coaching for Performance: Growing People, Performance and Purpose*, 4th edn. London: Nicholas Brealey.

11

COACHING IN HIGHER EDUCATION

IOANNA IORDANOU, AGNIESZKA M. LECH AND VERONICA BARNES

INTRODUCTION

As discussed in the previous chapter, interest in coaching is expanding rapidly in primary and secondary education. Taking into account the financial and economic situation (i.e. increases in tuition fees, challenges in sustaining levels of research funding) and its impact on universities, together with the various expectations from stakeholders, it is not surprising that universities are gearing themselves up to meet these challenges (Devine et al., 2013). This chapter provides an overview of how coaching can be used within the higher education sector. It considers a variety of methods and approaches to coaching and discusses the potential impact it might have on education at this level. It also explores the ideas of providing coaching not only to university staff members but also to university students in order to optimise individual and organisational performance.

Coaching tends to flourish in environments where the focus on continuous improvement and achieving the best outcomes is cultivated. Currently, due to various political and economic changes, Higher Education (HE) institutions are under growing pressure to succeed on a number of related fronts, i.e. student experience, research excellence and financial viability. This may be one of the reasons that coaching was given a 'green light to enter' educational institutions (Russo, 2004). According to the *Online Etymology Dictionary* the term itself comes from the Hungarian word *kocsi* (szekér), a carriage, which suggests that coaching is a means of 'transport' from one place to another. Therefore, in more practical terms, coaching allows a coachee to 'travel' from their current place in life to a more desirable place. Interestingly, the *Online Etymology Dictionary* reports that the term was used for the first time in the early nineteenth century at the University of Oxford to denote an educator who 'carried' a student through to exams.

As discussed in Chapter 1: The Importance of Understanding Professional Contexts, definitions of coaching seem to agree that its two main purposes are to support the development of a person, team or organisation and assist in formulating and achieving goals

(Segers et al., 2011; Segers and Vloeberghs, 2009). This process is based on the interaction between coach and coachee, where the coach motivates and inspires the coachee (Bax et al., 2011) to improve their performance and competencies so that they can make changes in their life. The key here is a variety of methods that can be applied in teaching and learning environments.

Universities have existed for centuries and have always been perceived as engines of progress in economic as well as in social spheres (Webb, 2005). Recently, however, HE institutions have become more like entrepreneurial companies and are therefore strongly results-driven (Webb, 2005). It seems interesting that both coaching and education can be defined in a variety of ways, but nevertheless both are quite closely related. Despite a variety of definitions, one can agree that coaching programmes can (or should) be implemented and embedded in HE institutions in order to help achieve better results in the performance of broadly defined professional duties. This can be done either by supporting 'the development of students, teachers, school leaders and the educational institutions of which they are part' (Devine et al., 2013: 1383) in achieving their goals and targets, or by helping them discover and release hidden potential. It must be stressed here that coaching is a relatively new field and there are still ongoing debates regarding its 'conceptual foundation' (Nelson and Hogan, 2009). Despite the fact that there is a limited body of research into the effectiveness of coaching in higher education (Devine et al., 2013), early research is already indicating some impressive outcomes not only in the executive world but also in educational environments (Marcus, 2013; van Nieuwerburgh, 2012).

WHAT IS UNIQUE ABOUT COACHING IN THIS CONTEXT?

HE is a learning environment. Staff in HE are witnesses to what education can do for students, whether those students are young school leavers or mature adults. So it is natural that staff would also want to develop and grow in order to realise their own full potential and achieve their aspirations. Like those in any other context, many staff in HE may want to enhance their career prospects. They might often wish to remain and advance their careers within this sector. Employers therefore have an interest in developing their staff to better motivate and retain them. It is moreover increasingly important to enhance the performance of HE staff to rise to the twin challenges of tightening budgets and meeting the increasing expectations of students who have been encouraged to see themselves as active consumers rather than merely passive recipients of education (Kotze and du Plessis, 2003).

Coaching has, until recently, not been used consistently as a means of developing staff within HE. However, it is now much more likely to be seen as one of a range of activities offered to staff by university Human Resource Development departments (see, for example, Thomson's (2012) case study). Coaching is becoming firmly established as an acceptable and effective form of development for university staff, whether academic or administrative, at all levels and in any job role. The credibility that coaching is now afforded was recently evidenced at the 2013 Staff Development Forum (SDF) conference (part of the UK's Leadership

Foundation for Higher Education), which focused on the topic of 'Coaching in Higher Education'.

Coaching, as a developmental tool, is not only suitable for staff in higher education. It is suggested that both mentoring and coaching are also an important part of introducing an aspiring researcher into successful careers in academia (Sorcinelli, 2000). However, there is an ongoing debate about the effectiveness of coaching within both private and professional areas of life. The research into the effectiveness of coaching has been steadily developing within the last twenty years (Fillery-Travis and Lane, 2008; Grant et al., 2010; Theeboom et al., 2014; see also Chapter 13: The Current State of Research). Interestingly, it seems that research into coaching PhD students is still in its early stages and therefore the empirical evidence of the impact of coaching on this sphere has yet to be fully supported. It is possible that this limited pool of studies is correlated with the assumption that 'well-qualified intellectuals do not need touchy-feely life coaching to get through a PhD' (Geber, 2010: 64). Or do they? It has been suggested that a positive relationship between doctoral students and their supervisor is essential for the successful completion of a doctoral thesis (Mainhard et al., 2009). However, the thesis itself is no longer perceived only as an academic piece of work. These days it has become a significant part of the process of becoming a researcher (Roland, 2007). Professor Matthew Lambon Ralph has suggested that 'a broadly-experienced PhD student will be better able to meet the demands of an ever-changing research landscape and for making an advanced contribution to the academic, commercial, charity and government sectors' (Bennett and Turner, 2013: 3).

Yet not every supervisor can provide the best opportunities for their doctoral students. Unsatisfactory situations can occur due to various factors (e.g. time constraints or a lack of proper training in supervisory skills). Moreover, the idea of completing empirical research while acquiring new knowledge and skills and under continuous pressure to publish a number of papers over the course of a three-year programme becomes an almost unachievable goal (Roland, 2007). However, coaches could support PhD students by 'getting them past obstacles and doing things to get going in the writing process' (Geber, 2010: 74), by improving their 'goal-setting and goal attainment' (Griffiths, 2005: 57) and by achieving 'life balance and lower stress levels' and 'better communication and problem-solving skills' (2005: 57). This is why coaching has the potential to become a key element in supporting doctoral students.

Taking into account that coaching is increasingly seen favourably as a developmental tool for university staff of all levels, one might be inclined to consider its usefulness for students. Research on this topic is scarce. A limited, yet growing literature has explored the potential of this option for secondary school students. The results that have sprung from the few relevant studies are very promising. Coaching, seen as a space for reflection and learning (Stelter, 2009), offers fertile ground for students to enhance their academic performance (Passmore and Brown, 2009; Shidler, 2009). Training secondary school students to be coaches has been shown to improve study skills and academic performance, while enhancing other significant abilities like communication and emotional intelligence (van Nieuwerburgh and Tong, 2013).

In this chapter we will explore the usefulness of coaching in HE in three distinct domains: coaching HE staff for performance enhancement and professional development; coaching PhD students for a fulfilling doctoral experience and increased career prospects; and training undergraduate students to be coaches for their peers, in an effort to increase the quality of learning and enhance employability and professional success.

HOW CAN COACHING BE USED IN THIS CONTEXT?

Coaching for staff development

Within the last decade, HE institutions in the UK have experienced many significant changes (e.g. the intensive development of higher education, an increase in the number of students, progressive economisation and the computerisation of processes). Such changes have led to additional demands and required new competencies from university staff. Surveys from 2013 indicate that stress levels among employees in post-compulsory education are comparatively high and that British academic employees are the least satisfied in Europe (Kinman and Wray, 2013). In response to this, a number of UK universities now have coaching as part of their staff development portfolio. These range from short 'bite-size' seminars helping managers to recognise opportunities when they might take a coaching approach during a conversation (and how to do this), to formalised and accredited coaching programmes that provide a 'pool' of internal coaches.

Gander et al. (2014) suggest that coaching can provide new insights into the way an individual is at work, how they respond to people and situations, and how they can achieve outcomes and goals. This provides that individual with increased self-awareness and self-confidence. This is particularly relevant for administrative roles. Universities in the twenty-first century are having to act more and more like commercial businesses. They need to do this to maintain their competitive advantage in an era of large-scale 'new' universities and an increasing number of private universities. Therefore administrators who support academics as well as the university's infrastructure are required to navigate complex problems and situations. Having a coach to listen, support, and challenge their work can lead to a more satisfactory, well-considered outcome for both an individual and their institution. Imperial College London, the University of Warwick and the Open University are amongst several UK universities now offering coaching to staff.

Coaching within the academic community can be more varied. It may feature as a component of a management development programme for academic managers, as described for administration managers above. In the USA, Canada and Australia 'peer coaching' has become very popular and successful within university contexts. This offers 'sufficient time and opportunity (for mid and senior faculty members) to explore the questions of greatest interest to them at [a particular] point in their career' (Huston and Weaver, 2008). One definition of peer coaching is 'a confidential process through which two or more professional colleagues work together to reflect on current practices; expand, refine and build new skills; ... or solve problems in the workplace' (Robbins, as cited in Slater and Simmons, 2001).

According to Mcleod and Steinert (2009) such a programme of peer coaching that took place at the University of Adelaide resulted in 'increased participant confidence in teaching … and improved sense of institutional support and collegiality'.

Whatever its role in the university sector, most authors and developers close to coaching programmes would agree that coaching provides time and a safe space for an individual to think about themselves. This takes place within a confidential 'cocoon' with a trained, experienced and professional coach. They may consider their role, behaviours, performance and aspirations. Coaching is not a panacea, but the experience of some of the universities cited above indicates that it is increasingly found to provide multiple benefits to individuals and their organisations.

COACHING FOR PHD STUDENTS

Being a PhD student is a very unique experience, because it combines many roles (e.g. being a student, an assistant lecturer, an early researcher etc.) and balances a huge variety of expectations (e.g. research-related, work-related, socially-related etc.) (Smith et al., 2008). This can often lead to conflicts, arguments and breakdowns in communication. Despite the fact that sometimes it is said to be a rather lonely journey, quite often PhD students receive support from family members and/or other friends and colleagues, with whom they share their 'frustrations' (Mewburn, 2011). Students are said to share their 'troubles while […] friends and family variously diagnose the trouble, make prognoses, report other relevant experiences and suggest remedies' (Mewburn, 2011: 13). It is worth stressing that those 'venting' sessions rarely take place in front of supervisors because such topics are deemed to be inappropriate. Unfortunately, due to reforms in HE and 'increased emphasis on efficiency and quality' (Pearson and Brew, 2002: 135), PhD students are under even more pressure to successfully progress through their research course in a minimum time (Kearns et al., 2008). Yet at the same time, they are expected to gain a set of broadly-defined employability skills because more and more students are finding employment outside of academia (Pearson and Brew, 2002).

In response to this situation, there seems to be a trend among HE institutions to introduce a variety of supervisor development opportunities (Pearson and Brew, 2002). If we accept that 'the supervisor can make or break a PhD student' (Lee, 2008: 1), the role of academic supervisor becomes an important focus. Therefore researchers' attention has turned to PhD supervision and the roles and competences of successful supervisors (Lee, 2008; Lepp et al., 2013). It is said that this should vary according to students' individual needs as well as students' stage of a career, hence some studies have also looked at students' expectations regarding their supervisors (Becker et al., 2010). For example, Lee (2008: 4) has suggested that there are five categories of supervisor tasks: functional (i.e. project management); enculturation (i.e. supporting new academics to join the disciplinary community); critical thinking (i.e. critical analysis); emancipation (i.e. individual development); and developing a quality relationship (i.e. inspiring and caring for doctorate students). In some publications supervisors are claimed to provide coaching to their doctorate students. However, this seems to relate to 'teaching' and mentoring strategies employed by them (Pearson and Brew, 2002) rather than to the non-directive approach to coaching discussed in this book.

The idea of offering coaching to PhD students is a relatively novel concept and therefore its effectiveness still needs to be placed under research scrutiny. However, the focus of coaching 'is on identifying opportunity for development based on individual strengths and capabilities' (Fazel, 2013: 386), and the main scope of these sessions is 'concerned with the enhancement of human functioning, achieved through the improvement of cognitive, emotional and behavioural self-regulation' (Spence and Oades, 2011). Therefore, it seems appropriate to recommend this opportunity to postgraduate students. Interestingly, it seems that students approach coaching with relatively similar 'difficulties' related to their career stages. Early PhD students seem to be concerned about their progression, planning and confidence, while those who are near completion are more focused on future career planning. Professor Mirjam Godskesen, who has been coaching doctoral students, has indicated that the main subjects they were coached on were 'time-management, handling the relation to the supervisor, motivation, stress and self-confidence' (James, 2014).

Feedback gained from PhD students who have already experienced coaching was nothing but positive (Geber, 2010). However, it is worth stressing here that despite any potential benefits coaching should not be considered to be a replacement of academic supervisors because these two roles are markedly different in their scope and focus. For example, some studies indicated that PhD students can actually engage in self-sabotaging behaviours (i.e. procrastination or overcommitting) which can negatively affect their research projects (Kearns et al., 2008). As mentioned previously, discussing such topics might not be suitable for the supervisor-supervisee relationship, with some mentors comparing such 'consultations' as 'whingeing' sessions which can have a negative effect on that relationship (Mewburn, 2011: 6). In contrast, analysing self-sabotaging behaviours seems to be appropriate within coaching sessions. Taking under consideration that coachees 'repeatedly report better reception and use of feedback, better understanding of consequences of actions, practical application of theory, more effective thinking strategies, changes in behaviour, increased awareness of wants, present-focus, the ability to identify challenges and blocks, a deeper sense of self and generally functioning' (Griffiths, 2005: 57), it seems that coaching has potential in supporting PhD students in terms of thesis completion and employability. Godskesen suggests that 'maybe we should accept that supervisors don't need to be experts at everything and that a coach can be a good way to complement a supervisor who is not that strong on communication and process? And that some doctoral students can be helped through the study with the right support from a coach' (James, 2014).

COACHING FOR UNDERGRADUATE STUDENTS

The increasing cost of university degrees has shifted the focus of students to employability and career prospects. As a result, intellectual stimulation has gradually given way to a growing interest in professional progress. While a critique of the current HE landscape is beyond the scope of this chapter, many of its strands, especially the realm of business and management education, have come under intense scrutiny due to the increasing preoccupation of students with networking, employability, and personal branding (Glenn, 2011; Middleton and Light, 2011). Academic programmes have also faced the critics' censure. These are accused of a limited cultivation of critical abilities and out-of-the-box thinking, traits that are deemed paramount by employers and corporations (Arum and Roska, 2011; Starkey and Tempest, 2009). Educational programmes that allow for the cultivation of subjectivity, sensitivity and responsibility through reflexive and experiential learning have been put forth as a solution to this issue (Cunliffe, 2002; Gray, 2007; Sutherland, 2013: 26). In this chapter, we will propose the undergraduate study and practice of coaching as a practical and rigorous response to this pressing issue.

A recent empirical study presented at the 2013 Coaching in Leadership and Healthcare conference, hosted by the Institute of Coaching in the USA, explored the usefulness of incorporating the study and practice of coaching in the undergraduate curriculum of a UK-based business school (Iordanou and Roberts, 2013). In practice, students from a variety of academic backgrounds were taught coaching theories and then encouraged to practise these by coaching younger university students. The initial findings of the study were promising. By engaging in coaching conversations, the student-coaches experienced first-hand the usefulness of active listening, a key tool in the coach's toolkit that has been argued to facilitate empathy, congruence and unconditional positive regard (Joseph, 2010). Through coaching conversations, the coaches practised recognising and respecting the beliefs, values, and assumptions of others (Iordanou and Roberts, 2013). The coaches were therefore deemed capable, and most importantly, keen to emotionally connect and empathise with their coachees.

Coaching not only sharpens one's listening abilities, it also offers fertile ground for questioning and reflection. Through the study and practice of coaching, students are not only trained in accepting and respecting the beliefs, values and assumptions of others; they are afforded the space to explore, question, and reflect on their own values, beliefs, and assumptions as well. Coaching can therefore be an avenue for critical reflection in action while the learning process is in progress (Schön, 1987, 1991; Yanow and Tsoukas, 2009). Scholars have long argued for the instrumentality of reflection in any form of learning. This is because reflection allows for several 'ways of seeing', at times different from those initially presented as the 'most evident explanation' (Yanow and Tsoukas, 2009: 1359). But can reflection be taught? Dewey (1933), one of the doyens of progressive education, asserted that it could. Consequently, embedding the study and practice of coaching in undergraduate HE curricula can provide fertile ground for cultivating an attitude of critical enquiry, one that extends from the individual to the collective (Gray, 2007).

Most students pursue university education with hopes of fulfilling and prosperous careers. Many aspire to managerial roles, where they will have to adapt and make sense of situations collectively, as part of a team. Indeed, entering contemporary corporate environments, individuals have to work within teams and departments, and at times, across continental borders.

Effective working relationships, increasingly reliant on virtual communication, depend on exchanges with people with diverse backgrounds, skills and qualities, and a speedy adjustment to *this is how we do things around here* (Deal and Kennedy, 1982). The ability, therefore, to make swift and collective sense of situations is crucial not only for professional development, but also for organisational learning (Gray, 2007). So is the capacity to effectively work with others, especially subordinate colleagues. The recent rise in HE fees in the UK increased the expectation, if not the need, of students to be adequately prepared for all the 'ill-defined, unique, emotive and complex issues' that the abstract world of work generates (Cunliffe, 2002: 35). As an immediate response to this pressing need, scholars have suggested approaches that place reflection and critical enquiry at the core of education (see, for instance, Cunliffe, 2002). As we have seen, coaching is conducive to this kind of learning. Through its study and practice from an undergraduate level, students can cultivate a 'coaching mind-set' that can potentially lead to effective working relationships (Hunt and Weintraub, 2002).

Overall, there is great value in embedding the study and practice of coaching in HE undergraduate curricula. Firstly, it has the potential to enhance students' affective capabilities, and especially empathy with the experience of others (Baker and Baker, 2012). This is because coaching conversations allow for the cultivation of active listening, and as a result, an appreciation and acceptance of one's beliefs, values and assumptions. Secondly, through questioning and reflecting, the student-coaches experience the value in enabling and facilitating the critical exploration of others and themselves. Finally, studying and practising coaching in HE are conducive to fostering coaching mind-sets that can lead to more effective interpersonal relationships in the world of work and beyond.

CONCLUSION

This chapter has investigated the various roles and benefits that coaching can bring to HE. Coaching is an invaluable tool and effective way to increase effectiveness, and it has been widely used within industrial environments for over 30 years. Despite this fact, using coaching in HE is still a relatively new area, and therefore it feels like more research is needed in order to fully support this innovation. Nevertheless, it is worth mentioning that empirical studies are already indicating the benefits of coaching for universities, not only on an organisational level but also for all involved individuals, ranging from executives and directors (Denton and Hasbrouck, 2009), through senior and new staff members, to graduates and undergraduates students. In some HE institutions coaching has already been established as an effective way of developing both academic as well as administrative staff. In addition, acknowledging the difficulties that PhD students can experience during their professional development, and understanding that not every supervisor is 'equipped' to adequately support their students on a personal level, is a key reason for introducing coaching to doctoral students. Furthermore, coaching should not only be considered as a form of 'intervention', it can also be a part of developing transferable and employability skills. As studies indicate, introducing coaching as a part of undergraduate curriculum allows students to develop skills (e.g. listening, critical reflection etc.) which they can later apply either in academic or non-academic professions. Therefore, we would argue that coaching has a natural place in HE and it seems only right that it becomes an integral part of the university experience.

Practical suggestions for those working in this sector

Coaching staff

- In universities that develop internal coaches, there should also be provision of coaching supervision for all 'active' internal coaches (see Chapter 15: Supervision for Learning, for a discussion about internal coach supervision).
- Management of 'pools' of internal coaches should lie with a qualified coach and/or supervisor who is a senior manager within the institution (e.g. in Imperial College London, this resides with the Talent Development Manager who manages the Coaching Academy).
- Provision of Continuing Professional Development for internal coaches (e.g. the Open University's Coaches Network which provides external speakers, interactive workshops and an opportunity to network with other coaches in their community of practice).
- As many of the developed internal coaches as possible should be given the opportunity to coach on a regular basis. This then enables them to maintain their practice.

Coaching for PhD students

- Make it clear to both PhD students and academic supervisors that the role of a coach is not to undertake thesis supervision, but to support students in achieving their goals both within and outside the academic setting.
- Consider who should be responsible for coaching provision within the institution (e.g. a person from a specific school, Student Union, HR, career services etc.) to avoid unnecessary confusion and dispute over the roles of departments.

Coaching for undergraduate students

- Consider the design and delivery of a basic and practical coaching module in undergraduate HE curricula.
- The coaching module should provide a risk-taking environment that allows learners to be 'human, in all our messiness, confusion and glory' (Ladkin and Taylor, 2010: 240).
- Allow time for critical reflection and self-reflection during the weekly classes.
- Show that emotions, empathy and feelings are okay; give permission that insights from the senses can help the learning process.

Visit the companion website, https://study.sagepub.com/coachingcontexts, to read the case studies that accompany this chapter:

- Case Study 17: Developing coaches and coaching staff
  Veronica Barnes

- Case Study 18: Coaching PhD students
  Agnieszka M. Lech

- Case Study 19: A student's perspective
  Olliver R. Lloyd

REFERENCES

Arum, R. and Roska, J. (2011) *Academically Adrift: Limited Learning on College Campuses.* Chicago, IL: University of Chicago Press.

Bachkirova, T. (2008) 'Coaching supervision: Reflection on changes and challenges'. Paper presented at the People and Organisations at Work conference, September.

Baker, D.F. and Baker, S.J. (2012) 'To "catch the sparkling glow": A canvas for creativity in the Management classroom', *Academy of Management Learning & Education, 11*(4): 704–21.

Barnes, V.M.E. (2013) 'Case study: Nurturing internal coaches at the Open University', *Coach & Mentor, The OCM Journal, 13*: 24–5.

Bax, J., Negrutiu, M. and Calota, T.O. (2011) 'Coaching : A philosophy, concept, tool and skill', *Journal of Knowledge Management, Economics and Information Technology,* (7).

Becker, P., Bengtsson, M., Nilsson, D., Nordquist, B., Thelander, C. and Toth-Szabo, Z. (2010) *Approaches to Doctoral Supervision in Relation to Student Expectations.* Available at: www.brand.lth.se/fileadmin/brandteknik/utbild/Pedagogik/resurser/Report_final_version.pdf (accessed September 2015).

Bennett, P. and Turner, G. (2013) *PRES 2013: Results from the Postgraduate Research Experience Survey.* pp. 1–53.

CIPD (2011) *The Coaching Climate.* London: CIPD.

Cunliffe, A.L. (2002) 'Reflexive dialogical practice in management learning', *Management Learning, 33*(1): 35–61.

Deal, T. and Kennedy, A. (1982) *Corporate Cultures.* Reading, MA: Addison-Wesley.

Denton, C.A. and Hasbrouck, J. (2009) 'A description of instructional coaching and its relationship to consultation', *The Journal of Educational & Psychological Consultation, 19*(2): 150–90.

Devine, M., Meyers, R. and Houssemand, C. (2013) 'How can coaching make a positive impact within educational settings?', *Procedia – Social and Behavioral Sciences, 93*: 1382–9.

Dewey, J. (1933) *How We Think. A Restatement of the Relation of Reflective Thinking to the Educative Process* (rev. ed.). Boston, MA: D.C. Heath.

Fazel, P. (2013) 'Teacher-coach-student coaching model: A vehicle to improve efficiency of adult institution', *Procedia – Social and Behavioral Sciences*, 97: 384–91.

Fillery-Travis, A. and Lane, D. (2008) 'Research: does coaching work?'. In S. Palmer and A. Whybrow (eds), *Handbook of Coaching Psychology: A Guide for Practitioners*. Hove, East Sussex: Routledge. pp. 57–70.

Gander, M., Moyes, H. and Sabzalieva, E. (2014) *Managing your Career in Higher Education*. Basingstoke: Palgrave.

Geber, H. (2010) 'Coaching for accelerated research productivity in Higher Education', *International Journal of Evidence Based Coaching and Mentoring*, 8(2): 64–79.

Glenn, D. (2011) 'The default major: Skating through B-school', *The New York Times*. Available from www.nytimes.com/2011/04/17/education/edlife/edl-17business-t.html?pagewanted=all&_r=0 (accessed 9 June 2014).

Grant, A.M., Passmore, Cavanagh, M. & Parker, H. (2010) 'The state of play in coaching', *International Review of Industrial & Organizational Psychology*, 25: 125–68.

Gray, D.E. (2007) 'Facilitating management learning: Developing critical reflection through reflective tools', *Management Learning*, 38(5): 495–517.

Griffiths, K. (2005) 'Personal coaching: A model for effective learning', *Journal of Learning Design*, 1(2): 55–65.

Hunt, J.M. and Weintraub, J.R. (2002) *The Coaching Manager: Developing Top Talent in Business*. Thousand Oaks, CA: Sage.

Huston, T. and Weaver, C.L. (2008)'Peer coaching: Professional development for experienced faculty in innovation in Higher Education', *Innovative Higher Education*, 33(1): 5–20.

Iordanou, I., and Roberts, A. (2013) 'Coach me if you can: Embedding the study and practice of coaching in undergraduate Higher Education Business School classrooms'. Paper presented at the Institute of Coaching's 'Coaching in Leadership and Healthcare' annual conference, Boston, MA.

James, E.A. (2014) 'Your opinion counts: Can Technology Help PhDs Finish Faster?', *Higher Education Teaching and Learning*. Available from www.linkedin.com/groupItem?view=&item=5875677522892451841&type=member&gid=2774663&trk=eml-b2_anet_digest-null-8-null&fromEmail=fromEmail&ut=0femtEbgWvi6g1 (accessed 25 May 2014).

Joseph, S. (2010) 'The Person-centred approach to coaching'. In E. Cox, T. Bachkirova and D. Clutterbuck (eds), *The Complete Handbook of Coaching*. London: Sage. pp. 68–79.

Kearns, H., Gardiner, M. and Marshall, K. (2008) 'Innovation in PhD completion: the hardy shall succeed (and be happy!)', *Higher Education Research & Development*, 27(1): 77–89.

Kinman, G. and Wray, S. (2013) 'Higher stress: A survey of stress and well-being among staff in Higher Education'. Available from www.ucu.org.uk/media/pdf/4/5/HE_stress_report_July_2013.pdf (accessed September 2015).

Kotze,T.G. and du Plessis, P.J. (2003) 'Students as "co-producers" of education: A proposed model of student socialisation and participation at tertiary institutions', *Quality Assurance in Education*, 11(4): 186–201.

Ladkin, D. and Taylor, S. (2010) 'Leadership as art: Variations on a theme, *Leadership*, 6(3): 235–341.

Lee, A. (2008) 'How are doctoral students supervised? Concepts of doctoral research supervision', *Studies in Higher Education*, 33(3): 267–81.

Lepp, L., Karm, M. and Remmik, M. (2013) 'Supervisors' activities in supporting PhD students in the supervisory process liina'. In E. Saar and R. Mõttus (eds), *Higher Education at the Crossroads: The Case of Estonia*. Berne: Peter Lange. pp. 1–21.

Mainhardt, T., Rijst, R. Van Der, Tartwijk, J. and Van Wubbels, T. (2009) 'A model for the supervisor–doctoral student relationship', *International Journal of Higher Education and Educational Planning, 58*(3): 1–23.

Marcus, J. (2013) '"Success coaches" prodding college students to graduate', *Community College Week*. Available from http://ccweek.com/article-3646-tracking-trends-%25E2%2580%2598success-coaches%25E2%2580%2599-prodding-college-students-to-graduate.html (accessed September 2015).

Mcleod, P.J. and Steinert, Y. (2009) 'Peer coaching as an approach to faculty development', *Medical Teacher, 31*(12): 1043–44.

Mewburn, I. (2011) 'Troubling talk: Assembling the PhD candidate', *Studies in Continuing Education, 33*(3): 321–32.

Middleton, D. and Light J. (2011) 'Harvard changes course: School's curriculum overhaul part of a push to alter elite B-School culture', *The Wall Street Journal*. Available from http://online.wsj.com/news/articles/SB10001424052748704124504576118674203902898 (accessed 9 June 2014).

Nelson, E. and Hogan, R. (2009) 'Coaching on the dark side', *International Coaching Psychology Review, 4*(1): 9–22.

Passmore, J. and Brown, A. (2009) 'Coaching non-adult students for enhanced examination performance: A longitudinal study', *Coaching: An International Journal of Theory, Research and Practice, 2*(1): 54–64.

Pearson, M. and Brew, A. (2002) 'Research training and supervision development', *Studies in Higher Education, 27*(2): 135–50.

Roland, M.C. (2007) 'Who is responsible? Supervisors and institutions need to focus on training in the responsible conduct of research and change the culture in the laboratory', *EMBO Reports, 8*(8): 706–11.

Russo, A. (2004) 'School-based coaching', *Harvard Education Letter Research Online* (August).

Segers, J., and Vloeberghs, D. (2009) 'Do theory and techniques in executive coaching matter more than in therapy?', *Industrial and Organizational Psychology, 2*: 280–3.

Segers, J., Vloeberghs, D., Henderickx, E. and Inceoglu, I. (2011) 'Structuring and understanding the coaching industry: The coaching cube', *Academy of Management Learning & Education, 10*(2): 204–21.

Schön, D.A. (1987) *Educating the Reflective Practitioner*. San Francisco, CA: Jossey-Bass.

Schön, D.A. (1991) *The Reflective Practitioner: How Professionals Think in Action*. Adlershot: Arena.

Shidler, L. (2009) 'The impact of time spent coaching for teacher efficacy on student achievement', *Canadian Journal of Education, 17*(1): 51–65.

Slater, C.L. and Simmons, D.L. (2001) 'The design and implementation of a peer coaching program', *American Secondary Education, 29*(3): 67–76.

Smith, G., Lech, A., DeCock, P. and Pennington, G. (2008) 'The hitchhiker's guide to the thesis – Life, PhDs and everything', *The Psychologist, 21*(12).

Sorcinelli, M.D. (2000) *Principles of Good Practice: Supporting Early-career Faculty.* Washington, DC: American Institute for Higher Education.

Spence, G.B. and Oades, L.G. (2011) 'Coaching with self-determination in mind: Using theory to advance evidence-based coaching practice', *International Journal of Evidence Based Coaching and Mentoring, 9*(2): 37–55.

Starkey, K. and Tempest, S. (2009) 'The winter of our discontent: The design challenge for business schools', *Academy of Management Learning and Education,* 8(4): 576–86.

Stelter, R. (2009) 'Coaching as a reflective space in a society of growing diversity – towards a narrative, postmodern perspective', *International Coaching Psychology Review, 4*(2): 209–19.

Sutherland, I. (2013) 'Arts-based methods in leadership development: Affording aesthetic workspaces, reflexivity and memories with momentum', *Management Learning, 44*(1): 25–43.

Thomson, B. (2012) 'Coaching in higher education'. In C. van Nieuwerburgh (ed.), *Coaching in Education: Getting Better Results for Students, Educators and Parents.* London: Karnac. pp. 205–14.

Theeboom, T., Beersma, B. and van Vianen, A.E.M. (2014) 'Does coaching work? A meta-analysis on the effects of coaching on individual level outcomes in an organizational context', *Journal of Positive Psychology, 9*(1): 1–18.

van Nieuwerburgh, C. (ed.) (2012) *Coaching in Education: Getting Better Results for Students, Educators and Parents.* London: Karnac.

van Nieuwerburgh, C. and Tong, C. (2013) 'Exploring the benefits of being a student coach in educational settings: A mixed methods approach', *Coaching: An International Journal of Theory, Research and Practice, 6*(1): 5–24.

Webb, R.B. (2005) 'Barriers to teacher education reform: Lessons from literature and from experience'. In E. Bondy and D.D. Ross (eds), *Preparing for Inclusive Teaching – Meeting the Challenges of Teacher Education Reform.* New York: SUNY Press. pp. 33–50.

Yanow, D. and Tsoukas, H. (2009) 'What is reflection-in-action? A phenomenological account', *Journal of Management Studies, 46*(8): 1339–64.

FRAMEWORK FOR PRACTITIONERS 1: COACHING FOR RESEARCH SUPERVISION

CATHIA JENAINATI

Prof. Cathia Jenainati, Academic Director for the BA in Liberal Arts and the BASc in Global Sustainable Development, University of Warwick

BACKGROUND

For the past five years I have used a non-directive coaching approach for supervising the research projects of undergraduate- and graduate-level students. My experience has shown that such an approach results in palpable positive change in the students' motivation, their approach to research and their commitment to projects. This brief framework document outlines the methodology that I have developed to enable a more independent, student-led process of undertaking research projects. I will specifically focus on undergraduate students although similar positive results have been noted at graduate- and postgraduate-level supervision.

Undergraduate students in the UK typically undertake a long research project (dissertation) in the final year of their degree. Most degree programmes offer training sessions that introduce students to research methods and academic writing. The assumption seems to be that final-year students should be able to work independently, with some guidance from their supervisors, to produce an original and critically engaging piece of work. In the Arts and Social Sciences, the supervisor initially takes on the role of mentor whose expertise and deep involvement in the initial stages of the project gradually give way to allow the student to 'fly the nest' and take charge of their project.

In my experience, the initial stages of mentoring students as they formulate a feasible research project that is both academically sophisticated and intellectually stimulating are well-embedded within academic practice. Most programmes ensure that students receive extensive guidance and research training at the start of the academic year and that supervisors are available at regular intervals to provide mentoring and support. Once the project is underway, supervisors expect their students to work independently, contacting them when specific queries arise, or when they require feedback on a particular problem. However, a significant number of students find this 'writing-up' period difficult to manage and they complain about feeling abandoned by their supervisor whose constant mentoring and close guidance are perceived as necessary for the success of the project. It became evident to me that there was a gap in our supervisory provision, and that a framework had to be put in place to facilitate students' transition from dependent disciples to creative, critical and independent producers of ideas.

While I would advocate the maintaining of rigorous training programmes at the start of a research project, and while I support reinforcing the mentoring role of the expert supervisor, I would also propose that a clear and carefully managed transition from mentoring to coaching is fully signposted and systematically implemented. I have been developing and refining such a structure and have achieved extremely positive outcomes for my students. The Tripartite Model for Research Supervision, incorporating the GROWTH model of coaching, is outlined below (see Figure F1.1). For more information about the GROWTH process, see Framework for Practitioners 2: The GROWTH Model.

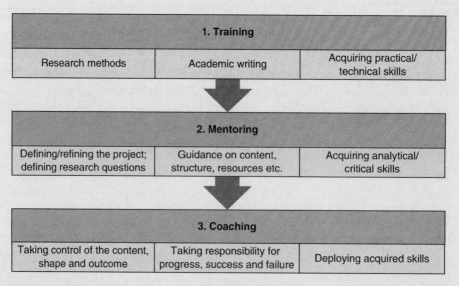

Figure F1.1   Tripartite Model for Research Supervision

TRIPARTITE MODEL FOR RESEARCH SUPERVISION

The tripartite, linear model for research supervision consists of three stages.

1. Training

This is led by an expert who may be the supervisor or a member of teaching staff, consisting of sessions on academic practice, archival research, reviewing the literature, locating information and avoiding plagiarism.

This kind of training is typically generic, even when it is discipline-specific and aims to develop the skills of researching and writing. This stage may be as brief as a few sessions or a month-long course. It should, ideally, be completed at the start of project in order to allow mentoring to begin.

2. Mentoring

This is led by the supervisor and consists of in-depth teaching and guidance.

In their role as mentor, the supervisor is expected to induct students into the subject area they are researching and help them define their research questions, refine the scope and limitations of the project, locate the most relevant primary and secondary sources, and offer advice and guidance on their project's structure and overall scholarly contribution. Through careful expert mentoring, the supervisor imparts valuable knowledge and models the critical tools that students need to deploy in their research. Mentoring sessions are managed by the supervisor who decides on their frequency and determines their content based on a student's academic need. The supervisor-mentor sets tasks and learning objectives, assessing progress and offering regular feedback. Once students have demonstrated a satisfactory level of subject knowledge and achieved the required analytical skills, the mentoring stage comes to an end (see van Nieuwerburgh, 2012, for a discussion of the differences between coaching and mentoring).

3. Coaching

This is led by the student and consists of structured sessions of one-to-one discussions governed by the principles of non-directive coaching. At this stage, the student is expected to draw up a schedule for meeting with their supervisor-coach as well as a detailed plan for progressing the project towards its completion. The supervisor-coach relinquishes control over all aspects of the project, retaining an intellectual and pastoral interest in its progress and affirming their availability to conduct coaching sessions as needed. The frequency and content of the coaching sessions are managed by the student and should be used strategically to check progress, discuss specific difficulties, enable or 'support sustainable change to behaviours or ways of thinking', or 'focus on learning and development' (van Nieuwerburgh, 2014: 5).

The benefits of adopting this tripartite model are as follows:

- It is not recursive: once a step is accomplished, student and supervisor progress to the next.
- Its parameters are clearly delineated: student and supervisor discuss the transition from one stage to the next and ensure that they are both ready for taking on the roles that each step demands of them.
- It can be mapped against the submission timeline to ensure timely completion of the project. For example, my students are allocated nine months (September–May) to complete their dissertation: we spend one month on Stage 1, three months on Stage 2, five months on Stage 3.
- It requires a continually shifting supervisor-student dynamic, whereby the locus of authority gradually transfers from supervisor to student (see Figure F1.2 below).
- It enables the student to progressively occupy the subject positions of recipient, protégé, and ultimately, producer of knowledge (see Figure F1.3 below).
- It requires the supervisor to progressively adopt the subject positions of trainer, mentor, and non-directive coach.

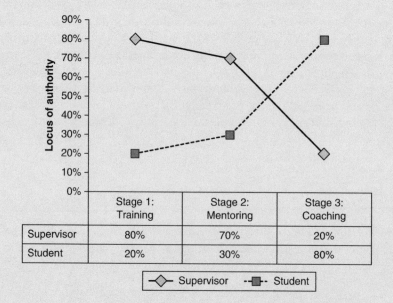

	Stage 1: Training	Stage 2: Mentoring	Stage 3: Coaching
Supervisor	80%	70%	20%
Student	20%	30%	80%

Figure F1.2 Dynamic shift in the locus of authority

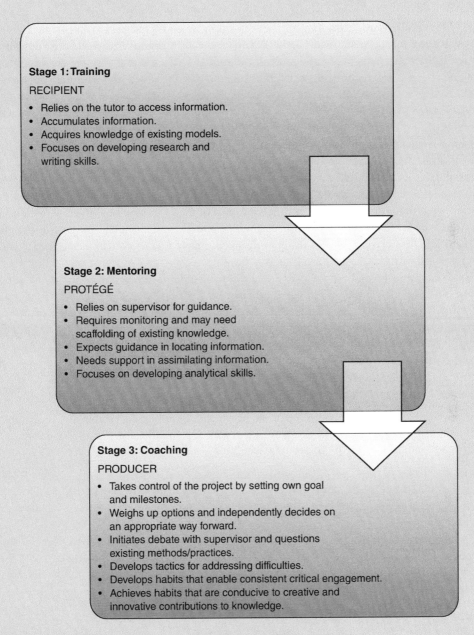

Stage 1: Training

RECIPIENT

- Relies on the tutor to access information.
- Accumulates information.
- Acquires knowledge of existing models.
- Focuses on developing research and writing skills.

Stage 2: Mentoring

PROTÉGÉ

- Relies on supervisor for guidance.
- Requires monitoring and may need scaffolding of existing knowledge.
- Expects guidance in locating information.
- Needs support in assimilating information.
- Focuses on developing analytical skills.

Stage 3: Coaching

PRODUCER

- Takes control of the project by setting own goal and milestones.
- Weighs up options and independently decides on an appropriate way forward.
- Initiates debate with supervisor and questions existing methods/practices.
- Develops tactics for addressing difficulties.
- Develops habits that enable consistent critical engagement.
- Achieves habits that are conducive to creative and innovative contributions to knowledge.

Figure F1.3   Progressive shift in subject positions (student)

GROWTH IN RESEARCH SUPERVISION

I have found that the GROWTH coaching model (Growth Coaching Online, 2014) provides an ideal framework for Stage 3 of the Tripartite Model of Research Supervision. The

GROWTH model is an adaptation of the well-known GROW process (Whitmore, 2009). It consists of the standard steps of Goals, Reality and Options and Will, with the addition of Tactics and Habits. This process has revolutionised the way in which we coach students by allowing space for reflection not only about how the set goal will be achieved but also in regard to how future success can be assured.

I have been using this model with my students and noticed that the addition of Tactics and Habits-related questions have enabled more focused attention being paid to the immediate and long-term outcomes. For example, when we address the 'Will' phase of the coaching conversation, the coachee is encouraged to commit to decisions and actions. Once they have assessed the extent to which each of their stated options 'will have the most impact on moving towards their goal', the conversation moves towards 'Tactics' and invites the coachee to demonstrate their commitment to their decisions and actions. At this point a question such as 'By when do you intend to complete this action?' followed by 'How will you ensure that this action will be undertaken within the timeframe you have identified?' invites the coachee to take responsibility for implementing their actions.

Research projects can be extremely demanding of students' intellectual and organisational abilities. I have often found that many students who exhibit talents in creative, imaginative and critical thinking are less 'talented' at managing their time and bringing their projects to completion. Therefore I believe that in addition to developing their learning capabilities and thinking skills, undertaking a research project while being coached through it provides an opportunity to develop habits that students will carry with them into their future careers. The GROWTH model's ethos aligns with this belief:

> 'It is recognised that looking into the future and building support for sustaining success ahead of time helps to keep the coachee on track and able to respond constructively to any interruptions and setbacks.' (Growth Coaching Online, 2014)

In this respect, the coaching conversation must necessarily conclude with questions about 'Do you need to make any changes in your current habits in order to ensure that you attain and sustain success?'

In addition to refining and expanding on the GROW model, the GROWTH model acknowledges the importance of building trust at the start of each coaching conversation, and of concluding by 'acknowledging the progress' that the coachee has made. These are crucial components of any supervision session, especially when the coach intends to be non-directive and non-judgmental. The coachee should understand that they are not being assessed on their progress, but that the coach is an enabler of progress. Therefore it is important that the coach frames the conversation through the use of rapport-building comments.

Reflective commentary on using GROWTH in research supervision

Adopting and implementing a coaching approach to research supervision has been an ongoing and gradually evolving process. It requires careful planning and a shift in culture that should be prudently managed. In the section below, I provide some recommendations on how the Tripartite Model for Research Supervision can be introduced into practice. The suggestions below are the result of my own experience, they are neither prescriptive nor directive. I am still learning to supervise and I develop my tactics and habits with every interaction.

1. *Communication*: this is perhaps the most important recommendation. It is essential that the three stages of the supervision process are clearly outlined to the student-researcher at the onset. The purpose and learning objectives should be articulated, and an indication of the typical duration of each stage should be clarified. Students may not be familiar with the difference between mentoring and coaching and could perhaps benefit from an explication of each process. In my experience, recording a short podcast that students can access prior to the briefing session produces a positive engagement with the process.

2. *Managing the dynamic shift in the locus of authority*: I attempted to illustrate, using rough percentages, the abrupt shift that needs to take place when the relationship between supervisor and researcher shifts from mentoring to coaching. As I stated in the introduction this shift already exists in current supervisory relationships, and it leads to a sudden expectation that the student is capable of undertaking independent research as the 'writing-up' period gets underway. The Tripartite Model gives structure to this writing-up period by developing the researcher's cognitive abilities through coaching conversations. There is, nonetheless, still an abrupt shift in the locus of authority and the site of responsibility that must be managed by the supervisor. I have found that a transition meeting helps pave the way for this shift. This meeting is the last milestone that I set for my students before handing over the reins. We discuss their progress to date and I reflect back to the student my assessment of the skills and capabilities they have acquired and which will position them favourably to steer the project towards completion. The transition meeting is also an opportunity to discuss the shift in our roles, as described in the next recommendation.

3. *Enabling the progressive shift in subject positions*: one of key accomplishments of the Tripartite Model of Research Supervision is that it recognises the necessity for the supervisor and the researcher to occupy different subject positions. The supervisor must signal to the researcher the necessity for and consequences of the shift from mentor to coach. The researcher is then invited to reflect on the effect that this shift will have on their learning, recognising (as described in Figure F1.3) that they have gradually been trained and mentored towards becoming a coachee who is capable of taking on the responsibility of completing their project.

4. *Ensuring that the coach cultivates a 'Way of Being' that is conducive to positive interactions with their coachee*: I am here explicitly referring to the concept of 'Way of Being' as articulated by van Nieuwerburgh (2014) and by Knight's (2011) 'partnership principles'. In brief, it is the supervisor-coach's responsibility to ensure that their interactions with the researcher-coachee are characterised by honesty, integrity, empathy and unconditional positive regard.

5. *'Creating Coaching Cultures for Learning'*: one of the unintended consequences of the success of the Tripartite Model for Research Supervision has been its widespread popularity among the student body. In the five years since I first began to implement it, I have noticed a marked improvement in my students' motivation and an increased recognition of their personal development. It is not possible to draw conclusions about the effect that this approach has had on the academic achievement (i.e. final mark) of each student, but based on the qualitative feedback I have collected it is possible to assert that the Tripartite Model enables students to achieve a higher level of independence in their thinking, project-management capability and confidence in their ability to reach solutions. This approach can be easily replicated and scaled up at all levels of an educational setting where it can support the creation of 'Coaching Cultures for Learning' (van Nieuwerburgh and Passmore, 2012).

6. *Reflecting on progress*: my final recommendation is that the supervisor should continually seek feedback on their performance from those they have been training, mentoring and coaching. Self-reflection is a powerful tool for educators but it can only reveal to us a limited amount of information. For the past couple of years I have invited students to coach me, using the GROWTH model, with a specific goal of understanding my own praxis and improving it. Although I have only been coached by two students so far, I have found the process invaluable, enabling, and deeply moving.

IDEAS FOR FUTURE CONSIDERATION

I continue to research and develop new ways to undertake supervision in Higher Education, and I believe that the Tripartite Model can be used to enhance relationships other than the supervisor-researcher. For example, I plan to introduce this model into the training programme we offer to newly recruited academics who are required to undertake a period of probation, and who would benefit from the combination of training, mentoring and coaching as they progress towards achieving tenure. The Tripartite Model allows for constructive peer-to-peer interaction, and would be conducive to productive long-term engagement between colleagues at various stages of their academic careers.

REFERENCES

Growth Coaching Online (2014) 'The GROWTH Model: An Overview'. Available at www.growthcoachingonline.com/ (last accessed 12 December 2014).

Knight, J. (2011) *Unmistakable Impact: A Partnership Approach for Dramatically Improving Instruction.* Thousand Oaks, CA: Corwin.

van Nieuwerburgh, C. (2012) 'Coaching in education: an overview'. In C. van Nieuwerburgh (ed.), *Coaching in Education: Getting Better Results for Students, Educators and Parents.* London: Karnac. pp. 15–17.

van Nieuwerburgh, C. (2014) *An Introduction to Coaching Skills: A Practical Guide.* London: Sage.

van Nieuwerburgh, C. and Passmore, J. (2012) 'Creating coaching cultures for learning'. In C. van Nieuwerburgh (ed.), *Coaching in Education: Getting Better Results for Students, Educators and Parents.* London: Karnac. pp. 153–72.

Whitmore, J. (2009) *Coaching for Performance: Growing Human Potential and Purpose*, 4th edn. London: Nicholas Brealey.

Professor Cathia Jenainati is the Academic Director of the BA Liberal Arts and the BASc Global Sustainable Development at the University of Warwick. In addition she leads on the development of Humanities and Social Sciences curricula for a range of international programmes. She has introduced coaching strategies into the teaching, assessment and personal development aspects of her practice and has been promoting the development of a coaching culture more widely in higher education.

12

INTEGRATING COACHING AND POSITIVE PSYCHOLOGY IN EDUCATION

CLIVE LEACH AND SUZY GREEN

INTRODUCTION

This chapter explores the application and integration of coaching and positive psychology within a context of 'Positive Education' (Seligman et al., 2009), with the intention of increasing levels of wellbeing, resilience and achievement in schools. This is particularly pertinent at this point in time when, despite the best efforts of the education system, increasing numbers of young people are experiencing mental illness and psychological distress with a subsequent devastating impact on their capacity to flourish and function at their optimal best. It sets a context for positive psychology, the science of wellbeing and the utilisation of Positive Psychology Interventions (PPIs), including evidence-based coaching as a means to flourishing. The chapter focuses on the application to date of PPIs in schools, the emerging field of Positive Education, and the unique role that evidence-based coaching can play in supporting wellbeing and flourishing in both adults and young people.

In recent years there has been exciting and innovative work occurring in schools, and more broadly education, through the applications of evidence-based coaching and positive psychology. Underpinning this is a growing research base for evidence-based coaching and positive psychology interventions. For example, studies have shown evidence-based coaching to be applicable with senior high school students, teachers and public sector workers, with significant increases in wellbeing, goal striving, resilience and hope, and reductions in depressive symptoms extending beyond the life of the coaching intervention (Green et al., 2006; Grant et al., 2007, 2009, 2010). Coaching has also been shown to impact positively on emotional intelligence, academic achievement and attitudes to learning, with benefits for those being coached and those delivering the coaching (van Nieuwerburgh and Passmore, 2012; van Nieuwerburgh and Tong, 2013; van Nieuwerburgh et al., 2012).

In regard to applications of positive psychology, there is also a growing research base on school-based Positive Psychology Interventions (PPIs) indicating that these are significantly related to the wellbeing of young people, the quality of their relationships and their academic performance (Waters, 2011). However there has been a call for a greater integration of these approaches, particularly when it comes to implementing the relatively new field of Positive Education, recently defined as 'the application of wellbeing science into an educational setting aimed at increasing the resilience and wellbeing of students, staff and the whole school community' (Green, 2014: 402).

WHY POSITIVE PSYCHOLOGY IN SCHOOLS?

Over the last two decades the science of positive psychology, often referred to as the science of wellbeing and optimal human functioning, has emerged (Gable and Haidt, 2005; Seligman and Cziksentmihalyi, 2000). Positive psychology has sought to identify the determinants of a flourishing life and to explore how wellbeing can be enhanced within individuals, organisations and communities through the use of PPIs (Sin and Lyubomirsky, 2009). Rather than focus on deficit and mental illness, positive psychology focuses on 'what works well' and shines a light on the strengths and characteristics that help people to thrive (Boniwell and Ryan, 2012; Waters, 2011). Whilst there are various theories and models of psychological wellbeing (Deci and Ryan, 2000; Keyes, 2007; Ryff, 1989), more recently, Seligman, through his multi-dimensional PERMA model (2011), has identified five key factors underpinning wellbeing: *Positive Emotions, Engagement, Relationships, Meaning* and *Accomplishment*. Although we would suggest most people aspire to live a flourishing life, in reality it is widely suggested that only approximately 20% of the population can be classified as truly flourishing, with the majority experiencing only moderate mental health, and upwards of 20% in distress or suffering from serious mental health problems (Huppert and So, 2009; Keyes, 2007).

From the perspective of young people, the future today is as full of opportunities, challenges, uncertainties and dangers as it has ever been. Some young people display remarkable resilience and achieve positive life outcomes and adapt well in the transition to adulthood despite the challenges and threats they experience. At the same time, others at little risk and with every opportunity to flourish fail to do so (O'Connor et al., 2014). Similarly to the adult population, research indicates that only a small proportion of adolescents are flourishing in life and that poorer states of mental health are associated with increased health-risk behaviour (Venning et al., 2013). Studies show that in Australia, the USA and UK levels of life satisfaction in young people are in decline, with one in ten young people living with a mental disorder, one in four young people regularly experiencing depressive symptoms, and one in three feeling constantly under strain, often related to school and examination stress, bullying or other forms of conflict, low body image, financial worries, or concerns about their future job prospects or career opportunities (Princes Trust, 2013; Resilient Youth Australia, 2014). There is a corresponding prevalence in behaviours relating to suicide, self-harm, drugs and alcohol use, anti-social behaviour and violence (Mission Australia, 2013; UK Centre Forum, 2014; Venning et al., 2013; Waters, 2011). The World Health Organization (WHO) predicts that by 2030 depression will be the largest global health burden facing the millennial generation (WHO, 2011).

Recognition of this reality has led to increasing calls for schools to take a proactive approach to building mental health and wellbeing, drawing on longitudinal evidence that it is a child's emotional health rather than academic success when young, or wealth when older, that leads to ongoing adult life satisfaction and happiness (Layard et al., 2014). Specifically, the application of PPIs within schools settings (Furlong et al., 2014) is being increasingly adopted with the primary aim of helping individuals shift from languishing and moderate mental health into more flourishing states, and to support those who are flourishing to continue to do so. Research has also shown increasing support for PPIs within school settings (Waters, 2011).

PPIs have been defined as 'intentional activities that aim to increase wellbeing through the cultivation of positive feelings, cognitions and behaviours' (Sin and Lyubomirsky, 2009). PPIs are also often activities that generate increased PERMA. A meta-analysis of 51 empirically tested PPIs involving over 4000 individuals concluded that they can significantly increase levels of wellbeing and decrease depressive symptoms (Sin and Lyubormirsky, 2009). More recently Bolier et al. (2013) conducted an analysis of 39 peer-reviewed studies into PPIs, concluding that these significantly enhanced both subjective wellbeing (SWB) and psychological wellbeing (PWB) and reduced depression. Although research into PPIs and young people remains limited (Norrish and Vella-Brodrick, 2009), Water's (2011) review of school-based PPIs confirmed these are significantly related to the wellbeing of young people, the quality of their relationships and their academic performance. Interventions featured in these meta-analyses included evidence-based coaching (Grant and Stober, 2006), goal training and setting, cultivating gratitude and hope, acts of kindness, mindfulness, learned optimism, character strengths identification and development, and best possible self exercises.

Supporting previous calls for the application of evidence-based coaching in schools (van Nieuwerburgh, 2012) and in support of Positive Education Programmes (Green, 2014), we would also argue based on our direct experience as evidence-based coaches and facilitators working with schools that evidence-based coaching is integral to the success of Positive Education programmes. Firstly, in terms of the sustainability of PPIs in general, but also and more powerfully where schools go beyond stand-alone coaching programmes and work towards the creation of 'coaching cultures for learning' (van Nieuwerburgh and Passmore, 2012) that support positive cultural change.

Positive Psychology Interventions (PPIs) for the purposes of this chapter are defined as initiatives to enhance wellbeing or build competence within a primary or high school context, and the term 'young people' refers to those between the ages of 5 and 18 years. A great deal of work in the Positive Education space is also taking place within higher and community education contexts, and the benefits described above have the potential to be equally as relevant for these providers, including those working in early childhood education, youth services or the adult education sector. There is also increasing interest from the higher education sector in terms of both the application of coaching through internal programmes (see Chapter 11: Coaching in Higher Education, for a further discussion), and the implicit integration of positive psychology and coaching into educational leadership and teacher training qualification courses.

WHAT IS UNIQUE ABOUT COACHING IN THIS CONTEXT?

Next to home and family life, schools are the most important development context in the lives of young people (Norrish et al., 2013). As such offering proactive mental health interventions, like evidence-based coaching and PPIs, may have a double benefit: in the short term they may improve the wellbeing, resilience and achievement of young people, and in the longer term they may give them psychological tools to help them deal with the stresses and adversities of life over time as they transition into adulthood and journey through the life span (Green et al., 2011, O'Connor et al., 2014).

Additionally, whilst there is a compelling argument for the provision of mental health promotion and prevention interventions for young people (which include both PPIs and evidence-based coaching), there is also wide recognition of significant stress on the adults in young people's lives. Hence, there is an urgent need to support the wellbeing of those who educate, guide and support young people, such as school leaders, teachers, youth workers and parents (Earle and Clough, 2014; Grant et al., 2010; Kern et al., 2014; Leach et al., 2011; Norrish et al., 2013). For example, building psychological capital comprising hope, optimism, self-efficacy and resilience in school leaders has been shown to lead to higher levels of workplace wellbeing, job satisfaction, organisational commitment, engagement and mental health (Luthans, 2012; Strauss et al., 2013). In support of this, it has been suggested that teachers with higher levels of mental toughness are better able to navigate a range of workplace stressors (Earle and Clough, 2014). We would argue that if adults do not themselves understand the prerequisites for wellbeing and resilience in life and experience at first hand how to enhance their own capacity to flourish, they cannot hope to support young people effectively.

Whilst schools have traditionally had 'welfare' policies and services in place to tackle mental distress for both students and teachers, there have been clear strides within education policy and curriculum to focus more pro-actively on 'wellbeing' by building personal, emotional and social capability in school communities (Boniwell and Ryan, 2012; Green, 2014; Green et al., 2011; Noble and McGrath, 2008; Waters, 2011). It has also been widely acknowledged that positive functioning and flourishing are more than just minimising stress and reducing mental illness. These are about thriving physically, mentally, socially and professionally (Kern et al., 2014; Green, 2014). O'Connor et al. (2014) make reference to longitudinal positive psychology studies in Positive Youth Development (Catalano et al., 1999), highlighting that interventions to reduce negative outcomes do not automatically produce positive ones. Research over a thirty-year span is showing that a focus on realising potential and promoting positive functioning in all young people relating to social competence, life satisfaction, civic engagement, building tolerance and trust is positively associated with the ongoing adult life-span experience of increased resilience, better physical health and higher quality relationships, combined with less anti-social behaviour and psychological distress.

This recognition is also being informed by a growing consensus that alongside academic achievement, schools have a duty of care to promote and enhance the wellbeing and character of young people (Resilient Youth Australia, 2014; Seldon, 2013; UK Centre Forum, 2014). Indeed, in Australia in 2008 in the Melbourne Declaration on Educational Goals for Young Australians there was a reference to schools playing 'a vital role in promoting the intellectual, physical, social, emotional, moral, spiritual and aesthetic development and wellbeing of young Australians, and in ensuring the nation's ongoing economic prosperity and social cohesion'. In 2013, the UK Positive Education Summit hosted at 10 Downing Street and attended by global leaders in the research and application of positive psychology endorsed PERMA and the promotion of flourishing in schools, with the aim of developing both the skills of wellbeing and the skills of achievement in young people (Positive Education Summit, 2013). In February 2014 the Positive Education Schools Association (www.pesa.edu.au) was formally launched in Australia and November 2014 saw the launch of IPEN – The International Positive Education Network which is at the vanguard of collating and sharing best practice examples of schools around the world who are striving to enhance achievement, character and wellbeing within their communities (www.ipositive-education.net).

To support these calls, the field of Positive Education has emerged from the growing global introduction and application of PPIs within primary and high school settings in both state-funded and private sector schools that have built upon and added value to programmes designed to promote social and emotional learning and pastoral care (Boniwell and Ryan, 2012; Green et al., 2011; Noble and McGrath, 2008). These have included a specific emphasis on positive educational practices, including evidence-based coaching and wellbeing curricula specifically designed to increase PERMA and enhance positive youth development (Boniwell and Ryan, 2012; Noble and McGrath, 2008; Norrish et al., 2013; O'Connor et al., 2014). Increasingly and in light of the need to support school leadership, teacher and parent wellbeing, Positive Education programmes are aimed at targeting the whole school community and creating a positive organisational culture (Green, 2014; Kern et al., 2014). Within Australia and globally, increasing numbers of schools are embracing Positive Education. In 2014 the Positive Education Schools Association (www.pesa.edu.au) was formally launched in Australia, and is at the vanguard of collating and sharing examples of best practice from schools around the world. Each and every school is unique and schools have taken on many varied approaches. These include applying ready-made Positive Education curricula or designing their own programmes; seeking to influence broad values-led and cultural change across the whole school; simply focusing on providing explicit wellbeing lessons; or prioritising student and staff wellbeing (Grenville-Cleave, 2013).

EVIDENCE-BASED COACHING AS AN APPLIED POSITIVE PSYCHOLOGY

In his seminal book *Coaching in Education: Getting Better Results for Students, Educators and Parents*, van Nieuwerburgh (2012) reviews the increasing support for and application of coaching in educational contexts, highlighting its efficacy as a stand-alone intervention to support leadership development, professional staff learning and development, instructional coaching supporting the implementation of teaching methods in the classroom, and the sharing of best practice in teaching and student learning. The book also showcases Positive Education and the potential for integrating coaching psychology and positive psychology in schools to facilitate a culture that has at its heart student, staff and whole school wellbeing (Green et al., 2012).

Whilst coaching within school settings has been historically utilised for enhancing teaching practice and leadership capability, it is coaching in this wellbeing and change context that is the focus of this chapter. The recognition of coaching as integral to Positive Education has been informed by both research and good practice, shared at two symposia on Positive Psychology in Education in 2009 and 2011 at the University of Sydney in Australia and the First International Conference on Coaching and Positive Psychology in Education in 2010 at the University of East London in the UK. Evidence-based coaching also featured heavily in the First Australian Positive Education Conference hosted by Knox Grammar School in Sydney in 2013. The approach was further endorsed by the launch of the first International Symposium for Coaching and Positive Psychology in Education (ISCAPPED) which took place at Sydney Business School in Australia in November 2014. As Green states (2014), some schools may use PPIs but have not specifically utilised coaching. For example, Geelong Grammar School, considered the world leader in the application of positive psychology in schools, has developed an applied framework for Positive Education drawing heavily on PERMA with an additional wellbeing domain of health (Norrish et al., 2013). This comprehensive model does not explicitly identify coaching as a prerequisite for the successful implementation of the framework. Although there is no 'one size fits all' approach, Green (2014) argues that it is the strategic integration of positive psychology and evidence-based coaching where the most power and potential lie. She refers to some recent whole-school studies that are subject to scientific evaluation from which it is hoped further evidence and support for coaching within Positive Education programmes will emerge. For example, in two large-scale Positive Education Programmes in Australian schools (Knox Grammar School and Loreto Kirribilli) evidence-based coaching was explicitly taught and implemented alongside other PPIs.

Evidence-based coaching is underpinned by the science of Coaching Psychology and has previously been described as an applied positive psychology (Biswas-Diener, 2010; Grant and Cavanagh, 2007; Green, 2014). Positive psychology coaching (PPC) is defined as 'a scientifically-rooted approach to helping clients increase wellbeing, enhance and apply strengths, improve performance, and achieve valued goals' (Kauffman et al., 2010: 158). It applies relevant psychological theories and techniques within a collaborative relationship that facilitates engagement, self-directed goal identification, striving and attainment and increased self-regulation within the normal or non-clinical population (Grant, 2007; van Nieuwerburgh, 2012).

We would suggest that evidence-based coaching can also be understood as a complementary partner to many other specific PPIs. It offers a sound methodology for building PERMA, a framework for the real-world application of learning and support in sustaining purposeful and positive change in both young people and adults. We suggest it is applicable in one-to-one, group and organisation-wide settings. In regard to PERMA, we would argue that evidence-based coaching has a direct impact across all five domains. It enhances and harnesses *Positive emotion*, for example by generating pride, inspiration, curiosity and hope as coachees are supported to set meaningful visions and goals and strive towards them. Enhancing positive emotions increases life satisfaction (Diener, 1984) and also broadens the capacity of coachees to think, be creative, and find solutions. It builds resilience through the development of emotional, physical, intellectual and psychological resources (Fredrickson, 2007). Coaching generates positive emotions at the same time as helping coachees to manage negative ones better (Sekerka and Fredrickson, 2010). It recognises that negative emotions have a place but the emphasis is on supporting emotional regulation, perspective taking, realistic or learned optimism (Seligman, 2004). This in turn engenders hope which facilitates intrinsic goal setting and pathways thinking to help coachees find ways to reach goals in the face of setbacks and the sense of agency, self-belief and confidence required for goal striving and attainment (Snyder et al., 2002). *Engagement* is supported through a focus on strengths discovery, identification and application that in turn correlates with wellbeing, resilience, achievement, mindfulness and flow (Czikszentmihalyi, 1991; Peterson and Seligman, 2004). Increasing positivity in *Relationships* is a coaching outcome achieved through its emphasis on asking rather than telling, building trust and space for reflection and collaboration. Benefits stem both in terms of the relationship between the coach and coachee and in the quality of relationships in the coachee's life. Coaching supports individuals to build social resources necessary for resilience by drawing on support from others and in pursuing goals that serve the wellbeing of others (van Nieuwerburgh and Tong, 2013). *Meaning* and purpose in life have been shown to be associated with high levels of wellbeing (Diener, 1984; Ryff, 1989) and coaching creates opportunities for coachees to reflect on their personal values and goals and identify opportunities to apply their strengths to become their best possible selves and make a wider contribution to the world (Sheldon and Lyubormirsky, 2006). Lastly through simple delivery models such as the GROW Model (Whitmore, 2002) coaching directly supports *Accomplishment* by providing a framework to support the coachees in intrinsic and self-concordant *goal* setting, the opportunity to assess current *reality*, exploration of *options* for both steps forward, and support and development of the *way forward* to act and commit to change.

Van Nieuwerburgh and Green (2014) also advocate the use of evidence-based coaching in building mental toughness in adults and young people which they argue falls under the umbrella of positive psychology. Mental toughness broadly comprises four key components – control, challenge, commitment and confidence. Control relates to the level of emotional control and self-efficacy an individual has. Commitment relates to persistence and the ability to stick at goal striving despite setbacks. Challenge relates to the way individuals perceive such setbacks as opportunities or threats and how proactive they are about seeking challenge. Confidence relates to the belief in self and the ability to achieve goals and also how these relate to and cope with others (Clough and Strycharczyk, 2012). Mental toughness, which can play a significant role in achieving academic outcomes and enhanced wellbeing, can be developed through coaching interventions (van Nieuwerburgh and Green, 2014).

HOW CAN COACHING BE USED IN A POSITIVE EDUCATION CONTEXT?

In this section we share some specific examples of how coaching has been and is being used in school contexts at organisational, group and individual levels. We draw upon good practice within the field and our professional experience as evidence-based coaches and facilitators in the Positive Education space. We are mindful that Positive Education is not a 'product' to be sold or promoted. We believe that it is by taking a coaching approach, i.e. the ability to 'be' with and listen to a school community, that we can facilitate a process of learning, awareness, growth and development within which the power and potential of Positive Education can be introduced and realised.

CREATING A CLIMATE FOR POSITIVE CHANGE

Many schools face increasing pressures in terms of scrutiny, academic expectations, bureaucracy, new government policy and initiatives, competing demands, a lack of resources, conflict resolution and staff retention. The risks of leadership and teacher stress and burnout are high (Green, 2014; Kern et al., 2014). It can be a challenge to introduce yet another educational initiative without attracting some level of cynicism and pushback. Therefore, creating the conditions and climate for positive change is important in order for Positive Education to be seen as an added value to existing priorities and commitments, and something that can be lived, taught and embedded within a school (Norrish et al., 2013). There are a number of organisational change approaches, informed by coaching principles, that can be utilised in this regard.

Traditional change models often focus on recognising or creating a sense of urgency for change (Kotter, 1996), for example the recognition of the rising global mental health burden we referred to in our introduction. This reactive approach acknowledges that this challenging situation needs to be addressed to avoid negative consequences and the focus is therefore on fears, deficits and what is wrong. Yet there is substantial research to suggest that people are more likely to be successful in achieving goals when they are intrinsically motivated to work towards them (Sheldon, 2002). Taking a proactive approach allows us to activate more positive energy by focusing on exploring and embracing what is right, what works well and why, and how much better the future would be if we build on our existing strengths and resources (Waters et al., 2012). Coaching schools to look toward this 'preferred future' can be informed by the Appreciative Inquiry 4D model (Cooperider and Srivastva, 1987) that has been used to great effect in engaging school leadership and whole school staff teams in the development of Positive Education programmes (Waters et al., 2012).

Developing intrinsic motivation for school communities to embrace Positive Education can also be supported by a model of change informed by Positive Organizational Scholarship

(Cameron et al., 2003). Mroz and Quinn's (2009) model is effective because it sits well with the idea of teaching, living and embedding coaching and positive psychology, harnessing the energy of those in schools with whom these ideas resonate and creating a 'coaching culture for learning' (van Nieuwerburgh and Passmore, 2012).

The model involves five stages:

1. *Creating a common understanding*: what is the goal and why?
2. *Selecting early adopters*: providing space for 'champions' to innovate and take risks.
3. *Creating pockets of success*: practical applications and reflection on what is working.
4. *Sharing across boundaries*: celebrating and building upon success stories.
5. *Adjusting across boundaries*: changing the 'way we do things' and embedding cultural change.

This approach is a great way to spot 'positive deviance' (Sekerka and Fredrickson, 2010) in a school. Positive deviance describes early adopters or 'champions' who step outside of the norm driven not by fear or anxiety but by a deep sense of positive meaning making. This can be marked by excitement, curiosity, optimism, hope, pride and many other positive emotions that foster creativity and innovation, whilst building the relational strengths, resourcefulness and resilience needed to face setbacks. Positive deviance is also exemplified by people who apply coaching characteristics such as positive high quality connections and the spirit of mutual trust, rigorous collaboration, an ability to take risks, positive regard, strengths use, active engagement, transparency and accountability that create resilient and flourishing relationships (Fredrickson, 2007).

In our experience, a powerful way to create a positive emotional climate and a common understanding on the goals for Positive Education is to introduce PERMA in the context of the flourishing, wellbeing and engagement of the school leadership team and teachers. This approach has been supported by a recent pilot study exploring teacher engagement in schools and demonstrating that when staff members are doing well across the domains of PERMA they have higher levels of life satisfaction, physical health and professional thriving (Kern et al., 2014). Our experience is that facilitating school leaders and teachers to self reflect when they are at their best helps them gain a unique and meaningful understanding of what it actually means to flourish. They often become more open to the exploration of PERMA, the key determinants of wellbeing, optimal functioning and how these relate to wellbeing and engagement in their school, work and life in general. The Wellbeing and Engagement Framework (WBEF) (Grant, 2012) is used to help establish a sense of the current reality in the areas of wellbeing and engagement. We have found school communities relate to WBEF (see Figure 12.1). The WBEF serves in this context to help school leadership, teachers, parents and students reflect upon where they and others within the school community might be on the matrix. This facilitates a greater appreciation and understanding of what they are already doing both personally and professionally to flourish, and where there is a need for improvement, support or greater emphasis. For example, in our direct experience as coaches and group facilitators it is common to find significant numbers of school leaders, teachers and parents resonating with the 'Distressed and Functional' quadrant. This encourages them to consider the personal responsibility they can take across the domains of PERMA to shift into a more flourishing state or to ensure mindful action is taken to sustain their current levels of optimal functioning. This personal and collective reflection provides further intrinsic motivation, helps identify champions, and also informs a wider debate about the unique needs and challenges within their school community. Actions might include an audit of existing activity that enhances PERMA (a Positive Education audit) followed by an exploration of opportunities to strategically introduce a range of additional PPIs. We also present a strong rationale as to how and why coaching, applied through external support or in-house peer networks, can help to apply learning to enhance wellbeing and sustain positive change.

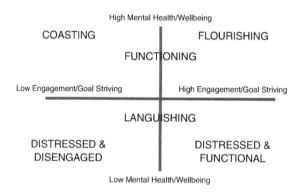

Figure 12.1   Wellbeing and Engagement

Adapted from Keyes (2007) and Grant (2012)

HOW COACHING IS APPLIED

As previously stated there is no 'one size fits all' approach to the application of positive psychology and coaching in schools, but we share here some initiatives that have been applied to serve as examples of good practice. As the development and implementation of positive psychology and coaching-based wellbeing programmes in schools continue to gain momentum, the need for a disciplined and structured method to evaluate the efficacy and outcomes of these approaches is critical.

Professional coaching

Evidence-based coaching has been shown to have the potential to contribute to the professional development and wellbeing of school leaders and teachers. Grant, Green and Rynsaardt (2010) studied the impact of development coaching on teachers at Sydney Girls High School.

A randomised control design was used to explore the impact of coaching on wellbeing, workplace wellbeing, resilience and leadership style. Forty-four teachers were randomly assigned to either a 20-week evidence-based coaching programme or a wait-list control group. Participants in the programme received 360-degree feedback on their leadership behaviours and with the support of a professional coach set goals to develop more positive and constructive behavioural styles. The pre- and post-test findings indicated that teachers experienced significant increases in dimensions of constructive leadership, goal attainment, wellbeing and resilience, and a significant reduction in stress as compared to the control group.

Formal coaching interventions can be also delivered as part of leadership training programmes, or offered to provide space for leadership team members to individually reflect on practical ways to build their own psychological capital and mental toughness in order to better support and sustain the wellbeing, resilience and sustained engagement of themselves and others within the school community. These programmes often draw upon tools such as the WBEF, strengths-based approaches using tools such as the VIA Character Strengths Survey (Seligman and Peterson, 2004), the Realise2 strengths assessment (Linley et al., 2010), or existing school leadership capability frameworks to support personal, professional and leadership development. Whilst focused on supporting leaders on the attainment of individual development goals, such programmes often bring leadership teams together for a facilitated group session which can include sharing their individual strengths, a review of their collective team strengths profile in light of the current and future school strategic plan, and the adoption of an Appreciative Inquiry approach to consider the future application of Positive Education within a school.

Teacher coach training

The ground-breaking study by Green, Grant and Rysaardt (2007) gave the first preliminary support for the application of evidence-based coaching for high school students delivered by teachers. A randomised waitlist control group study saw Year 10 students (16 year olds) access a 10-week solution-focused cognitive-behavioural life coaching programme delivered by teachers trained in evidence-based coaching models and techniques. Each coaching session involved working through a self-regulatory cycle of setting personal and school-related goals, reviewing progress towards these, developing self-generated actions plans, and monitoring and evaluating their progress. The post-test findings indicated that the coaching significantly increased cognitive hardiness and hope and significantly decreased depressive symptoms.

Schools embracing Positive Education in Australia, such as Knox Grammar, The Peninsula School, Scotch College, Ballarat Grammar and Loreto Kirribilli, are increasingly training their teachers in coaching skills to better facilitate wellbeing, learning and achievement. Through formal coaching programmes, teachers charged with offering support to peers and students are trained in coaching skills, processes and principles. These teachers can then apply the principles of Positive Education and coaching within their work to develop professional teaching practice, academic achievement and wellbeing. They are able to facilitate an 'asking as opposed to telling' environment and to encourage individual and group goal setting by both colleagues and students. From a teaching perspective, coaching challenges the status quo and shifts the emphasis of responsibility to the student as learner, helping to build greater self-determination. The introduction of positive psychology and coaching is therefore seeing a shift in pedagogy where teachers are creating more collaborative learning environments with greater student autonomy, and this has led to higher levels of wellbeing and the engagement in students, staff and leadership (Waters, 2011).

Coaching conversations

On a less formal basis, GROW (Whitmore, 2002) coaching conversations are being introduced to whole staff groups or faculties as part of Positive Education professional development events. The aim has been to facilitate ongoing peer support for applying PPIs to both teacher and student wellbeing. Using a simple coaching conversation model, staff and students are supported to have solution- and goal-focused conversations often with an emphasis on discovering, igniting and building on strengths and other personal resources that can help them pursue their goals.

CONCLUSION

Positive education adds value to traditional educational approaches to support and prevent negative impacts on the mental health and wellbeing of young people and adults in schools. More critically it also informs and validates the emerging emphasis on the role of schools to enable their communities to thrive rather than just survive. We have argued that evidence-based coaching as an applied positive psychology is integral to Positive Education programmes in schools because it can positively impact on the wellbeing, resilience and achievement of adults and young people individually to make positive and sustained changes in their lives. But the impact of coaching can also be felt more widely by informing a shift in pedagogy from telling to asking, transforming the culture of the institution, and creating a safer, richer and more conducive learning and working environment for all involved.

Equally important in the context of this book, we see the development of these approaches in schools today as a way of preparing and equipping young people for tomorrow to make the successful transition into adulthood. As the professionals of the future they are the people who will need to manage their personal and professional lives, albeit in corporate or public sector settings, in ways that will indeed allow them to flourish and maintain their resilience and wellbeing in the face of the challenges and threats that are the reality of the twenty-first century. We also believe that beyond the world of work Positive Education has the potential to lay the foundations for creating a healthier, kinder, more tolerant, equal and caring society.

Practical suggestions for those working in this sector

- Learn from those who are doing it or who have done it before: join PESA (www.pesa.com. au) and investigate existing good practice around the world as the pioneering schools share their learning and open themselves up to scrutiny and review.
- Look out for national and international conferences and symposia to attend.
- Engage senior leaders first and get buy-in, and then think about the unique context and needs of your school.
- Invest in one-to-one professional coaching for your senior leadership team to ensure they address their own wellbeing and engagement.
- Bring your school up to speed with developments and research in the fields of coaching and positive psychology and provide an experiential introduction.
- Allow for teachers to explore the benefits of positive psychology and coaching for their own wellbeing and engagement through continuing professional development events.
- Provide specific events for staff wellbeing.
- Create a Positive Education programme team of champions who are intrinsically motivated and ensure that there is identified and on-going sponsorship and support from within the senior leadership team.
- Conduct an audit of current activity across your school that relates to PERMA.
- Engage a positive education coach or consultant to work with the team and keep their focus on accountable outcomes and to provide expertise and resources over an extended period.
- Adopt Appreciative Inquiry and coaching approaches to engage stakeholders to proactively think about building on what works well.
- Think strategically about how to embed positive psychology and coaching within the culture of the school.
- Engage with parents through briefings and opportunities to participate in PPIs. Consider coaching conversation training for parents as part of the whole school approach.
- Use validated measures to benchmark wellbeing and engagement.

Visit the companion website, https://study.sagepub.com/coachingcontexts, to read the case studies that accompany this chapter:

- Case Study 20: A strategic approach to enhance wellbeing
  Claire Dale and Clive Leach

- Case Study 21: A strength-based coaching programme
  Wendy Madden and Suzy Green

REFERENCES

Biswas-Diener, R. (2010) *Practicing Positive Psychology Coaching Assessment, Diagnosis and Intervention.* New York: Wiley.

Bolier, L., Haverman, M., Westerhof, G.J., Riper, H., Smit, F. and Bohlmeijer, E. (2013) *Positive Psychology Interventions: A Meta-analysis of Randomized Control Studies.* BMC Public Health Online.

Boniwell, I. and Ryan, L. (2012) *Personal Well-being Lessons for Secondary Schools.* Maidenhead: Open University Press.

Cameron, K.S, Dutton, J.E. and Quinn, R.E. (2003) *Positive Organisational Scholarship.* San Francisco, CA. Barrett Koehlers. pp. 3–13

Catalano, R.F., Bergland, M.L., Ryan, J.A.M., Lonczak, H.S. and Hawkins, J.D. (1999) *Positive Youth Development in the USA.* Research findings on evaluations of Positive Youth Development Programs. Available at https://www.aspe.hhs.gov

Cheavens, S., Feldam, D., Gun, A., Scott, T.M. and Snyder, C.R. (2006) 'Hope therapy in a community sample: A pilot study', *Social Indicators Research, 77:* 61–78.

Clough, P. and Strycharczyk, D. (2012) *Developing Mental Toughness: Improving Performance, Well-being & Positive Behaviour in Others.* London: Kogan Page.

Cooperider, D.L. and Srivastva, S. (1987) 'Appreciative inquiry in organisational life'. In R.W. Woodman and W.A Passmore (eds), *Research in Organisational Change and Development.* Stamford, CT: JAL. pp. 129–169.

Csikszentmihalyi, M. (1991) *Flow.* New York: Harper.

Deci, E.L. and Ryan, R.M. (2000) 'The "what" and "why" of goal pursuits: Human needs and the self determination of behaviour', *Psychological Inquiry, 11*(4): 227–68.

Diener, E. (1984) 'Subjective well-being', *Psychological Bulletin, 95:* 542–75.

Earle, F. and Clough, P. (2014) 'Mental toughness: Its relevance to teaching'. In D. Strycharczyk and P. Clough (eds), *Developing Mental Toughness in Young People.* London: Karnac

Emmons, R. (2003) 'Personal goals, life meaning and virtue: Wellsprings of positive life'. In C.L.M. Keyes and J. Haidt (eds), *Flourishing: Positive Psychology and the Life Well Lived.* Washington, DC: APA. pp. 105–28.

Fredrickson, B. (2007) *Positivity.* Oxford: Oneworld.

Furlong, M.J., Gilman, R. and Huebner, E.S. (2014) 'Towards a science and practice of Positive Psychology in schools: A conceptual framework'. In M.J. Furlong, R. Gilmanand E.S. Huebner (eds), *The Handbook of Positive Psychology in Schools,* 2nd edn. New York: Routledge/Taylor & Francis.

Gable, S.L. and Haidt, J. (2005) 'What (and why) is positive psychology?', *Review of General Psychology, 9:* 103–10.

Grant, A.M. (2003) 'The impact of life coaching on goal attainment, metacognition and mental health', *Social Behavior and Personality: An International Journal, 31*(3): 253–66.

Grant, A.M. (2007) 'Past, present & future: The evolution of professional coaching and coaching psychology'. In S. Palmer and A. Whybrow (eds), *Handbook of Coaching Psychology.* Hove: Routledge. pp. 23–39.

Grant, A.M. (2012) 'ROI is a poor measure of coaching success: Towards a more holistic approach using a wellbeing and engagement framework', *Coaching: An International Journal of Theory, Research and Practice*, 5(2): 74–85.

Grant, A.M. and Cavanagh, M.J. (2007) 'Evidence-based coaching flourishing or languishing?', *Australian Psychologist*, 42(4): 239–54.

Grant, A.M. and Stober, D.R. (2006) 'Introduction'. In D.R. Stober and A.M. Grant (eds), *Evidence-based Coaching Handbook: Putting Best Practices to Work for Your Clients*. Hoboken, NJ: Wiley. pp. 1–14.

Grant, A.M., Curtayne, L. and Burton, G. (2009) 'Executive coaching enhances goal attainment, resilience and workplace well-being: A randomized controlled study', *Journal of Positive Psychology*, 4(5): 396–407.

Grant, A.M., Green, L.S. and Rynsaardt, J. (2010) 'Developmental coaching for high school teachers: Executive coaching goes to school', *Consulting Psychology Journal: Practice and Research*, 62(3): 151–68.

Green, L.S. (2014) 'Positive Education: An Australian perspective'. In M.J. Furlong, R. Gilman and E.S. Huebner (eds), *The Handbook of Positive Psychology in Schools*, 2nd edn. New York: Routledge/Taylor & Francis. pp. 401–15.

Green, L.S. and Spence, G.B. (2014) 'Evidence-based coaching as a positive psychology intervention. In A.C. Parks (ed.), *The Wiley Blackwell Handbook of Positive Psychology Interventions*. London/Oxford: Wiley and Blackwell.

Green, L.S., Oades, L.G. and Robinson, P.I. (2011) 'Positive Education: Creating flourishing students, staff and schools', *InPsych, the bulletin of the Australian Psychological Society*, April.

Green, L.S., Oades, L.G. and Robinson, P.I. (2012) 'Positive Education programs: Integrating, coaching and positive psychology in schools'. In C. van Nieuwerburgh (ed.), *Coaching in Education: Getting Better Results for Students, Educators and Parents*. London: Karnac. pp. 115–32.

Green, S., Grant, A.M. and Rynsaardt, J. (2007) 'Evidence-based coaching for senior high school students: Building hardiness and hope', *International Coaching Psychology Review*, 2(1): 24–31.

Green, S., Oades, L. and Grant, A.M. (2006) 'Cognitive-behavioural, solution-focused life coaching: Enhancing goal striving, well-being and hope', *Journal of Positive Psychology*, 1(3): 142–9.

Grenville-Cleave, B. (2013) Positive Education: Making successful schools', *Positive Psychology News Daily*. Available at www.ppnd.com

Hefferon, K. and Boniwell, I. (2011) *Positive Psychology Theory, Research and Applications*. Maidenhead: Open University Press.

Huppert, F.L. and So, T. (2009). 'What percentage of people in Europe are flourishing and what characterizes them?' Presentation to the First World Congress on Positive Psychology, Philadelphia, June 18–21.

IPEN (2014) International Positive Education Network. Available at www.ipositive-education.net

ISCAPPED (2014) International Symposium for Coaching and Positive Psychology in Education. Available at www.iscapped.com

Kauffman, C. (2006) 'Positive Psychology: The science at the heart of coaching'. In D. Stober and A.M. Grant (eds), *Evidence Based Coaching Handbook*. Hoboken, NJ: Wiley. pp. 219–254.

Kauffman, C., Boniwell, I. and Silberman, J. (2010) 'The positive psychology approach to coaching'. In E. Cox, T. Bachkirova and D. Clutterbuck (eds), *The Complete Handbook of Coaching*. London: Sage. pp. 158–71.

Kern, M.L., Waters, L., Adler, A. and White, M. (2014) 'Assessing employee well-being in schools using a multifaceted approach: Associations with physical health, life satisfaction and professional thriving', *Psychology*, 5: 500–13.

Keyes, C. (2007) 'Promoting and protecting mental health and flourishing', *American Psychologist*, 62(2): 95–108.

Kotter, J. (1996) *Leading Change*. Harvard: Harvard Business Press.

Layard, R., Clarke, A.E., Cornaglia, F., Powddthavee, N. and Vernoit, J. (2014) 'What predicts a successful life?: A life course model of well-being', *Economic Journal*, 123(580): 720–38.

Leach, C.J.C., Green, L.S. and Grant, A.M. (2011) 'Flourishing youth provision: The potential role of positive psychology and coaching in enhancing youth services', *International Journal of Evidence Based Coaching and Mentoring*, 9(1): 44–58.

Linley, P.A. and Harrington, S. (2006) 'Strengths coaching: A potential-guided approach to coaching psychology', *International Coaching Psychology Review*, 1: 37–46.

Linley, A., Williams J. and Biswas-Diener, R. (2010) *The Strengths Book: Be Confident, Be Successful & Enjoy Better Relationships by Realizing the Best You*. London: CAPP Press.

Luthans, F. (2012) 'Psychological capital: Implications for HRD, retrospective analysis and future directions', *Human Resource Development Quarterly*, 23(1): 1–8.

Madden, W., Green, L.S. and Grant, A.M. (2011) 'A pilot study evaluating strengths-based coaching for primary school students: Enhancing engagement and hope', *International Coaching Psychology Review*, 61: 71–83.

Mission Australia (2014) 'Annual Youth Survey 2014'. Available at www.missionaustralia.com

Mroz, D. and Quinn, S. (2009) 'Positive organisational scholarship leaps into the World of Work'. In N. Garcia, S. Harrington and P.A. Linley (eds), *Oxford Handbook of Positive Psychology and Work*. Available at Oxford Handbooks online.

Noble, T. and McGrath, H. (2008) 'The positive educational practices framework: A tool for facilitating the work of educational psychologists in promoting pupil well-being', *Education and Child Psychology*, 25(2): 119–34.

Norrish, J.M. and Vella-Brodrick, D.A. (2009) 'Positive Psychology and adolescents: Where are we now? Where to from here?', *Australian Psychologist*, 1: 1–9.

Norrish, J.M., Williams, P., O'Connor, M. and Robinson, J. (2013) 'An applied framework for positive education', *International Journal of Wellbeing*, 3(2): 147–61.

Nowack, K. (1990) 'Initial development of an inventory to assess stress and health', *American Journal of Health Promotion*, 4: 173–80.

O'Connor, M., Sawson, A.V., Toumbourou, J.W., Hawkins, M.T., Letcher, P., Williams, P. and Olsson, C. (2014) 'Positive development and resilience in emerging adulthood'. In J. Jensen-Arnett (ed.), *Oxford Handbook of Emerging Adulthood*. Oxford: Oxford University Press.

Palmer, S. and Whybrow, A. (2007) 'Coaching psychology: An Introduction'. In S. Palmer and A. Whybrow (eds), *Handbook of Coaching Psychology*. Hove: Routledge. pp. 1–20.

Peterson, C. and Seligman, M. (2004) *'Character Strengths and Virtues: A Handbook Classification.* New York: Oxford University Press.

Positive Education Summit (2013) Available at www.positiveeducationsummit.com/the-summit/ (last accessed 4 September 2014).

Prince's Trust Youth Index (2013) Available at www.princes-trust.org.uk/pdf/youth-index-2013.pdf (last accessed 31 August 2014).

Resilient Youth Australia (2014) *'Resilience Survey and Report'.* Available at www.reslientyouth.org.au

Ryff, C. (1989) 'Explorations on the meaning of PWB', *Journal of Personality and Social Psychology,* 57: 1069–81.

Sekerka, L. and Fredrickson, B. (2010) 'Working positively towards transformational cooperation'. In P.A. Linley, S. Hangka and N. Garcea (eds), *Handbook of Positive Psychology.* Oxford: Oxford University Press. pp. 81–94.

Seldon, A. (2013) *Why the development of good character matters more than the passing of exams.* Priestly Lecture, University of Birmingham, 23 November.

Seligman, M. (1998) *Learned Optimism.* New York: Simon & Schuster.

Seligman, M. (2004) *Learned Optimism: How to Change your Mind and your Life.* New York: Pocket Books.

Seligman, M. (2011) *Flourish: A Visionary New Understanding of Happiness and Well-being.* New York: Simon & Schuster.

Seligman, M. and Csikszentmihalyi, M. (2000) 'Positive Psychology: An introduction', *American Psychologist,* 55(1): 5–14.

Seligman, M. and Peterson, C. (2004) *Character Strengths & Virtues: A Handbook Classification.* APA/Oxford University Press.

Seligman, M., Randal, M.E., Gilman, J., Reivich, K. and Linkins, M. (2009) 'Positive education: Positive psychology and classroom interactions', *Oxford Review of Education,* 35: 293–311.

Sheldon, K.M. (2002)' 'The Self-concordance model of healthy goal striving: When personal goals correctly represent the person'. In E.L. Deci and R.M. Ryan (eds), *Handbook of Self-determination Research.* Rochester: University of Rochester Press. pp. 65–88.

Sheldon, K.M. and Lyubormirsky, S. (2006) 'How to increase and sustain positive emotion: The effects of expressing gratitude and visualising best possible selves', *Journal of Positive Psychology,* 1: 73–82.

Sin, N.L. and Lyubormirsky, S. (2009) 'Enhancing well-being and alleviating depressive symptoms with positive psychology interventions: A practice-friendly meta analysis', *Journal of Clinical Psychology,* 65(5): 467–87.

Snyder, C.R., Michael, S.T. and Cheavens, J. (1999) 'Hope as a psychotherapeutic foundation of common factors, placebos and expectancies'. In M.A. Hubble, B. Duncan and S. Miller (eds), *Heart & Soul of Change.* Washington DC: APA. pp. 179–200.

Snyder, C.R., Rand, K.L. and Sigmon, D.R. (2002) 'Hope theory: A member of the positive psychology family'. In C.R. Snyder and S.J. Lopez (eds), *Handbook of Positive Psychology.* Oxford: Oxford University Press. pp. 257–276.

Spence, G.B. and Grant, A.M. (2007) 'Professional and peer life coaching and the enhancement of goal striving and well-being: An exploratory study', *Journal of Positive Psychology*, 2(3): 185–94.

Strauss, G.E, Waters, L.E. and Somech, A. (2013) 'An investigation of the relationship between psychological capital and school leaders workplace well-being'. Presentation at the IPPA World Congress, Los Angeles, July.

Strycharczyk, D. (2014) 'What is mental toughness?'. In D. Strycharczyk and P. Clough (eds), *Developing Mental Toughness in Young People*. London: Karnac. pp. 81–97.

UK Centre Forum (2014) *Character and Resilience Manifesto: The All-Party Parliamentary Group on Social Mobility*. Available at www.centreforum.org/assets/pubs/character-and-resilience.pdf (accessed September 2015).

UK Government (2013) *Improving Children and Young People's Health Outcomes: A System Wide Response*. Available at www.gov.uk/9328-TSO-2900598-DHSystemWideResponse.pdf

van Nieuwerburgh, C. (2012) *Coaching in Education: Getting Better Results for Students, Educators and Parents*. London: Karnac.

van Nieuwerburgh, C. and Green, S. (2014) 'Developing mental toughness in young people: Coaching as an applied positive psychology'. In D. Strycharczyk and P. Clough (eds), *Developing Mental Toughness in Young People*. London: Karnac. pp. 81–97.

van Nieuwerburgh, C. and Passmore (2012) 'Coaching in secondary or high schools'. In C. van Nieuwerburgh (ed.), *Coaching in Education: Getting Better Results for Students, Educators and Parents*. London: Karnac. pp. 63–74.

van Nieuwerburgh, C. and Tong, C. (2013) 'Exploring the benefits of being a student coach in educational settings: A mixed-method study', *Coaching: An International Journal of Theory, Research and Practice*, 6(1): 5–24.

van Nieuwerburgh, C., Zacharia, C., Luckham, E., Prebble, G. and Browne, L. (2012) 'Coaching students in a secondary school'. In C. van Nieuwerburgh (ed.), *Coaching in Education: Getting Better Results for Students, Educators and Parents*. London: Karnac. pp. 191–8.

Venning, A., Wilson, A., Kettler, L. and Eliot, J. (2013) 'Mental health amongst youth in South Australia: A survey of flourishing, languishing, struggling and floundering', *Australian Psychologist*, 48(4): 299–310.

Waters, L. (2011) 'A review of school-based Positive Psychology interventions', *The Australian Educational and Development Psychologist*, 28(2): 75–90.

Waters, L., White, M. and Murray, S. (2012) 'Towards the creation of a positive institution', *International Journal of Appreciative Inquiry*, 14(2).

White, M.A. and Waters, L.E. (2014) 'A case study of "The Good School": Examples of the use of Peterson's strengths-based approaches with students', *Journal of Positive Psychology*. doi: 10.1080/17439760.2014.920408

Whitmore, J. (2002) *Coaching for Performance: GROWing people, performance and purpose*, 3rd edn. London: Nicholas Brealey.

WHO (2011) *Global burden of mental disorders and the need for a comprehensive, coordinated response from health and social sectors at country level*. Available at www.apps.who.int/gb/ebwha/pdf-files/EB130/B130_9-en.pdf (last accessed 8 October 2014).

13
THE CURRENT STATE OF RESEARCH
TIM THEEBOOM

INTRODUCTION

Coaching, which can be broadly defined as a dialogue-based change methodology, has become increasingly popular in the last three decades (Passmore and Fillery-Travis, 2011). During this time, the status of coaching in organisational settings has changed significantly. Today, coaching is no longer seen as a socially accepted form of therapy for dysfunctional managers, but is now understood as an opportunity to invest in one's own professional and/ or personal development. Further, coaching is no longer exclusively available to high-level executives but is also for people 'on the floor' such as nurses and teachers. To summarise, coaching has come of age and is now big business: the global revenue of coaching is estimated to be around US$2 billion and the International Coach Federation counts more than 22,000 members in over 100 countries (see www.coachfederation.org). Coaching Psychology is also now taught at undergraduate and postgraduate level at universities throughout the world (e.g. the University of East London in the UK, the University of Sydney in Australia, and the University of Amsterdam in the Netherlands).

Along with this increasing popularity of coaching as a developmental tool, the body of research on coaching is growing steadily. This chapter will briefly discuss the development of the literature, provide a summary of what is currently known about the application of coaching interventions in organisational settings, and outline some of the major challenges that need to be addressed by future research.

THE DEVELOPMENT OF THE COACHING LITERATURE

Although the first article on coaching was published as early as 1937 (by Gorby), use of the term 'coaching' has only become a common occurrence in the academic literature during the

1990s (Passmore and Fillery-Travis, 2011). From that time onwards, the coaching literature has evolved into several streams of research that have emerged over the past three decades. Initially, there was a strong focus on theoretical investigations that addressed definitions of coaching and boundaries with other developmental interactions such as mentoring, counselling and therapy. Gradually, the focus shifted from the question 'What is coaching?' to 'Does coaching work?' In regard to this latter question, the literature on coaching follows the typical development of research on other phenomena in the social sciences (and especially psychology). Initially there was a strong focus on case studies and surveys which were followed by qualitative studies, and later on small-scale randomised controlled trials (Passmore and Theeboom, 2015).

WHAT THE RESEARCH TELLS US ABOUT SPECIFIC COACHING INTERVENTIONS

Of all the different approaches to coaching, relatively few have been systematically studied. The large majority of studies has focused on cognitive-behavioral approaches such as solution-focused coaching (see Theeboom et al., 2014). This is hardly surprising: the structured nature of cognitive-behavioural (solution-focused) approaches is relatively easy to capture in standardised protocols, and therefore most convenient to study. In fact, one could (somewhat provocatively) argue that this might be one of the reasons why the cognitive-behavioural paradigm is currently considered the 'gold standard' in the field of psychotherapy.

Empirical support for other approaches to coaching can be found if one looks beyond the narrow definition of coaching and broadens the scope to include research on psychotherapy and counselling. Whereas there are notable differences between these 'developmental interactions and coaching, all of these interventions essentially deal with the facilitation of human development and change and could potentially be incorporated in organizational settings' (D'Abate et al., 2003). For example, several psychotherapeutic interventions such as motivational interviewing (Rollnick and Miller, 1995) and acceptance and commitment therapy (e.g. Bond et al., 2008) have been successfully applied in both public (e.g. education, healthcare) and private organisations (e.g. Bond et al., 2010; Brinkborg et al., 2011). Similarly, the evidence for approaches rooted in positive psychology (e.g. a strengths-based approach) and narrative approaches is accumulating steadily (e.g. Stelter et al., 2011). Thus, the good news is that multiple approaches can be translated to organisational settings.

On the other hand, however, it is quite worrisome that some of the most popular (and extensively marketed) approaches such as Neuro-Linguistic Programming (NLP) have received little empirical support (Witkowski, 2012). Further, it is not (yet) known how the different approaches to coaching compare to each other in terms of effectiveness, and to what degree this depends on the topic that the coaching intervention needs to address (e.g. is motivational interviewing as effective for increasing performance as it is for changing health behaviours?).

To our knowledge, there is not a single study that compares the effectiveness of various approaches to coaching. Whether this would be a fruitful area for future research is hard to say. On the one hand, results of such studies could potentially help clients of coaching (individuals and organisations) to decide on which approach of coaching to invest in. On the other hand, similar questions have been raised about psychotherapeutic interventions, and meta-analyses consistently point out that a) different approaches have comparable effects and b) that 'common factors' (such as the therapist–client relationship and the expectations of both therapist and client) are far more important than the use of specific techniques (e.g. Messer and Wampold, 2002).

OVERALL EFFECTS OF COACHING AND LIMITATIONS OF THE CURRENT LITERATURE

To sum up, there is an increasing amount of research which indicates that (some approaches to) coaching can be applied effectively in professional settings. Recently, a quantitative summary of the overall effects of coaching (regardless of the specific approach) was published (Theeboom et al., 2014). Specifically, the meta-analysis included all (quantitative) studies in which the coaching intervention matched Grant's (2003: 254) definition of coaching ('a result-oriented, systematic process in which the coach facilitates the enhancement of life experience and goal-attainment in the personal and/or professional lives of non-clinical clients') and considered its impact using five individual level outcome categories: skill development/performance, wellbeing, coping, work-related attitudes and self-regulation.

The results of the meta-analysis indicate that coaching can indeed have significant positive effects on all of these outcomes (see Table 13.1). Thus research seems to support the notion that coaching (and related interventions) can be applied effectively in organisational settings and this is encouraging for individual clients, organisations and coaches alike.

Table 13.1

Outcome	Effect size
Performance/skills	.60
Wellbeing	.46
Coping	.43
Goal-attainment	.74
Work/career attitudes	.54

However, the meta-analysis also shows that the field of coaching research is in its infancy, as has been noted by several scholars in the field (e.g. Grant et al., 2010; Passmore and

Fillery-Travis, 2011). Specifically, it points to several methodological issues that need to be addressed in future research in order to further develop the field. First, the results show that effect sizes in studies that incorporate a control group (and thus control for additional sources of bias such as the natural maturation of coachees) are much smaller than those that do not incorporate a control group. Second, the outcomes of coaching interventions are almost exclusively assessed by self-report questionnaires. This is problematic, since Peterson (1993) found that there are significant discrepancies between the self-reported progress of coachees (who tend to overestimate their progress) and the progress as reported by others such as the coach and/or the manager of the coachee. Third, the large majority of studies assessed the effectiveness of interventions directly after the last coaching session without further follow-up measures. As a result, very little information about the long-term effectiveness of coaching interventions is currently available. Taken together, these methodological shortcomings underline the need for more methodologically rigorous research in order to gain a realistic (rather than overly optimistic) perspective on the sustainable effectiveness of coaching interventions.

As a result, despite the encouraging results of the meta-analysis it should be considered a starting point rather than a definitive answer to the question 'Does coaching work?' There is a strong need for future research that addresses the methodological issues outlined above. In addition to these methodological issues, however, there are three broader challenges that need to be met if Coaching Psychology truly wants to develop as an academic discipline. First, research needs to shift its focus from the question 'Does coaching work?' to 'How does coaching work?' by grounding future research in strong theoretical foundations. Second, scholars need to (continue to) actively think about and debate the conceptualisation and measurement of coaching effectiveness. Third, and especially important from an organisational perspective, future research should consider the role of coaching in broader human resource development (HRD) systems in organisations. Thinking about these issues is crucial for building the cumulative knowledge base that is needed to further develop coaching interventions.

BALANCING EVALUATIVE VS. FORMATIVE RESEARCH IN COACHING AND THE NEED FOR STRONG THEORETICAL FOUNDATIONS

Why do we study coaching? The answer to this question might depend on who you ask. Typically, four potential stakeholders of coaching interventions in organisational settings can be identified: the organisation itself, the coachee, individual coaches, and organisations that provide coaching services (Ely et al., 2010). Together, the organisation and the coachee can be considered to be the two clients of coaching: they are the ones who invest their time and financial resources in coaching services because they expect a return in the form of improved wellbeing and/or the performance of the coachee. Thus, for these stakeholders, the most important question that needs to be addressed by coaching research is whether coaching can meet these expectations. In other words, 'Does coaching work?' Within the current literature on coaching, this type of *evaluative* research has received most attention from scholars. While an answer to this question can also provide feedback (and potential marketing opportunities) for individual coaches and the providers of coaching services, there is another question that begs our attention: 'How does coaching work?'

To date, this latter question has been largely ignored. To give an example, there are an increasing amount of studies indicating that coaching approaches that build on a coachee's strengths and successes can be applied effectively in organisations (Theeboom et al., 2014). But what makes this approach effective? Answering this question is crucial for the development of new approaches and the refinement of existing coaching interventions. Since coaching is in essence a change methodology aimed at facilitating human adaptation and change (Grant, 2012), future research that aims to answer these questions could benefit from incorporating seminal theories and constructs that have been studied in academic disciplines such as psychology, education and management.

To refer back to the example above, it might be that the positive emotions elicited by coaching approaches that encourage reflection on strengths and successes increase a coachee's creative problem-solving capabilities as predicted by the broaden-and-build theory of positive emotions (Fredrickson, 1998, 2001). Yet it might also be the case that reflecting on strengths and successes increases a coachee's feelings of self-efficacy (i.e. the belief in one's own ability to complete a task successfully), which in turn are strongly related to a coachee's motivation (Deci and Ryan, 2008). As opposed to evaluative research, *formative* research aims to uncover the causal mechanisms underlying effective interventions and it is this type of research that will allow coaches to target and time their coaching interventions more accurately. In order for Coaching Psychology to grow as an academic discipline, future research needs to find an adequate balance between evaluative and formative research in order to serve all stakeholders of coaching interventions in organisational settings.

THE CONCEPTUALISATION AND MEASUREMENT OF EFFECTIVENESS

The question of how to measure the effectiveness of coaching is one of the most salient discussions among scholars and practitioners alike. The major difficulty is that coaching is often a non-linear, organic and confidential process that deals with unique individuals with unique problems who work in unique environments. As such, the targeted outcomes of each coaching intervention tend to differ significantly (e.g. one coachee wants to improve their leadership while the other aims to find a balance between their work and family life). Research on the effects of coaching interventions, however, requires the standardisation of as many variables as possible. In order to compare two different coaching interventions, it is crucial that these are targeted at similar individuals, with similar topics, who work in similar environments, and to measure the same outcome for each individual.

A solution that has been advocated previously is the use of generic outcome measures that are broad enough to capture a wide array of problems and results. Two such measures have been discussed extensively: Return on Investment (ROI) measures and Goal-Attainment Scaling (GAS). ROI measures aim to relate the financial investments of coaching to beneficial (often financial) outcomes for the organisations. ROI measures are appealing, because they promise to provide insight into the tangible effects of coaching. However, these measures also have some serious limitations (see Grant et al., 2010, for an extensive discussion on ROI measures). Most importantly, direct (financial) performance measures are seldom available (e.g. how do you express improved work–family balance in financial terms?) and ignore the fact that performance measures can be influenced by multiple variables that cannot be attributed to coaching interventions (e.g. the financial climate).

In the search for another broadly applicable measure, GAS has received increasing attention in the literature. In GAS, the coachee selects a specific goal to work on (e.g. a better work–family balance) and rates themself on this goal before and after the intervention (see Spence, 2007). GAS measures hereby avoid the first problem of ROI measures, namely the questionable translation of intangible results into financial benefits that look deceivingly accurate. Further, when goals are chosen and defined carefully in terms of what the coachee themself can do (e.g. decrease work-related communication at home to increase the work–family balance) it also can (partially) avoid the second problem of ignoring contextual variables.

However, GAS has its own limitations. First, not all coaching is about (or can be translated into) achieving specific goals (e.g. choosing between two equally attractive career paths). In these situations, it might be most important to bring (yet) unconscious feelings, motivations etc. into awareness so that the coachee can reflect on these and then use this information to make a choice. Second, goals may change during the coaching process. For example, a manager who wants to improve their leadership skills might change their view of effective leadership during conversations with a coach and perhaps find out that they are already doing an excellent job and do not need to change anything (is coaching effective in this case?). Third, GAS measures are often unable to capture the degree to which the coachee actually learned from the coaching process and will be able to solve similar problems in future (without the help of a coach). It might be that the coach helped the coachee to prepare an excellent presentation for their managers, but did not gain insight into how to present effectively so that they will then face the same problem for the next big presentation.

The manager as coach?

Whereas coaching is traditionally seen as an activity that is only performed by specialised and highly trained professionals who work outside the client organisation (external coaching), internal coaching by managers and/or HR staff is gaining ground as can be seen in this book. Can managers be effective coaches? While the research is scarce, some initial findings suggest that they can. For example, Kim et al., (2013) found that managerial coaching was

positively correlated with role clarity, work satisfaction, commitment and (self-rated) performance. Likewise, Ellinger et al. (2010) found that intermediate levels (rather than the
exhaustive application) of managerial coaching were positively related to job performance,
commitment, and organisational citizenship behaviours. While the correlational and cross-
sectional nature of both of these studies requires cautious interpretation, the results look
promising. However, more research on this topic is needed – not only in order to see whether
these results can be replicated when controlling for potential sources of bias (e.g. common
source and common method bias), but also because the manager–employee relationship
differs significantly from the (external) coach–coachee relationship in terms of power and
status, which in turn might impact on the issues that can be addressed by coaching (see
Chapter 3: Manager as Coach, for a comprehensive discussion). For example, a coachee might
be willing to share her doubts about the quality of her manager with an external coach, but
not with the manager herself. On the other hand, an internal coach might be much more able
to help a coachee identify steps to take in order get promoted because she (the coach) is
familiar with the political climate in the organisation. In other words, the applicability and
scope of coaching interventions might differ depending on whether the coaching is provided
by an internal or external coach.

In sum, both ROI and GAS measures have the potential to partially uncover the degree to
which coaching can be applied effectively in organisational settings. One could argue, however, that neither of them (or any other generic standardised measure for that matter) is
sufficient to capture the full potential of coaching as a change methodology. Therefore, it
might be beneficial for future studies on coaching to include additional (quantitative and
qualitative) measures that can capture the (potential) increase of self-regulatory capacities
('the learning') of coachees, and that both quantitative and qualitative measures will be combined to capture the richness and organic nature of coaching interventions.

THE ROLE OF COACHING IN HUMAN RESOURCE DEVELOPMENT (HRD) SYSTEMS

Currently, coaching is mostly studied as a stand-alone intervention in organisations. From an
academic perspective, this approach is understandable. Studying coaching as an isolated
intervention reduces the chance that effects can be ascribed to factors (interventions) other
than coaching, and such clean and 'context-free' research is often preferred by academics and
more likely to get published in high-impact academic journals (Johns, 2006). However, such
an approach does not necessarily align with contemporary HRD practice. In most (large)
organisations, human resource development interventions (such as coaching, mentoring and
training) are embedded in broader strategic HRD systems that are aligned with those organisations' missions and goals. For example, a typical leadership development programme could

include training programmes to develop specific skills (e.g. project-management), courses aimed at developing the knowledge of specific topics (e.g. about the product or service that the organisation delivers), and individual coaching to deal with the daily challenges that young leaders need to meet in competitive and highly dynamic working environments.

Assuming that a major aim of research on coaching is to inspire evidence-based practice, future research needs to find a balance between fundamental/context-free research and more holistic approaches. While the fundamental and context-free research is needed to broaden our understanding of the causal mechanisms underlying effective coaching, a more holistic and integrative approach is needed to understand coaching as a part of integrated HRD systems. In this regard, one topic of future research that seems especially promising is the potential synergy between training and coaching. Previous work by Olivero et al. (1997) showed that eight weeks of coaching following a one-day training programme helped to increase the productivity of managers by 88% as compared to 22% by just the one day of training. This is hardly surprising considering that coaching can facilitate active reflection which in turn is the most important prerequisite for deep-level ('transformative') learning (Mezirow, 1997). Furthermore, coaching could help the coachees to implement their newly acquired knowledge and skills (through training and courses) in their daily work through feedback, goal-setting and planning how to deal with potential obstacles.

The synergy between coaching and training is just an example of an area that requires (additional) investigation. For similar reasons, coaching could also prove a welcome addition to organisational change efforts (e.g. by fostering change readiness and helping to smooth difficult transitions; see Stober, 2008). In this light, the currently predominant investigation of coaching as a standalone intervention does not suffice. Thus the integration and combination of multiple (quantitative and qualitative) research methodologies is needed not only to improve our measurement of coaching effectiveness but also to be able to study coaching as a part of larger HRD systems.

CONCLUSION

Overall, the research discussed in this chapter paints an encouraging picture. Approaches such as solution-focused coaching, motivational interviewing, acceptance and commitment therapy, strengths coaching and narrative coaching have all been applied effectively in professional settings. However, this chapter also points out that our current answers around to the questions 'Does coaching work?' are indefinite and that there are other questions that deserve the attention of future research.

First, research needs to shift its focus from the question 'Does it work?' to 'How does it work?' in order to uncover the causal mechanisms underlying effective coaching, so that both existing and new coaching interventions can be refined and developed. In order to answer this latter question, research needs to be grounded in strong theoretical foundations. Second, scholars (and practitioners) need to continue their search for ways to (both quantitatively and qualitatively) measure coaching effectiveness in the broadest sense, especially in order to be able to capture the lasting effects of coaching. Third, in order to ensure that research can (continue to) inform practice, coaching needs to be considered as a part of larger HRD systems rather than a standalone intervention. Considering this last point it is crucial that scholars and practitioners (continue to) work together in order to ensure that future research is both methodologically rigorous and practically relevant.

Despite the open questions and the concerns addressed in this chapter, there is reason to be optimistic about the future of coaching research. The academic community is growing rapidly, and seems to become increasingly aware of the multitude of challenges lying before us. It is only by our collective effort and constructive (yet critical) cooperation that we can advance the field of coaching research and facilitate its transition from infancy to adulthood.

REFERENCES

Bond, F.W., Flaxman, P.E. and Bunce, D. (2008) 'The influence of psychological flexibility on work redesign: Mediated moderation of a work reorganization intervention', *Journal of Applied Psychology*, 93(3): 645–54.

Bond, F.W., Flaxman, P.E., van Veldhoven, M.J.P.M. and Biron, M. (2010) 'The impact of psychological flexibility and acceptance and commitment therapy (ACT) on health and productivity at work', *Contemporary Occupational Health Psychology: Global Perspectives on Research and Practice*, 1: 296–313.

Brinkborg, H., Michanek, J., Hesser, H. and Berglund, G. (2011) 'Acceptance and commitment therapy for the treatment of stress among social workers: A randomized controlled trial', *Behaviour Research and Therapy*, 49(6): 389–98.

D'Abate, C.P., Eddy, E.R. and Tannenbaum, S.I. (2003) 'What's in a name? A literature-based approach to understanding mentoring, coaching, and other constructs that describe developmental interactions', *Human Resource Development Review*, 2(4): 360–84.

Deci, E.L. and Ryan, R.M. (2008) 'Self-determination theory: A macrotheory of human motivation, development, and health', *Canadian Psychology/Psychologie Canadienne*, 49(3): 182–5.

Ellinger, A.D., Ellinger, A.E., Bachrach, D.G., Wang, Y.L., and Baş, A.B.E. (2010) 'Organizational investments in social capital, managerial coaching, and employee work-related performance', *Management Learning*, 42(1): 67–85.

Ely, K., Boyce, L.A., Nelson, J.K., Zaccaro, S.J., Hernez-Broome, G. and Whyman, W. (2010) 'Evaluating leadership coaching: A review and integrated framework', *The Leadership Quarterly*, 21(4): 585–99.

Fredrickson, B.L. (1998) 'Cultivated emotions: Parental socialization of positive emotions and self-conscious emotions', *Psychological Inquiry*, 9(4): 279–81.

Fredrickson, B.L. (2001) 'The role of positive emotions in positive psychology: The broaden-and-build theory of positive emotions', *American Psychologist*, 56(3): 218–26.

Gorby, C. (1937) 'Everyone gets a share of the profits', *Factory Management and Maintenance*, *95*: 82–3.

Grant, A.M. (2003) 'The impact of life coaching on goal-attainment, metacognition and mental health', *Social Behavior and Personality*, *31*: 253–64.

Grant, A.M. (2012) 'The efficacy of coaching'. In J. Passmore, D. Peterson and T. Freire (eds), *Wiley Blackwell Handbook of the Psychology of Coaching and Mentoring*. Chichester: Wiley. pp. 15–39.

Grant, A.M., Passmore, J., Cavanagh, M.J. and Parker, H.M. (2010) 'The state of play in coaching today: A comprehensive review of the field', *International Review of Industrial and Organizational Psychology*, *25*(1): 125–67.

Johns, G. (2006) 'The essential impact of context on organizational behavior', *Academy of Management Review*, *31*(2): 386–408.

Kim, S., Egan, T.M., Kim, W. and Kim, J. (2013) 'The impact of managerial coaching behavior on employee work-related reactions', *Journal of Business and Psychology*, *28*(3): 315–30.

Messer, S.B. and Wampold, B.E. (2002) 'Let's face facts: Common factors are more potent than specific therapy ingredients', *Clinical Psychology: Science and Practice*, *9*(1): 21–5.

Mezirow, J. (1997) 'Transformative learning: Theory to practice', *New Directions for Adult and Continuing Education*, *74*: 5–12.

Olivero, G., Bane, K.D. and Kopelman, R.E. (1997) 'Executive coaching as a transfer of training tool: Effects on productivity in a public agency', *Public Personnel Management*, *26*(4): 461–9.

Passmore, J. and Fillery-Travis, A. (2011) 'A critical review of executive coaching research: A decade of progress and what's to come', *Coaching: An International Journal of Theory, Research and Practice*, *4*(2): 70–88.

Passmore, J. and Theeboom, T. (2015) 'Coaching Psychology: A journey of development in research'. In L.E. Van Zyl, M.W. Stander and A. Oodendal (eds), *Coaching Psychology: Meta-theoretical Perspectives and Applications in Multi-cultural Contexts*. New York: Springer.

Peterson, D.B. (1993) *Measuring change: A psychometric approach to evaluating individual training outcomes*. Symposium conducted at the Eighth Annual Conference of the Society for Industrial and Organizational Psychologists, San Francisco.

Platt, G. (2001) 'NLP: Neuro Linguistic Programming or No Longer Plausible?', *Training Journal*, 10–15.

Rollnick, S. and Miller, W.R. (1995) 'What is motivational interviewing?', *Behavioural and Cognitive Psychotherapy*, *23*(4): 325–34.

Sharpley, C.F. (1984) 'Predicate matching in NLP: A review of research on the preferred representational system', *Journal of Counseling Psychology*, *31*(2): 238.

Spence, G.B. (2007) 'GAS powered coaching: Goal Attainment Scaling and its use in coaching research and practice', *International Coaching Psychology Review*, *2*(2): 155–67.

Stelter, R., Nielsen, G. and Wikman, J.M. (2011) 'Narrative-collaborative group coaching develops social capital – a randomised control trial and further implications of the social impact of the intervention', *Coaching: An International Journal of Theory, Research and Practice*, 4(2): 123–37.

Stober, D.R. (2008) 'Making it stick: Coaching as a tool for organizational change', *Coaching: An International Journal of Theory, Research and Practice*, 1(1): 71–80.

Theeboom, T., Beersma, B. and van Vianen, A.E. (2014) 'Does coaching work? A meta-analysis on the effects of coaching on individual level outcomes in an organizational context', *Journal of Positive Psychology*, 9(1): 1–18.

Witkowski, T. (2012) 'A review of research findings on Neuro-Linguistic Programming', *Scientific Review of Mental Health Practice*, 9(1): 29–40.

14

COACHING FOR WELLBEING AT WORK

LINDSAY G. OADES

INTRODUCTION

This chapter examines the use and potential of coaching for wellbeing at work. The workplace is an important context for many adults, providing an opportunity for policy makers to introduce wellbeing initiatives as part of the aim to improve the overall wellbeing of the population and not only treat illness. Conversely, from an employer's perspective, the improved wellbeing of employees can have business and performance benefits including increased personal productivity, improved work performance and decreased staff turnover. Within this context, this chapter describes the unique issues and potential advantages of coaching for wellbeing as an evolution of existing workplace wellbeing programmes.

How coaching for wellbeing at work should be used is explored based on the two key types of wellbeing: *hedonic wellbeing* (feeling good) and *eudaimonic wellbeing* (functioning well). Firmly established theories of wellbeing are described, before providing practical suggestions for those coaching in this sector or setting up coaching programmes within these settings. The chapter concludes with ten common workplace challenges to wellbeing.

WELLBEING AT WORK

Adults spend much of their time working (Morgan, 2014). For this reason, the workplace is a key leverage area to improve the wellbeing of a population. Moreover, there is evidence that increasing the wellbeing of employees can improve the productivity and performance of individuals. At the same time, it can decrease staff turnover and reduce the costs of people being absent from work (absenteeism) and people being at work but not productive, often due to illness (presenteeism). The use of coaching in this context can provide benefits due to its personalised and responsive nature, as it can be tailored to meet individual needs.

Whilst coaching for wellbeing may be seen as similar to health coaching, coaching for wellbeing tends to be more psychological in nature, and emphasises subjective experiences. The approaches however overlap significantly. To understand coaching for wellbeing, it is first important to understand the concepts of wellbeing, known as hedonic and eudaimonic wellbeing (Waterman, 1993).

Short-term or hedonic wellbeing, often measured through Subjective Wellbeing, is one type of wellbeing. This is derived from the Bentham philosophy of utility, related *to maximising pleasure and minimising pain*. This is what a hedonist does, hence the term 'hedonic wellbeing'. This is the type of wellbeing most closely related to the commonly understood notion of happiness. Sustainable wellbeing or eudaimonic wellbeing, literally *eu* (wellbeing – or good) and *daimonia* (demon or spirit) – and virtuous action, is often measured by Flourishing or Psychological Wellbeing. This is derived from Aristotlean philosophy and is related to *reaching one's true potential or having a life well lived*, and has an explicit ethical component. For explanatory purposes, the analogy of 'cash flow' is used to describe hedonic wellbeing (i.e. more positive emotions than negative emotions, analogous to more income than expense). The analogy of an 'asset' is used to describe eudaimonic wellbeing, as assets can be built or eroded but usually in a manner that is slower than the changes of cashflow. Moreover, having more assets makes cashflow easier to gain. Hence, rather than an either/or approach to which type of wellbeing, in coaching it may be understood as a dynamic and dual process.

ESTABLISHED THEORIES OF WELLBEING

Strengths theory

Strengths theory (ST) can be considered a family of theories or a unifying proposition. The central proposition is that people will perform, feel and function better if they are using their strengths. Consequently, strengths researchers and practitioners have developed strengths assessment tools to assist people to gain knowledge of their strengths and then use these and spot the strengths of others. Two different conceptualisations of personal strengths are relevant to coaches. The first is character strengths which constitute a person's values put into action. These have been developed largely by Petersen and Seligman (2004). Character strengths cluster as virtues and represent things that are 'good' in an ethical sense, based on virtue ethics. The assessment tool Values in Action (VIA), often referred to as the 'signature strengths survey', is used to assess character strengths (Kaufman et al., 2008).

Performance strengths are different from character strengths in that they relate to something a person feels good at, and something a person feels energised by doing. Related to coaching for wellbeing at work, Proctor et al. (2011) report the relationship between strengths use and wellbeing. By enabling people to use more of their strengths at work, coaches are indirectly enabling employees to improve their personal wellbeing too.

Broaden-and-build theory

Broaden-and-build theory (BBT) helps to answer the question 'What is the function of positive emotion?' (Fredrickson, 1998, 2001). The theory proposes that experiences of positive emotions *broaden* people's momentary thought-action repertoires, i.e. a 'menu of choices' of thinking and acting is broader when a person is experiencing positive emotions. The theory holds that this serves to *build* enduring personal resources including physical, intellectual, social and psychological resources. Positive emotions are central to coaching for wellbeing at work, as illustrated in Table 14.1, and form the starting point for discussions underpinning subjective wellbeing.

Self-determination theory

Self-determination theory (SDT), often referred to as meta-theory, examines the effects of different types (rather than solely amounts) of motivation (Deci and Ryan, 2000). Expanding on the distinction between intrinsic and extrinsic motivation, the theory posits that external regulation can become internalised and be experienced as autonomous. Hence two key types of motivation are autonomous and controlled. SDT posits three universal psychological needs: (a) autonomy; (b) relatedness; and (c) competency. Hence people need to make their own choices, connect with others and feel competent as they exercise and grow their capacities. If these three needs are met, a person will have increased autonomous motivation. Autonomous motivation leads to greater perseverance at tasks that have originally been from an external origin (e.g. something from the organisation one works for becomes more internalised). Coaching for wellbeing at work may use components of SDT (Spence and Oades, 2011) to assist employees to meet their needs to feel autonomous, relate to others and have a sense of competency at work. This will improve employee sense of wellbeing and authenticity at work.

Wellbeing theory

Wellbeing theory (Diener, 2000) is similar to aspects of SDT (Seligman, 2011). It posits that there are five domains of life which both constitute and may be instruments towards wellbeing, and they each have a unique contribution. The five components are **P**ositive Emotions, **E**ngagement, **R**elationships, **M**eaning and **A**ccomplishment. Wellbeing theory is sometimes referred to simply as PERMA theory (the acronym making up the five components). PERMA is an evolution of Seligman's previous work on authentic happiness which included Positive Emotions, Engagement and Meaning with relationships and accomplishment added. The reader is encouraged to examine how PERMA is dispersed across the objectives outlined in Table 14.1.

WHAT IS UNIQUE ABOUT COACHING FOR WELLBEING AT WORK?

Coaching for wellbeing at work is different from life coaching, health coaching, executive coaching, business coaching and skills coaching (Green et al., 2006; Martin et al., 2014). The purpose is to improve wellbeing, and in this context, wellbeing at work and related to work. Whilst coaching may improve performance and productivity at work, this is a secondary benefit. The primary benefit is improvements to 'feeling good' and 'functioning well'. While there is an overlap with health coaching, the broad aim is to improve wellbeing. This can have mental and physical components (to feel good and do well), over and above managing illness or distress. Moreover, coaching for wellbeing is broader than health coaching by including issues of relationships, belonging and meaning, which would not typically feature within traditional health coaching.

Coaching for wellbeing will often be embedded within workplace wellbeing programmes or linked to employee assistance programmes. Coaching for wellbeing is somewhat different from counselling for the same reasons coaching is often differentiated from counselling. Importantly, coaching has an approach motivation (i.e. it assists people to move towards something positive, not solely move away from something negative, that is escape or avoidance motivation). Therefore it is important for coaching for wellbeing not to be reduced to 'illness prevention.' While important, this would not be a complete conceptualisation of coaching for wellbeing at work, as illustrated in Table 14.1.

Myth:	Wellbeing is about positive thinking and feeling good all of the time.
Myth buster:	Wellbeing involves good functioning, which at certain times involves negative emotions, like fear. Coaching for wellbeing at work can involve helping people to feel good, but importantly also to function well by managing the common challenges to wellbeing in the workplace.

GUIDANCE FOR THOSE WORKING TO IMPROVE WELLBEING AT WORK

Spence and Grant (2013) summarised the limited evidence on coaching for wellbeing. Oades and Passmore (2014) describe positive psychology coaching in terms of methods to achieve hedonic wellbeing ('feeling good') and eudaimonic wellbeing ('functioning well'). In this sense, positive psychology coaching is the type of coaching most explicitly linked to coaching for wellbeing (Biswas-Diener, 2010). Hence, Table 14.1 uses an adapted version of the Oades and Passmore (2014) schema, applied specifically to the work context. This provides a broad framework for guiding coaching for wellbeing at work.

Table 14.1   Coaching aims to improve different types of wellbeing at work

Short-term wellbeing (hedonic wellbeing) *'the cashflow'*	Sustainable wellbeing (eudaimonic wellbeing) *'the asset'*
1. Coaching to modulate the ratio of positive to negative emotions at work	1. Coaching to increase sense of meaning and purpose at work
2. Coaching to ensure basic psychological needs are satisfied at work	2. Coaching to assist people to live authentically in line with strengths and values at work
3. Coaching to foster positive relationships at work	3. Coaching to increase the sense of autonomy at work
4. Coaching for strengths knowledge and use to assist people to gain mastery and feel energised at work	4. Coaching to live in line with 'true self' and strive to achieve perceived potential at work
5. Coaching to increase experiences of flow at work	5. Coaching to build resilience resources at work (e.g. optimism, functional social support, mindfulness skills, willpower)

Coaching to modulate the ratio of positive to negative emotions at work

As described, the understanding of positive emotions and their importance has been greatly assisted by the work of Fredrickson (1998, 2001, 2009) and broaden-and-build theory. It is important for coaches to understand positive and negative emotions in terms of ratios. For a well-functioning person, positive emotions are more frequent but less intense, whilst negative emotions are less frequent and more intense. By thinking in terms of ratios it is useful to help employees understand that they can aim to have more positive emotions than negative emotions. However, a ratio implies that there should still be some negative emotions as they also serve an important function (Kashdan and Biswas-Diener, 2014). There are numerous ways to assist people to experience positive emotions, ranging from gratitude exercises (e.g. counting blessings and gratitude diaries; Emmons and McCullough, 2003) to maintaining and enhancing positive relationships by increasing socialising amongst employees (de Carvalho et al., 2012).

Coaching to ensure basic psychological needs are satisfied at work

As mentioned, the three psychological needs of autonomy, relatedness and competency serve as useful touchpoints for a coach when coaching for wellbeing at work. Stated simply, does the person have a sense of enough choices at work? Does the person experience positive relationships at work? Does the person feel competent at work? If that answer is 'no' or 'not much' to any of these questions, the person will likely have lowered levels of wellbeing at work. Like positive emotions above, there are numerous different and individualised ways that this may be improved.

Coaching to foster positive relationships at work

Positive relationships are closely related to positive emotions. This is one reason many people enjoy socialising. Teaching employees approaches of active constructive responding (Passmore and Oades, 2014), sharing positive events (Gable et al., 2004, 2006) and strengths spotting in others (Linley, 2011) will all improve relationships at work. In the organisational context it is necessary to think of the network of relationships and not just the relationships of an individual coachee. Coaching for wellbeing at work should also include working with managers and leaders on how they foster the positive relationships of their employees. Cameron's (2012) model of positive leadership includes fostering positive relationships as a key role of a positive leader.

Coaching for strengths knowledge and use to assist people to gain mastery and feel energised at work

Linley (2006) describes strengths coaching as a way to assist coaches to know and use their strengths. The three parts of strengths knowledge, strengths use and strengths spotting form the basis of the strengths coaching endeavour (Govindji and Linley, 2007; Linley et al., 2010). The Realise2, developed by Linley and colleagues, is an example of an assessment tool used to measure performance strengths. The Realise2 includes four components: realised strengths, unrealised strengths, weaknesses and learned behaviours. Strengths coaching will often focus on how to realise unrealised strengths. The result is that people feel more energised and will persevere longer under adversity. Strengths use may also lead to an experience of flow and engagement.

Coaching to increase experiences of flow at work

Csikszentmihalyi (1990) described flow as an optimal experience, which involves full absorption in a feedback-providing goal-directed activity that is matched to one's level of skill. Similar to strengths use, there is a relationship between time spent in a flow state and wellbeing. For this reason, assisting employees to understand and maximise experiences of flow is important for wellbeing at work. Given that it is a goal-directed activity, there are often work opportunities for people to experience flow (Csikszentmihalyi and LeFevre, 1989). Salanova et al. (2006) reported evidence for an upward spiral at work resulting from people experiencing flow states over time. Coaching in this area may include assisting people to job craft to increase tasks in which they experience flow whilst working. For example, some may experience flow whilst working with numbers on spreadsheets. Coaching may explore how they can increase time spent in this state.

Coaching to increase a sense of meaning and purpose at work

Meaning and purpose are closely related to the definition of eudaimonic wellbeing. Work can provide people with a great sense of meaning, and it can often be a key part of a broader purpose in life (Steger et al., 2014). Conversely, work disengagement may be a product of a lack of meaning in work tasks. Coaching for wellbeing is highly likely to include some discussion of the meaning that work provides to the person and how they may increase a sense of meaning.

Coaching to assist people to live authentically

Like strengths, there is evidence that people who live in line with their values will have higher levels of wellbeing (Veage et al., 2014). Strengths coaching has already been discussed, but coaching using values is also important. This relates also to assisting employees to find meaning in their work. Coaching using values may draw on recent literature from Acceptance and Commitment Therapy (ACT) which emphasises living in line with values (Hayes et al., 1999).

Coaching to build resilience resources at work

Resilience has become a popular term in wellbeing literature, and to a lesser extent the coaching literature. Grant et al. (2009) report an executive coaching study that builds resilience. Several positive psychology constructs have been related to resilience including optimism (Lyubmomirksy, 2008), mindfulness (Kabat-Zinn, 2013) and willpower (self-regulation) (Baumeister and Tierney, 2012). Lyubmomirksy (2008) and Magyar-Moe (2009) provide useful overviews of positive psychological interventions that can build resilience.

Common challenges to wellbeing at work

Table 14.2   Ten common challenges to wellbeing at work

1.	Work–life interference	Individuals experiencing work issues interfering with home and family life, directly or indirectly (e.g. having to work late instead of eating with the family or seeing young children before they are in bed)
2.	Turning up to work but not being productive (presenteeism)	Individuals physically turning up ('presenting') at work, but being unproductive due to illness, emotional or motivational issues (e.g. staring at a computer screen aimlessly due to drowsiness from hayfever allergies)
3.	Sitting too much	Weight gain and increased risk of cardiovascular problems due to long periods of sitting
4.	Sleep quality	Loss of productivity and related problems due to poor quality of sleep (e.g. too much caffeine due to work stress compounding sleep issues)
5.	Managing your energy at work	Issue of long work days requiring concentration and self-regulation impacted by diet and movement (e.g. having too little energy to concentrate in the afternoon)
6.	Time management/information management or 'busyness'	Having an overwhelming sense of loss of personal control due to amount of tasks or information at work (e.g. feeling overwhelmed by emails)
7.	Workplace conflict	Experiencing destructive conflict at work (e.g. workplace bullying)
8.	Not feeling valued at work	Feelings and thoughts that you and your work are undervalued by workmates, superiors or the employer (e.g. manager provides no positive feedback and only identifies problems)
9.	Speed of change and uncertainty	A sense of lack of stability at work (e.g. third upgrade of information technology and related systems within 18 months)
10.	Procrastination	A repeated pattern where one avoids commencing or consistently working on key tasks or projects (e.g. writing an overdue report)

Table 14.2 illustrates ten common challenges to wellbeing at work. While it is preferred that employees will work to improve their wellbeing for its own sake, they will often be motivated to attend coaching due to some current problems or puzzles. Each of these challenges impacts on both hedonic and eudaimonic types of wellbeing and hence there are also many of the general coaching aims to improve wellbeing. More broadly, the key theories of wellbeing are also relevant to these tangible challenges. Generally speaking, by increasing one's positive relationships at work and positive emotions at work, by knowing one's strengths and values and improving one's willpower (self-regulation) many of these challenges will be easier to master. When considering the case study of Barry (visit the companion website, https://study.sagepub.com/coachingcontexts, to read this case study), the reader is encouraged to systematically think about the relevant theories, the two types of wellbeing and the five ways each to improve them, and the ten common challenges which relate to the case study.

CONCLUSION

Coaching for wellbeing at work forms part of the evolution of broader workplace wellbeing programmes. By providing a summary of wellbeing theories and coaching approaches to improve the two different types of wellbeing, it was possible to illustrate a coaching example with Barry who was experiencing several of the ten challenges to wellbeing at work described. Those coaching or developing coaching programmes are encouraged to explore the established theories, use the distinction between the types of wellbeing, and keep in mind the ten examples of common wellbeing challenges at work.

Practical suggestions for those working in this sector

There are numerous differences across work contexts and individuals, hence a one-size-fits-all formula for coaching for wellbeing at work is not possible. The following are however some practical suggestions and pitfalls to avoid for those starting coaching for wellbeing at work, or setting up programmes to assist others to do so.

1. Psychological and physical

Many workplace wellbeing programmes have been weighted towards physical health issues and often focus solely on preventing physical illness. Whilst these are clearly important, the role of psychological factors and wellbeing requires equal weighting. There is a converse risk of neglecting physical factors. Hence a key recommendation for coaching for wellbeing at work is to ensure there is a coverage of both psychological and physical issues, and also that the goals are not only to reduce or prevent illness but also to promote and enable wellbeing for its own sake.

2. Co-production and participation

Whilst most coaches will seek to tailor coaching sessions to individuals this has not always been the case for the implementation of workplace wellbeing programmes. Many programmes have been somewhat top-down in nature, and not eliciting the skills and ownership of the teams and employees who have local contextualised expertise about day-to-day challenges. A key recommendation is to include employees in the design, implementation and evaluation of the coaching programmes in conjunction with the first recommendation above.

3. Differentiate coaching from counselling

As mentioned, people will often present to coaching with a problem. For this reason, there is still the challenge that people (including managers) may see coaching as solely about problem solving or the alleviation of distress. It is important to educate employees,

(Continued)

(Continued)

managers and other stakeholders in the vital differences between coaching and counselling. This is magnified for coaching for wellbeing even more so than executive, business or skills coaching.

4. Explain the rationale for coaching to employees

In addition to differentiating coaching from counselling, many people may not understand the rationale for coaching. Whilst coaches can describe this easily, there remains the challenge of communicating this for coachees in understandable ways. This may seem an obvious or assumed recommendation, however it is often overlooked.

5. Develop a coaching culture, not just coaching

Further to the previous recommendation about providing a rationale for coaching, it is useful for organisations to think beyond individual formal coaching sessions. If coaching is considered a style of relationship, coaching style interactions can become pervasive across an organisation (Crowe et al., 2011). A key recommendation when implementing coaching for wellbeing at work is to enable peer coaching opportunities throughout the social network. This moves from coaching wellbeing programmes to coaching wellbeing cultures (see Chapter 16: Towards Coaching Cultures, for a discussion of coaching cultures).

6. Justify the returns to employers

The relationships between employee wellbeing and staff productivity are still not fully known, understood or accepted by employers. Likewise the benefits of coaching remain varied in their acceptance with employers. Hence, it is important to provide a justification to employers for (a) improving wellbeing, (b) using a coaching modality, and (c) combining the two in terms of coaching for wellbeing. Some employers may be interested in the wellbeing of employees per se, whilst others may require return on investment (ROI) calculations and will ask for the financial cost and benefits ratios of the costs of coaching for wellbeing. A combination of evidence for the costs of illness and lost productivity at work, combined with the general evidence on coaching effectiveness (see Chapter 13: The Current State of Research), can form part of a justification to employers.

Visit the companion website, https://study.sagepub.com/coachingcontexts, to read the case study that accompanies this chapter:

- Case Study 22: Coaching for wellbeing
  Lindsay G. Oades

REFERENCES

Baumeister, R. and Tierney, J. (2012) *Willpower: Rediscovering the Greatest Human Strength.* New York: Penguin.

Biswas-Diener, R. (2010) *Practicing Positive Psychology Coaching: Assessment, Activities, and Strategies for Success.* Hoboken, NJ: Wiley.

Cameron, K. (2012) *Positive Leadership: Strategies for Extraordinary Performance*, 2nd edn. San Francisco, CA: Berrett-Koehler.

Crowe, T.P., Oades, L.G., Deane, F.P., Ciarrochi, J. and Williams, V.C. (2011) 'Parallel processes in clinical supervision: Implications for coaching mental health practitioners', *International Journal of Evidence Based Coaching and Mentoring*, 9(2): 56–66.

Csikszentmihalyi, M. (1990) *Flow: The Psychology of Optimal Experience.* New York: Harper & Row.

Csikszentmihalyi, M. and LeFevre, J. (1989) 'Optimal experience in work and leisure', *Journal of Personality and Social Psychology*, 56(5): 815–22.

de Carvalho, J.R.B. et al. (2012) 'Practicing and validating positive psychology coaching: Empowering strengths, positive emotions, hope and well-being', *International Journal of Psychology*, 47: 626–46.

Deci, E.L. and Ryan, R.M. (2000) 'The "what" and "why" of goal pursuits: Human needs and the self-determination of behaviour', *Psychological Inquiry*, 11(4): 227–68.

Diener, E. (2000) 'Subjective well-being: The science of happiness, and a proposal for a national index', *American Psychologist*, 55: 34–43.

Emmons, R. and McCullough, M.E. (2003) 'Counting blessings versus burdens: An experimental investigation into gratitude and subjective well-being in daily life', *Journal of Personality and Social Psychology*, 84: 377–89.

Fredrickson, B.L. (1998) 'What good are positive emotions?', *Review of General Psychology*, 2: 300–19.

Fredrickson, B. (2001) 'The role of positive emotions in positive psychology: The broaden-and-build theory of positive emotions', *American Psychologist*, 56: 218–26.

Fredrickson, B. (2009) *Positivity: Groundbreaking Research Reveals how to Release the Hidden Strength of Positive Emotions, Overcome Negativity and Thrive.* New York: Random House.

Gable, S.L., Gonzaga, G.C. and Strachman, A. (2006) 'Will you be there for me when things go right? Supportive responses to positive event disclosures', *Journal of Personality and Social Psychology*, 91: 904–17.

Gable, S.L., Reis, H.T., Impett, E.A. and Asher, E.R. (2004) 'What do you do when things go right? The intrapersonal and interpersonal benefits of sharing positive events', *Journal of Personality and Social Psychology*, 87: 228–45.

Govindji, R. and Linley, P.A. (2007) 'Strengths use, self-concordance and well-being: Implications for strengths coaching and coaching psychologists', *International Coaching Psychology Review*, 2(2): 143–53.

Grant, T., Curtayne, L. and Burton, G. (2009) 'Executive coaching enhances goal attainment, resilience and workplace well-being: A randomised controlled study', *Journal of Positive Psychology*, 4(5): 396–407.

Green, L.S., Oades, L.G., and Grant, A.M. (2006) 'Cognitive-behavioural, solution-focused life coaching: Enhancing goal striving, well-being and hope', *Journal of Positive Psychology*, 1(3): 142–9.

Hayes, S.C., Strosahl, K.D. and Wilson, K.G. (1999) *Acceptance and Commitment Therapy: An Experiential Approach to Behavior Change*. New York: Guilford.

Kabat-Zinn, J. (2013) *Full Catastrophe Living: Using the Wisdom of Your Body and Mind to Face Stress, Pain, and Illness*, 2nd edn. New York: Random House.

Kashdan, T.B. and Biswas-Diener, R. (2014) *The Upside of Your Dark Side: Why Being Your Whole Self–Not Just Your 'Good' Self–Drives Success and Fulfillment*. New York: Hudson Street.

Kaufman, C., Silberman, J. and Sharpely, D. (2008) 'Coaching for strengths using VIA'. In J. Passmore (ed.), *Psychometrics in Coaching*. London: Kogan Page. pp. 239–53.

Linley, A., Willars, J.L. and Biswas-Diener, R. (2010) *The Strengths Book: Be Confident, Be Successful, and Enjoy Better Relationships by Realising the Best of You*. London: Capp.

Linley, P.A. (2006) 'Strengths coaching: A potential-guided approach to coaching psychology', *International Coaching Psychology Review*, 1(1): 37–46.

Linley, P. A.G. (2011) 'The strengths of the strengthspotter: Individual characteristics associated with the identification of strengths in others', *International Coaching Psychology Review*, 6(1): 6–15.

Lyubomirsky, S. (2008) *The How of Happiness: A Practical Approach to Getting the Life You Want*. London: Piatkus.

Magyar-Moe, J.L. (2009) *Positive Psychological Interventions. Therapist's Guide to Positive Psychological Interventions*. San Diego, CA: Academic. pp. 73–176.

Martin, L.S., Oades, L.G. and Caputi, P. (2014) 'Intentional personality change coaching: A randomised controlled trial of participant selected personality facet change using the Five-Factor model of personality', *International Coaching Psychology Review*, 9(2): 182–95.

Morgan, J. (2014) *The Future of Work*. Hoboken, NJ: Wiley.

Oades, L.G. and Passmore, J. (2014) 'Positive Psychology coaching'. In J. Passmore (ed.), *Mastery in Coaching: A Complete Psychological Toolkit for Advanced Coaching*. London: Kogan Page. pp. 15–40.

Passmore, J. and Oades, L.G. (2014) 'Positive Psychology techniques – Active constructive responding', *Coaching Psychologist*, 10(2).

Peterson, C. and Seligman, M.E.P. (2004) *Character Strengths and Virtues: A Handbook and Classification*. Oxford: Oxford University Press.

Proctor, C. et al. (2011) 'Strengths use as a predictor of well-being and health-related quality of life', *Journal of Happiness Studies*, 12(1): 153–69.

Rath, T. (2013) *Eat Move Sleep: How Small Choices Lead to Big Changes*. Arlington, VA: Missionday.

Ryan, R.M. and Deci, E.L. (2000) 'On happiness and human potentials: A Review of research on Hedonic and Eudaimonic Well-Being', *Annual Review of Psychology*, 52: 141–66.

Salanova, M., Bakker, A.B. and Llorens, S. (2006) 'Flow at work: Evidence for an upward spiral of personal and organizational resources', *Journal of Happiness Studies*, 7: 1–22.

Seligman, M.E.P. (2011) *Flourish*. New York: Simon and Schuster.

Spence, G.B. and Grant, A.M. (2013) 'Coaching and well-being: A brief review of existing evidence, relevant theory and implications for practitioners'. In S. David, I. Boniwell, and A. Ayers (eds), *Oxford Handbook of Happiness*. Oxford: Oxford University Press. pp. 1009–25.

Spence, G.B. and Oades, L.G. (2011) 'Coaching with self-determination theory in mind: Using theory to advance evidence-based coaching practice', *International Journal of Evidence Based Coaching and Mentoring*, 9(2): 37–55.

Steger, M.F., Dik, B.J. and Duffy, R.D. (2014) 'Measuring meaningful work: The Work and Meaning Inventory (WAMI)', *Journal of Career Assessment*.

Thompson, N. and Bates, J. (2009) *Promoting Workplace Wellbeing*. London: Palgrave Macmillan.

Veage, S., Ciarrochi, J., Deane, F.P., Andresen, R.., Oades, L.G. and Crowe, T.P. (2014) 'Value congruence, importance and success in the workplace: Links with well-being and burnout amongst mental health practitioners', *Journal of Contextual Behavioral Science*, 3: 258–64.

Waterman, A.S. (1993) 'Two conceptions of happiness: Contrasts of personal expressiveness (eudaemonia) and hedonic enjoyment', *Journal of Personality and Social Psychology*, 64: 678–91.

15

SUPERVISION FOR LEARNING

MARY WATTS, ESTHER CAVETT AND SARAH DUDNEY

I'm sitting in a room with three other people. We are all coaches and we're all here to learn. One of us is designated the supervisor, the other three as supervisees. Our backgrounds, professionally and personally, are very different. Our area of coaching practice and the range of our experience are equally varied. What we share is a perspective that professionally and ethically we have a responsibility to our clients to continue our learning and to personalise this in ways which will enhance both our coaching practice and our personal wellbeing. We believe that the forum we have created is one of several ways of enhancing our personal and professional learning and practice. We also share a perspective which suggests that the process of engagement, making sense of, reflecting and learning, that we collaboratively engage in, is reflexive – meaning that whether we are supervisor, supervisee, coach or client, the process of engagement and interpretation is relevant to each of us. We are all, whatever our role and personal history, engaging in a process of learning, albeit in distinctive, individual ways.

INTRODUCTION

The focus of this chapter is on coaching supervision with a particular slant towards those working in an organisational context, either as internal staff coaches or external coaches employed to work within an organisation. The core themes, models, case vignette and learning activities are relevant to all coaches whether or not they work in organisational settings. The chapter raises a number of issues and perspectives relating to supervision and contextualises these within practical experience and examples. It encourages you, the reader, to explore and develop your own perspective on supervision. Throughout the chapter we draw attention to the notion of perspective-taking and its centrality to how we think and what we do. We argue that meaning comes not just from what we see or observe, but also from the interpretations and constructions that we place on these (Carroll, 2008; Kelly, 1955, 1970). Perspectives are often implicit and may influence our own and others' behaviours in subtle but significant ways. We introduce a range of literature, some relating directly to supervision. Other literature has a broader relevance to the issue of enhancing learning and professional practice in a range of contexts. Questions are posed at a number of places in the text, encouraging you to reflect upon coaching supervision in general and coaching supervision within an organisational context in particular. We would encourage you to add your own questions to these. Our short vignette is designed to raise a number of questions about coaching supervision.

The statements below (Whybrow and Watts, 2013; Watts, 2014) all reflect perspectives on learning and supervision and are of course open to challenge by those holding alternative views:

- Supervision is about learning.
- We can engage in it alone and with others.
- It benefits from creative and flexible thinking.
- Learning is ongoing and never ending.

It is very usual in professional and training programmes for trainees to have a practical, supervised period of training. This is the case in medicine, law, teaching and psychology, for example. Supervision is taken as an integral part of learning to practice, and often takes the form of live supervision where one works alongside and is prompted and observed by a more experienced colleague. The roots and history of supervision vary considerably between professions. Coaching finds itself in an interesting position – influenced to a large degree by counselling and psychotherapy, yet applied generally in very different contexts and drawing frequently on a much wider knowledge base. For example, psychology has considerable relevance to coaching but this includes areas of psychology not commonly focused on in clinical and counselling psychology training. Organisational psychologists find that much of their training has direct relevance to coaching. In addition, coaches frequently draw on knowledge and experience from a wide range of theoretical disciplines and areas of practice, including finance and economics, law, business, education, physiology and neurology. This leads to some interesting dilemmas and debates in relation to supervision:

- What should supervision look like?
- What are its primary purposes? Who should do it?
- What background should supervisors have?

This chapter is not the place to answer all these questions. It may not even be possible to give definitive answers to these questions. However this chapter takes the perspective that supervision is fundamentally about learning, and in particular personal learning. The personal learning approach to supervision outlined and illustrated in action below has a number of roots, in particular education, including the work of Jarvis (2006, 2012), Argyris and Schön (1974), Kolb (1984), Mezirow (2000), and psychology, drawing on many ideas and perspectives but in particular those linked to the work of George Kelly (1955, 1970) and his work on personal constructs. Some features of personal learning link closely to the ideas of John Mayer (2014) and his work on personal intelligence.

The learning cycle presented in this chapter is based upon a conceptual model of personal learning that is reflexive in nature and applicable to our learning whether we are in the role of client, coach, supervisor or supervisee. But what of non-learning (Jarvis, 2012)? Very often, if someone does not learn what another person, such as a supervisor or a teacher, thinks they should be learning they label this as non-learning. However, it may be the case that learning may well have occurred although it might not be the learning that was expected or prescribed. In these situations, the term 'non-learning' is somewhat misleading and may indicate a power imbalance between the learner and the labeller. There are two other contexts in which non-learning may occur. The first is where there are internal or external constraints that have an impact upon an individual's learning. When these are removed, learning may progress. The second is where we are so familiar with our world, living in harmony with it, that we presume upon it – meaning we take it for granted and do not ask the kinds of questions that would lead us to experience discomfort. It is the heightened awareness that comes from this discomfort that creates a potential personal learning situation (Jarvis, 2012; Watts, 1994). When considering learning in the context of supervision we need to be constantly aware of each of these three situations. Learning and non-learning both need consideration whether we are in the role of client, coach, supervisee or supervisor.

PERSONAL LEARNING

The scenario presented at the start of this chapter centres on an example of small group supervision with one supervisor and three supervisees. It draws attention to the learning element of supervision and suggests that personal learning is an important part of the supervision activity whether you are the supervisor or supervisee. The scenario also suggests that learning is important regardless of prior experience and professional background. However much we 'know', each time we step into new territory, including coaching a new client, entering a new organisational context, or maybe just focusing on changing aspects of our client's world, some of what we 'know' will be relevant. However, we have to reflect on how what we 'know' applies to these new situations. It may not be new learning (in the sense of abstract formal learning) that is important. It may be more to do with learning about a particular client and their situation. Or it may be about knowing how to integrate our own previous learning and experience in order to apply these to the current coaching situation. Or it may relate to knowing how to effectively reflect upon our practice in ways that will continue to enhance it. Importantly, our learning may help us recognise how to nurture our ongoing learning in ways that make sense to ourselves, helping us sustain our personal wellbeing as well as that of our clients. Shared learning is vital, whether one-to-one or in a group. However, the need for personal learning of the type described above is ongoing, constant, and occurs on a day-by-day and minute-by-minute basis. To defer all learning until we meet with others is unrealistic. Before, during and after coaching sessions there is a place for thoughtful reflection designed to help us makes sense of what we 'know' and reformulate our thinking where necessary. These activities, designed to increase our personal 'knowing', can be described as personal learning activities.

It is likely we will all engage in these on a regular basis, in ways that are more or less effective and more or less planned and consciously undertaken. The starting place for supervision in this chapter is reflective practice, i.e. the undertaking of personal learning activity that is consciously planned and carried out on a regular basis. The intention of this reflective practice is to increase personal knowledge in order to enhance the individual's professional activity as a coach and the wellbeing of clients.

Personal knowing and personal learning are critical to the way we think, feel and act in private and professional capacities. What follows is the depiction of a cycle that has personal learning at its centre. Figure 15.1 depicts the cycle which is not closed. It shows the person as learning and changing and moving into a new place as their learning progresses. The Personal Learning Cycle highlights five action points, all of which have a role to play in the promotion and support of personal learning. The cycle is elaborated using the five activities of listening using all of your senses, engaging (which also includes exploring, experimenting, and evaluating), applying, reflecting and nurturing. You can use the cycle putting yourself in the centre, whether you are the supervisee, the supervisor, or the coachee.

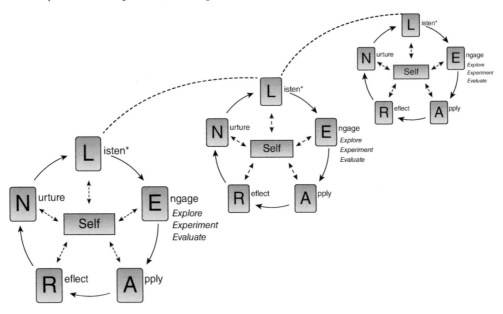

Figure 15.1   Personal LEARNing Cycle

*"'Listen' with all your senses

© MHWA Ltd

Personal learning is not just something that our client engages in, we do it too! Learning does not take place in a vacuum. It is influenced by many factors including social, geographical, organisational and cultural contexts. Nevertheless, the Personal Learning Cycle proposes that each of us has a significant element of choice in respect of our learning and behaviour. We can choose, for example, to focus on particular areas of activity and increase our understanding of these. We can control aspects of our environment, and we can act upon as well as be acted upon. George Howard refers to the core construct of human action as personal agency. In his book *Understanding Human Nature* (1996), he stands much of psychology writing on its head when he challenges third person accounts which he says usually leave personal agency out. In contrast, he argues, a first person account asks for the role of personal agency in our actions.

The two constructs of learning and personal agency are core to the discussion of supervision in this chapter and are combined within the concept of personal learning. These are represented within the Personal Learning Cycle presented in Figure 15.1 which is based on a previous model developed by Watts (2013, 2014) for use in coaching supervision workshops.

A vignette

Mark, who is currently in coach training, has just finished his second coaching session with his client. He is writing notes and reflecting on what happened in the session. He feels it did not go as he had planned. He had thought through the session carefully in advance. In his training there is a focus on using the GROW model (Whitmore, 2002). Mark had intended to elicit his client's goal for the session early on. This didn't happen. In fact the client had talked and talked and Mark had spent most of the time listening. He felt he had no clear idea of how and when to intervene or slow his client down. When his client eventually stopped talking, very near to the end of the session, he felt he had to think on his feet about how to draw the session to a close.

By reflecting on and engaging with his experience, Mark is creating a personal learning opportunity. He had intended to apply what he had been learning and practising in his coaching tutorials. Things had gone differently which had caused him a degree of discomfort, and he listened to his feeling of discomfort and engaged with it. He spent time reflecting and trying to make sense of it. Interestingly, within the coaching session, Mark had done something very similar. He had listened to his client and engaged with what he was saying rather than trying to shift him to the place where he, Mark, had thought his client ought to be – and rather than then applying his formal learning in a mechanistic way he had chosen to go with what he heard, including hearing and noting his own instincts. He continued to listen intently.

Listening, engaging, applying and reflecting all feature heavily in this brief scenario. All are equally important in this instance. The personal reflections that Mark made after the coaching session were the trigger for his learning relating to the session. In this instance he knew that he needed additional input to help him understand more about what had happened. He was worried that he had gone too far 'off piste'. Engaging in reflective practice of this kind can enable deep personal learning that can transform personal understanding and subsequent practice. Often it is the trigger for discussions with a supervisor, or maybe for further reading or other approaches to taking personal learning and understanding forward.

In the Personal Learning Cycle, the activity of engagement features three further elements or activities – exploration, experimentation and evaluation. Engagement suggests giving broad attention and energy to something. Exploration, experimentation and evaluation are more specific types of activity. We can engage in supervision, whether one-to-one or in groups. In fact, there is a range of ways in which coaches can access supervision depending on their personal circumstances or needs (see, for example, van Nieuwerburgh, 2014: 177). During this time we explore ideas, different ways of making sense of something, our own feelings and so on. We can experiment with ideas and approaches to something in our imagination before we try it out in practice, and we can hypothesise what might have happened had we done such and such or if we were to do a particular thing in the next coaching session. We can also evaluate the implications of certain actions and potential outcomes and consider both the advantages of these and the possible risk factors, always being aware of our ethical code of practice. At the same time that we engage in this process, our supervisor will be engaging in their own personal learning process, as will our colleagues if we are in group supervision. What we each take from the learning situation will be different but the process itself is reflexive.

In relation to the example above, Mark engaged first with reflective practice, thinking about, listening and questioning his approach in the session outlined. Collaboratively with his supervisor he explored further, considering the possible implications of both the approach he took and also alternative approaches. He engaged in mental experimentation and an evaluation of possible alternative approaches. The significance of timings became a key area for further exploration for Mark, i.e. when to intervene, when to let someone talk, when to identify a goal early in the session, and when it may stand in the way of meaningful learning and progress on the part of the client. Mark had engaged both independently and collaboratively with four of the activity elements of the learning cycle. At this stage it is very easy to get 'bogged down' with life and other areas of work and not to nurture the seeds of the new learning. In this case, Mark nurtured it well through continued supervision, ongoing reading and reflecting and also through keeping a learning log, which captured significant learning points and areas for ongoing exploration. The learning was also nurtured within his ongoing client work. It was then pulled together and integrated at the end of his coaching programme in the form of a very thoughtful essay on the significance of timings in coaching.

The brief scenario above shows an individual in motion as they actively engage in the pursuit of personal learning. The individual happens to be a coach in supervision but the cycle is relevant also to the client who is actively seeking to learn and change through being in a coaching relationship. Learning moves us to a different place, hence the depiction of the learning cycle as a series of linked cycles with the person at their centre. The activity points in the cycle are linked but learning can start at any point and does not necessarily follow a neat or uniform order.

The cycle shows five learning activity points but it is not meant to imply that these are the only ones that have an impact on personal learning. It also does not indicate the kinds of activities that facilitate each of the five occurring. For example, reflective writing may be a powerful tool for one person (Mair with Dudley, 2008) while drawing may resonate for another. These activities may trigger reflection or engagement with a recent event or facilitate 'listening' to personal feelings. They may also be a powerful way of nurturing learning and personal wellbeing.

The cycle also does not presume a particular theoretical approach to making sense of people and their world, nor to approaches to change. The theoretical perspectives of the coach and supervisee will have an impact on their meaning making, the hypotheses they make and the approaches to change that they generate. For example, a coach or supervisor taking a cognitive approach (Palmer and Szymanska, 2008) would look at the possible impact of the cognitions held by their client, identify 'faulty' cognitions, and work with their client to change these. By contrast, a coach using a personal construct approach (Pavlović and Stojnov, 2011) would be seeking to understand the constructs an individual uses to make sense of their world and how these together form a comprehensive system of personal meaning making. By definition, these are not faulty. They have a purpose and to change them requires a deep understanding of their interrelationship. The language used by the cognitive coach and the personal construct coach would be different, as would the approach to engaging, exploring, experimenting and evaluating. There would also be a difference in respect of the listening element of the cycle. Each would listen well but what each hears and the sense each makes of it would be different. The questions asked and the hypotheses made are also likely to be rather different.

Often, coaches and their supervisors will not adhere to a single model. It is likely that they will have implicit personal beliefs and ideas that will have an impact on what they hear and the way they practise as coaches. One purpose of coaching supervision is to create an opportunity to explore these and their possible impact on our clients and ourselves. Where the perspectives of supervisor and supervisee are different, skillfully handled by the supervisor, this can lead to some interesting and creative reflection and debate.

SUPERVISION FOR COACHES WORKING IN AN ORGANISATIONAL CONTEXT

All that has been written so far in this chapter is applicable to a wide range of coaching supervision situations. In all cases, external and cultural factors can have an impact on our learning, and one place where the coach and coach supervisor need to be extremely sensitive to this is in an organisational context.

As Towler put it:

'The influence of the organization is an ever-present reality in the room in organizational supervision. This influence is usually mediated through the values, beliefs and behaviours of significant organizational personnel and can be expressed through the beliefs of the organizational culture. For supervisees and supervisors managing this presence can be both hindering and facilitating.' (Towler, 2008: 38)

This statement was made in the context of counselling supervision in organisational contexts, but Towler's research and its findings may be applicable to coaching supervision. Towler concludes that organisational supervision requires working with both an individual and a systemic lens. He draws attention to the necessity for clear contracting with organisational third parties (e.g. managers and supervisees) to clarify respective roles and responsibilities.

Supervision can help supervisees to develop an awareness of the impact of organisational culture and systems on both their own behaviour and that of their clients. It can help them consider ways of establishing good relationships with an organisation, to understand not only key elements of the culture and related practices, but also ways of 'standing back', of retaining independence of thought, of considering alternative ways of doing and being within that institution. All of these factors are important within the context of the relationship that the coach supervisee has with their client and the organisation. It is likely that in the same way that the learning styles of individuals can be different (Jarvis, 2006; Watts, 2012) so too can their preferred approaches to supervision. Stage of training, experience of the area of work and characteristics of the client and the organisation are also likely to impact upon preference, which may vary from time to time. For example, again within the context of counsellor supervision, González-Doupé (2008: 48) concluded from her research that 'workplace group supervision actually helps workplace counsellors work better in crisis management settings'.

An interesting perspective comes from Gale and Alilovic (2008) who challenge the often-held belief that managers should not supervise those that they manage. They conclude that in some situations (but not all) dual relationships of this kind can lead to creativity and development. What seems clear is that learning through supervision can take many forms and it is not possible to argue that a particular type of supervision is always best for certain supervisees in certain situations. In fact, to try to do this and to dictate appropriate supervision to meet all needs would be to impersonalise learning through supervision. It would move away from the core principles of coaching, with its emphasis on empowering clients and recognising that they know more about themselves and their needs. It would create a situation where the supervision of coaching was incongruent with the principles and ethics of coaching. Further research into coaching supervision is much needed. In the same way that the application of research into real-life coaching situations is as much an art as a science, this also applies to the application of research into coaching supervision.

What follows are a number of questions to encourage you to draw on your personal experience of being a supervisee, supervisor, manager, or employer of coaches. There are no right answers to these questions. Their purpose is to encourage creative thought, challenge the status quo, and aid your personal reflection about what works for you. At the heart of all of this, we must remember to maintain a clear focus on what is in the best interest of our clients. As you debate these questions, either alone or with others, bear in mind the statements made by George Kelly:

'[People do] not always think logically. Some take this as a serious misfortune. But I doubt that it is … human progress depends also upon the selective creation of uncertainties; that is to say, the pinpointing of preposterous doubts, and the formulation of new questions and issues … A pat answer is the enemy of a fresh question.' (Kelly, 1969: 114)

Some questions

Can you think of a situation where your client, your organisation or you benefited from supervision?

What was it about the supervision that enabled this to happen?

How could you demonstrate this benefit to others?

Can you think of a situation where non-learning occurred for you in supervision?

Why do you think this happened?

What could have been more helpful to your learning?

PROFESSIONAL ASSOCIATIONS

One significant area relates to accreditation of programmes and registration of individuals with professional bodies. This could be a chapter in itself. There are many such professional organisations in coaching, each with their own training and continuing professional development requirements (see list below for some of these), and you would be advised to carefully consider the guidelines and requirements of any organisation you are thinking of joining. You may find differences between them that influence you in terms of the organisation you wish to be part of.

Some of the major professional and accrediting coaching organisations

Association for Coaching www.associationforcoaching.com

The British Psychological Society www.bps.org.uk

European Mentoring and Coaching Council www.emccouncil.org

International Coach Federation www.coachfederation.org

World Association of Business Coaches www.wabccoaches.com

Coaches, both those in training and experienced practitioners, often ask 'How much supervision do I need?' There are at least two approaches to answering this. Firstly, one can focus on the individual's perceived learning and development needs which will vary from time to time and in different coaching situations. Secondly, one can take an impersonal, 'rule bound' stance. As indicated, professional training programmes frequently follow strict guidelines regarding the form and frequency of supervision and its associated assessment. These 'rules' are generally established and upheld by professional bodies. In the 'listening and talking' helping professions, which include coaching, the guidelines and rules will vary among the various professional bodies both in terms of what is needed for initial qualification purposes and what is needed for ongoing practice, continuing professional development and re-accreditation purposes. It is not always easy for the trainee or even the more experienced practitioner to understand the 'rules' or the implicit assumptions behind them. Research can raise issues, challenge ideas and practices and make thoughtful suggestions, but it is unlikely to ever provide emphatic answers to individuals or organisations about what is the right or best type and frequency of supervision. Perhaps it is time for professional and accrediting bodies to recognise this and engage in a shared and challenging debate about supervision and its place in coaching practice. To do this, the current anomalies, implicit beliefs and practices in this area need to be acknowledged and questioned.

CONCLUSION

The focus of this chapter has been on learning through supervision with a particular focus on personal learning. The Personal Learning Cycle has been introduced as an aid to promoting and reflecting on personal learning and associated action. Real-life supervision material has been used to demonstrate the cycle in action. The questions posed throughout the chapter were designed to encourage reflective and creative thought that can be engaged in individually or with others in a range of contexts. Their purpose is not to elicit definitive answers but to draw on the richness of individuals' experiences in ways that can enhance coaching supervision and practice, with the purpose of promoting the wellbeing of the client, their organisation and the coach. Coaching makes many demands on coaches and has the capacity to both contribute to and detract from a coach's wellbeing. It is in our clients' as well as our own interest as coaches to identify and engage in activity that supports and enhances our personal wellbeing.

We have considered some perspectives on supervision, namely that it is about learning and that it can benefit from creative and flexible thinking. It is an ongoing process. These statements are based upon a perspective that views coaching as occurring within an ever-changing world in which solutions are considered temporary and learning as only ever partial. However knowledgeable we are, the situations we find ourselves in can never be totally predictable or understood, not least because of the uniqueness of the individuals that populate our world and with whom we interact. Many types of knowing and learning are required for living, and also for supporting people in this endeavour in ways that will enhance their personal understanding and personal agency in life. There are very strong links between the concept of personal learning and the theory of personal intelligence recently developed by

Mayer (2014). Both have a relevance to coaching, supervision, and living in a complex and changing world.

Finally, supervision is just one approach to facilitating personal learning on an ongoing basis. The word 'supervision' is a generic term, i.e. a construct we use to refer to a range of activities and purposes. It is helpful to remember this as we listen, engage, apply, reflect and nurture both our own personal learning and that of others.

Practical suggestions for those setting up supervision arrangements

Having discussed the current context, it becomes clear that it is no easy task for those responsible for the provision of coaching in organisations to determine how best to ensure that their coaches, whether internally employed or external to it, are engaged in appropriate ongoing supervision. Recommendations in this area can only be viewed as broad guidance as they relate to the type of work being undertaken, the experience of the coach, and their familiarity with the particular organisation.

Supervision is more than guidance on 'what to do' with individual clients. It is a whole package of coaching learning and development. Individual client issues are a part of this. It cannot be assumed that guidance in relation to coaching in an organisation best comes from one person – a supervisor. Therefore, as an employer of coaches for your organisation what are your responsibilities? These may vary from time to time and in different organisations but will include the following:

- Ensuring the coaches' experience is relevant and appropriate for the work you wish them to undertake. This does not mean knowing your organisation and area of practice inside out. It may be better not to. Genuine curiosity, openness to learning and flexible thinking are equally important. Appropriate experience may take many forms. What is important is that the coach can coherently articulate their approach and its relevance to the particular work.
- Ensuring the coach has had sufficient, appropriate levels of training in coaching, including supervised practice, some of which has been observed.
- Ensuring the coach has access to and uses appropriate ongoing learning and development opportunities. This would include formal knowledge, coaching practice, networking, organisational and personal development learning.
- Making a decision about what can be offered internally and what is sought externally. In addition a decision must be made regarding whose responsibility it is to seek out and pay for the supervision, learning and development. Some organisations, for example, take responsibility for providing and paying for this if a coach is an internal employee whereas others may part-fund it. If the coach is external to the organisation and is responsible for finding and funding their own learning and development this does not absolve the organisation from

(Continued)

(Continued)

all responsibility – it is appropriate to discuss this with the coach when offering a contract to ensure that it meets with the needs and high standards of your own organisation.

- Considering and making decisions regarding professional indemnity insurance. For example, is the coach covered by the organisation's professional indemnity insurance? If not, do they have their own?
- Expecting adherence to a relevant coaching code of ethics and encouraging membership of a relevant professional body.

ACKNOWLEDGEMENTS

Thank you to our clients, supervisors, colleagues and peers for your challenges to our thinking and contributions to our learning.

Thank you to Julia Clarke, John Hornby and Jason Rabinowitz, for conversations that have helped to shape the ideas in this chapter.

Thank you to Helen Herd for reading drafts of the chapter and your patience and skill in drawing the Personal Learning Cycle.

Visit the companion website, https://study.sagepub.com/coachingcontexts, to read the case studies that accompany this chapter:

- Case Study 23: Reflections on coaching supervision
  Esther Cavett

- Case Study 24: Finding time to think
  Sarah Dudney

REFERENCES

Argyris, C. and Schön, D. (1974) *Theory in Practice: Increasing Professional Effectiveness.* San Francisco, CA: Jossey-Bass.

Bachkirova, T., Jackson, P. and Clutterbuck, D. (eds) *Coaching and Mentoring Supervision: Theory and Practice.* Maidenhead: McGraw-Hill. pp. 230–38.

Carroll, M. (2008) 'Supervision, creativity and transformational learning', *Occasional Papers in Supervision*, British Psychological Society Division of Counselling Psychology, August.

Gale, N.K. and Alilovic, K. (2008) 'Relationships between supervision and management', *Occasional Papers in Supervision*, British Psychological Society Division of Counselling Psychology, August.

Garvey, R., Stokes, P. and Megginson, D. (2009) *Coaching and Mentoring: Theory and Practice.* London: Sage.

González-Doupé, P. (2008) Group supervision in crisis management organizations', *Occasional Papers in Supervision*, British Psychological Society Division of Counselling Psychology, August.

Howard, G.S. (1996) *Understanding Human Nature: An Owner's Manual.* Notre Dame, IN: Academic Publications.

Jarvis, P. (2006) *Towards a Comprehensive Theory of Human Learning.* New York: Taylor and Francis Group.

Jarvis, P. (2012) 'Non-learning'. In P. Jarvis with M.H Watts (eds), *The Routledge International Handbook of Learning.* Oxford and New York: Routledge.

Kelly, G. (1955) *The Psychology of Personal Constructs*, Vols 1 and 2. New York: Norton.

Kelly, G. (1969) 'The strategy of psychological research'. In B. Mayer (ed.), *Clinical Psychology and Personality: The Selected Papers of George Kelly.* Abingdon: Wiley. pp. 114–32.

Kelly, G. (1970) 'A brief introduction to Personal Construct Psychology'. In D. Bannister (ed.), *Perspectives in Personal Construct Theory.* London: Academic Press. pp. 1–30.

Kline, N. (2009) *More Time To Think.* Carmel, CA: Fisher King.

Kolb, D. (1984) *Experiential Learning.* Englewood Cliffs, NJ: Prentice-Hall.

Mair, M. with Dudley, H. (2008) 'Seeing in the dark or writing as lighting', *Occasional Papers in Supervision*, British Psychological Society Division of Counselling Psychology, August.

Mayer, J.D. (2014) *Personal Intelligence: The Power of Personality and How it Shapes Our Lives.* New York: Scientific American/Farrah, Straus and Giroux.

Mezirow, J. and Associates (2000) *Learning as Transformation: Critical Perspectives on a Theory in Progress.* San Francisco, CA: Jossey-Bass.

Palmer, S. and Szymanska, K. (2008) 'Cognitive Behavioural Coaching: An integrative approach'. In S. Palmer and A. Whybrow (eds), *Handbook of Coaching Psychology: A Guide for Practitioners.* Hove: Routledge. pp. 278–92.

Pavlović, J. and Stojnov, D. (2011) 'Personal construct coaching: A "new/old" tool for personal and professional development'. In D. Stojnov, V. Džinović, J. Pavlović and M. Frances (eds), *Personal Construct Psychology in an Accelerating World.* Belgrade: Serbian Constructivist Association, EPCA Publications.

Rogers, J. (2004) *Coaching Skills: A Handbook*, 2nd edn. Maidenhead: McGraw-Hill.

Towler, J. (2008) '"The Influence of the Invisible Client": A crucial perspective for understanding counselling supervision in organizational contexts', *Occasional Papers in Supervision*, British Psychological Society Division of Counselling Psychology, August.

Watts, M.H. (1994) 'Professional Education, Ideology and Learning: A Study of Student Nurses' Construing of Patients and Their Care'. Unpublished PhD thesis, City University, London.

Watts, M.H. (2012) 'Autism spectrum conditions and learning'. In P. Jarvis with M.H. Watts (eds), *The Routledge International Handbook of Learning*. Oxford: Routledge.

Watts, M.H. (2014) 'LEARN: A new tool for supervision and self-supervision'. First Annual Welsh Coaching Conference: Fresh perspectives and Professional Development, Glamorgan Conference Centre, University of South Wales, 18 March.

Whitmore, J. (2002) *Coaching for Performance*, 3rd edn. London: Nicholas Brealey.

Whybrow, A. and Watts, M.H. (2013) 'Super-Vision in Coaching Psychology Workshop: A mini skills session'. British Psychological Society Special Group in Coaching Psychology 4th European Conference, 12–13 December, Herriot Watt University, Edinburgh, Scotland.

16

TOWARDS A COACHING CULTURE

CHRISTIAN VAN NIEUWERBURGH

INTRODUCTION

As a consequence of the widescale adoption of coaching interventions in professional contexts in many of the world's leading economies (Sherpa Executive Coaching Survey, 2015), attention has turned to finding ways of sustaining the positive effects of coaching and broadening out its impact across organisations. The phrase 'coaching culture' is often used within organisational settings, despite the fact that there seems to be little shared understanding of what this means (Gormley and van Nieuwerburgh, 2014). This chapter considers the key characteristics of a coaching culture and provides some practical ideas for organisations interested in leveraging the benefits of coaching. The chapter concludes with some thoughts about the future of coaching cultures within organisational settings.

There seems to be growing agreement that coaching has a positive role to play within organisational settings. For example, Penny Valk, Chief Executive of the Institute of Leadership and Management (ILM), noted that 'coaching is a particularly powerful tool in the modern workplace – one that has proven to be a highly effective way of developing individual and organisational performance by unlocking capability. At its best, this key management tool can deliver considerable benefits, helping managers get the most from their teams, boosting employee engagement and developing high performing workplaces' (Institute of Leadership and Management, 2011: 1).

According to a survey commissioned by the ILM, coaching is widely used in professional contexts within the UK (see Table 16.1).

Table 16.1   Responses to ILM survey

What proportion of organisations use coaching as a development tool?	80%
What proportion of organisations make coaching available to all staff?	52%
What proportion of organisations provide ongoing support and development for internal coaches?	66%
How many respondents saw the direct benefits of coaching to the organisation?	96%
What proportion of organisations use coaching for the personal development of staff?	53%
What proportion of organisations use coaching for improving organisational performance?	26%
What proportion of organisations measure the outcomes of coaching?	93%

Created from data gathered from an ILM report that was based on telephone interviews with learning and development managers at 250 large organisations (Institute of Leadership and Management, 2011).

WHAT IS A COACHING CULTURE?

This widescale use of coaching has raised questions and interest about how organisations can leverage the most value out of coaching interventions. Peter Hawkins, Professor of Leadership at Henley Business School (UK), sees the creation of coaching cultures as the 'next phase in the development of coaching' (2012: 2). Clutterbuck and Megginson, both leading figures in the area of coaching and mentoring, propose that a coaching culture is one in which 'coaching is the predominant style of managing and working together … where a commitment to grow the organization is embedded in a parallel commitment to grow the people in the organization' (2005: 19). The phrase 'parallel commitment' is very helpful in this context. In other words, if we are interested in pursuing a coaching culture, we should note that a dual focus is required: the organisation's goals on the one hand and the growth of people within the organisation on the other. Coaching interventions can be planned and implemented in ways that fully support both aims.

Following a comprehensive review of the literature, Gormley and van Nieuwerburgh developed a revised definition of coaching cultures based on a 'bringing together' of existing ideas and concepts: ' … coaching cultures exist when a group of people embrace coaching as a way of making holistic improvements to individuals *and* the organisation through formal and informal coaching interactions. This can mean a large proportion of individuals adopting coaching behaviours to relate to, support, and influence one another and their stakeholders' (2014: 92).

WHAT ARE THE KEY ELEMENTS OF A COACHING CULTURE?

Gormley and van Nieuwerburgh (2014) identified some consistent features of prevailing theories about coaching cultures.

- Coaching can form an integral part of how organisations develop their people.
- Coaching can be embedded within regular performance management processes.
- Coaching can demonstrate a commitment to support the professional growth of individuals within an organisation.
- Creating a coaching culture requires investment and can take time.
- Creating a coaching culture can lead to changes in the organisation with rewards for staff, stakeholders and clients.

WHAT ARE THE PROPOSED BENEFITS OF COACHING CULTURES?

The proposed benefits of coaching cultures are manifold. Bringing together the results of a number of research projects, evaluations and case studies of internal coaching programmes, it is possible to reflect on some of the consistently noted positive outcomes.

According to an evaluation undertaken by Carter et al. (2009), an internal coaching programme for managers resulted in enhanced emotional intelligence, increased self-awareness, improved relationships between staff, enhanced interpersonal skills, increased workplace confidence, an improved ability to manage and better work-life balance. In a similar study, McKee et al. (2009) found that coachees reported increased loyalty to their organisation, development in their leadership abilities, improved communication with peers, an enhanced ability to resolve conflicts, and a renewed passion to support the development of others. In a study based in India, Mukherjee (2012) proposed that there were both direct and indirect benefits for managers trained to act as coaches within the organisation. Mukherjee concluded that 'coaching is one of the most effective tools in building leadership capacity' within organisations. These findings are presented in Table 16.2.

Table 16.2   The proposed benefits of coaching interventions within organisations

Proposed Benefit	Studies
Enhanced emotional intelligence	Carter et al.
Increased self-awareness	Carter et al.
Better relationships/communication with colleagues	Carter et al., McKee et al.
Enhanced interpersonal skills	Carter et al.
Increased confidence	Carter et al.
Better ability to manage/lead	Carter et al., McKee et al., Mukherjee
Better work-life balance	Carter et al.
Increased loyalty to organisation	McKee at al.
Enhanced ability to resolve conflicts	McKee at al.
Renewed passion to support development of others	McKee at al.

HOW CAN WE KNOW THAT A COACHING CULTURE EXISTS?

Many organisations now use coaching within a range of learning and development, and organisational development interventions. However, it is not always clear when a coaching culture can be said to exist within an organisation. According to a leading expert in this field, 'a coaching culture exists in an organisation when a coaching approach is a key aspect of how the leaders, managers, and staff engage and develop all their people and engage their stakeholders' (Hawkins, 2012: 21). In other words, the existence of a coaching culture can be determined if most people within an organisation use a coaching approach. While this is a good measure, it is a difficult variable to observe and record. Furthermore, questions could be raised about who makes the decisions about whether the managers and staff are employing a coaching approach in their interactions. Having said this, it seems appropriate to judge whether an organisation has a coaching culture based on the experiences of its people and its clients or stakeholders. The 'Framework for Practitioners 3: Coaching Cultures' presented at the end of this chapter provides an example of a helpful way of assessing the existence of coaching cultures.

HOW CAN WE WORK TOWARDS A COACHING CULTURE?

Even though there has been little clarity within the field about the exact definition of a coaching culture, there have been many attempts to identify ways of creating, developing and embedding coaching cultures. Early writers on the topic, Clutterbuck and Megginson (2005), proposed that there were four stages of development towards a coaching culture:

1. *Nascent*: almost no commitment to the concept of a coaching culture.
2. *Tactical*: some recognition that a coaching culture may be desirable but only a vague understanding of the concept.
3. *Strategic*: investment has been made towards developing a coaching culture and leaders start to model best practice.
4. *Embedded*: people across the organisation are involved in coaching and these initiatives align with organisational objectives.

While Clutterbuck and Megginson's four stages related to the phases that organisations might go through en route to a coaching culture, Passmore and Jastrzebska (2011) recommended a 'journey' comprising of five stages.

A journey towards a coaching culture

1. Informal external coaching.
2. Professional external coaching.
3. Coaching as a management style.
4. Coaching for all.
5. Coaching across the network.

Hawkins (2012) suggests a more comprehensive seven-step process.

The seven steps towards a coaching culture

1. Procuring external coaches.
2. Developing internal coaching capacity.
3. Leaders supporting coaching initiatives.
4. Developing team coaching/organisational learning.
5. Embedding coaching in performance management.
6. Coaching becoming the dominant style of managing.
7. Coaching used to do business with stakeholders.

Discussing the creation of coaching cultures in educational settings, van Nieuwerburgh and Passmore propose an integrated process for working towards a coaching culture. They recommend aligning the process to the Appreciative Inquiry stages of Discovery, Dream, Design and Destiny (4-D cycle) (Srivastva et al., 1990) in order to gain buy-in for the move towards a coaching culture from all stakeholders. The 4-D cycle is then followed up by the leadership team who would take responsibility for ensuring that:

- Suggestions and proposals for moving towards a coaching culture were incorporated into the organisation's strategic plans.

- Leaders across the organisation model the new behaviours.

- They were available to support the implementation of action plans.

- Challenges and difficulties were engaged with quickly and efficiently.

- Successes were regularly celebrated.

(van Nieuwerburgh and Passmore, 2012: 171)

WHAT CONCLUSIONS CAN BE DRAWN?

Having considered a number of proposed routes towards coaching cultures, it seems that, generally speaking, the following broad stages seem to be supportive of the creation of coaching cultures. It seems that it is helpful to have an initial stage of *assessment*. How well is the organisation doing already? What is in place? What is the appetite for a coaching culture? Who will support it? How will leadership buy-in be secured? This initial stage may need to be followed by some *championing*. This may include enlisting the support of influential thought leaders who are enthusiastic about the proposed coaching culture. It also requires leaders to 'champion' the benefits of coaching, particularly by modelling best practice and getting involved in coaching initiatives. The authors in this book have consistently argued for the provision of high-quality *training* for those who will be involved in coaching others. This training should be offered to those who volunteer to take on coaching roles within the organisation. Following the training, an *internal coaching resource* should be set up. The existence of internal coaches seems to be one of the principal ways of leveraging the benefits of coaching within professional contexts (Gormley and van Nieuwerburgh, 2014). A key to the long-term success of coaching within professional contexts is *organisational alignment*. The use of coaching interventions and approaches should be integrated into existing schemes, projects and objectives. Coaching should not be seen as a 'bolt-on' initiative. The final stage necessary for embedding coaching within organisations is *normalisation*. Formal coaching sessions, managers using a coaching approach and informal coaching conversations should become part of 'the way we do things round here'.

ACTION planning for a coaching culture

Assessment

Championing

Training

Internal coaching resource

Organisational alignment

Normalisation

For those who like acronyms and checklists, the ACTION plan may provide a way of working towards a coaching culture. However, it should be acknowledged that the development of a coaching culture is a complex, albeit valuable, undertaking. We believe that the process of working towards a coaching culture is ongoing. The ethos of a coaching culture demands continual improvement and an openness to new ideas about creating a better environment in which to work.

For readers who are less comfortable with acronyms and checklists, we would propose an alternative approach. This comprises of three questions that should be addressed by those wishing to move towards a coaching culture.

Three Questions

- What is the case for a coaching culture?
- How can we transfer what is most powerful about coaching conversations into our workplace?
- What will be different in our organisation as we work towards a coaching culture?

The principle of *democratic voluntary involvement* is a necessary part of the process and should underpin initiatives to support the development of coaching cultures. 'Democratic' means that everyone has the opportunity to participate. 'Voluntary' means that each person is given a choice about whether or not to engage in coaching-related activities. 'Involvement' means that those who volunteer should be able to contribute positively in one way or another. By addressing the three questions listed above and adhering to the principle of democratic voluntary involvement, organisations can develop their own unique ways of pursuing coaching cultures.

Practical ideas for consideration before embarking on a journey towards a coaching culture

- Creating a coaching culture will require a significant investment of time and money.
- It is important to make sure that the people involved see some value in working towards a coaching culture.
- From the start, it is helpful to think about how the benefits of a coaching culture will flow beyond the organisation's staff to clients and stakeholders.
- Coaching initiatives and programmes should be co-created based on the principle of democratic voluntary involvement.

REFERENCES

Carter, A., Fairhurst, P., Markwick, C. and Miller, L. (2009) 'Evaluation of West Midlands Regional Coaching Pool'. IES Paper, West Midlands Regional Improvement and Efficiency Partnership.

Clutterbuck, D., and Megginson, D. (2005) *Making Coaching Work: Creating a Coaching Culture.* London: CIPD.

Gormley, H. and van Nieuwerburgh, C. (2014) 'Developing coaching cultures: A review of the literature', *Coaching: An International Journal of Theory, Research and Practice,* 7(1): 90–101.

Hawkins, P. (2012) *Creating a Coaching Culture.* Maidenhead: Open University Press.

Institute of Leadership and Management (2011) *Creating a Coaching Culture.* London: ILM.

Lindbom, D. (2007) 'A culture of coaching: The challenge of managing performance for long-term results', *Organization Development Journal,* 25(2): 101–6.

McKee, A., Tilin, F. and Mason, D. (2009) 'Coaching from the inside: Building an internal group of emotionally intelligent coaches', *International Coaching Psychology Review,* 4(1): 59–70.

Mukherjee, S. (2012) 'Does coaching transform coaches? A case study of internal coaching', *International Journal of Evidence Based Coaching and Mentoring,* 10(2): 76–87.

Passmore, J. and Jastrzebska, K. (2011) 'Building a coaching culture: A development journey for organizational development', *Coaching Review,* 1(3): 89–101.

Sherpa Coaching (2015) *Executive Coaching Survey: Full Report.* Cincinnati, OH: Sherpa Coaching.

Srivastva, S., Fry, R.E. and Cooperrider, D.L. (eds) (1990) *Appreciative Management and Leadership: The Power of Positive Thought and Action in Organizations.* San Francisco, CA: Jossey-Bass.

van Nieuwerburgh, C. (2014) *An Introduction to Coaching Skills: A Practical Guide.* London: Sage.

van Nieuwerburgh, C. and Passmore, J. (2012) 'Creating coaching cultures for learning'. In C. van Nieuwerburgh (ed.), *Coaching in Education: Getting Better Results for Students, Educators, and Parents.* London: Karnac. pp. 153–172.

van Nieuwerburgh, C. and Tong, C. (2013) 'Exploring the benefits of being a student coach in educational settings: A mixed-method study', *Coaching: An International Journal of Theory, Research and Practice,* 6(1): 5–24.

Whitmore, J. (2009) *Coaching for Performance: Growing People, Performance and Purpose,* 4th edn. London: Nicholas Brealey.

FRAMEWORK FOR PRACTITIONERS 2: THE GROWTH MODEL

JOHN CAMPBELL

John Campbell, Executive Director, Growth Coaching International

As interest in various forms of workplace based coaching has developed in recent years, the number of opportunities for learning coaching skills has also increased. In many of these coaching skill development programmes, both those offered by universities, and those offered by commercial providers, various coaching models or coaching conversation frameworks have been proposed.

It is argued that such coaching models provide a structure to help coaches 'on the ground' during coaching interactions. The most widely used of these coaching models is GROW, popularised by Sir John Whitmore in an early edition of *Coaching for Performance* (2009). GROW is a mnemonic suggesting four key steps or components of a coaching conversation:

G – Goal (setting a goal in relation to a preferred future in an identified area of change)

R – Reality (exploring the current situation or reality so as to establish a starting point on the journey towards the goal)

O – Options (generating possible strategies and options for achieving the goal)

W – Wrap up (next steps and actions that can be undertaken to move towards the goal)

Various other coaching models and frameworks including REGROW and CIGAR (Grant, 2005) have been proposed, sometimes with similar components and sometimes with differing points of emphasis. All have been designed, however, to provide the novice coach, in particular, but also more experienced coaches, with a scaffold to help ensure coaching interactions are structured, purposeful and that they ultimately lead to action.

Models such as GROW have attracted some criticism (Cavanagh, 2013) for being too linear and simplistic to cope with the complex nature of the coaching interaction. If used without skill, subtlety and flexibility such models can be less helpful. Used skilfully and with a 'light touch' they provide a valuable way to help a coach and coachee navigate the coaching conversation.

GROWTH is another of these coaching frameworks. A variation on GROW, it was developed originally by Mandy O'Bree, the Founder of Australian Growth Coaching (now Growth Coaching International), a coaching consulting practice based in Sydney, Australia. It was originally published and described in the original, self-published edition of *The Leadership Coaching Guide: Growing You and Your Organisation* (O'Bree, 2002).

Figure F2.1

THE GROWTH MODEL

While adapted from GROW, the GROWTH model has a number of additional dimensions that have proved popular with many practising coaches.

It begins by emphasising the critical importance of the *Relationship* between coach and coachee in any coaching interaction. If levels of trust and rapport are strong it is much more likely that the conversation will be purposeful and helpful (Bluckert, 2005). If this is not the case any coaching conversation will be more challenging.

Identifying a clear and specific *goal* is an important part of the coaching process. Helping the coachee get clear on what is wanted can take some time but is always worth the effort. Indeed it is essential. It is not uncommon that more time will be spent in this part of the

GROWTH model than any other. There is considerable literature emphasising the central place of goal setting within coaching (Grant, 2006; Locke, 1996; van Nieuwerburgh, 2014).

Once a goal has been clarified and agreed it is helpful to establish the current *Reality*. This is important for several reasons – it helps to establish a clear starting point, but even more significantly, within the GROWTH model approach, it involves an exploration of 'what's already working', and helps direct attention to current resources that might assist in achieving the goal. At this point concepts from Solutions Focused theory (Jackson and McKergow, 2007; Shennan, 2014) influence how this step is explored. Emphasis is given to an exploration of strengths, positive past experiences, and any other personal or social environment resources that could assist in goal attainment. Consequently, in the GROWTH model R also stands for *Resources* since it is at this stage that the coach can specifically direct attention and tease out any skills, experiences, practices, policies or people – any of which can support progress towards the goal.

A focus on any strengths or resources that can be identified helps to build a sense of self-efficacy in the coachee – the sense of 'I can do this!' A growing sense of self-efficacy is a component of Agency Thinking, one of the key ingredients in building hope (Rand & Cheavens, 2009). Agency Thinking refers to the level of intention, confidence and ability to follow various pathways towards the desired future. Helping to establish a strong sense of hope in relation to the identified goal is an important influence contributing to goal attainment.

When the reality and resources have been explored the conversation moves towards exploring *Options* – identifying various possible strategies and actions that can move the coachee towards the goal. This is typically done as a form of brainstorming – to generate a range of possible strategies. At this point an additional element of Hope Theory, Pathways Thinking, becomes important (Rand and Cheavens, 2009). 'Pathways Thinking' refers to the ability to generate various routes from the present to the desired future. It is argued that a cyclical relationship exists between Agency Thinking and Pathways Thinking – increasing the sense of Agency helps to generate more Pathways and more options helps to increase Agency – both contributing to a growing sense of hope.

At this point the model moves from exploration towards action and the *Will* step invites a choice from among the various options. This is a clear signal that the conversation will require decision and action. Exploration is helpful but new actions will be required to begin movement towards the goal. The simple question, 'What will you do?' can be quite confronting at this point. An additional helpful question here can often be 'Which of these options do you have most energy around pursuing?' This allows the coachee to follow the 'energy path' – a helpful way to create some momentum.

Once a particular strategy has been chosen identifying specific next actions in the *Tactics* step moves the coachee towards identifying and committing to simple and do-able small next step actions. Again the influence of the Solutions Focus perspective is significant here (Jackson and McKergow, 2007). These are small, even tiny, steps creating initial movement towards the goal. Small steps increase the chances of success and allow for a flexible, more nimble, response as the initial actions begin to create change. It also helps if these next step actions are tied to specific times, they are more likely to happen if that is the case.

It is helpful at this point to invite some reflection on sustaining progress and the *Habits* step in the GROWTH framework emphasises this aspect. 'What might help ensure that you continue the momentum on this?' is a good question to help identify support mechanisms that can ensure that progress towards the goal is sustained.

Golwitzer's (1999) research on implementation intentions supports the value of giving explicit focus and time to thinking into the future to identify ways to continue striving towards goal attainment even in the face of unexpected twists and turns in the journey.

Finally the model recognises that *celebrating* progress and success is an important component that helps build and sustain motivation. Gable and colleagues' (2004) work on Positive-Constructive responses to success, however small, is helpful in highlighting the motivational and relational impact of intentionally and explicitly celebrating progress towards the goal.

The GROWTH model develops and extends a number of the key elements of GROW. In addition, the increasing application of positive psychology and Solutions Focused theories and research provides a stronger evidence base for various elements and enables a more nuanced application.

REFERENCES

Bluckert, P. (2005) 'Critical factors in executive coaching – the coaching relationship', *Industrial and Commercial Training, 37* (7): 336–40.

Cavanagh, M. (2013) 'The coaching engagement in the twenty-first century: New paradigms for complex times'. In S. David, D. Clutterbuck and D. Megginson (eds), *Beyond Goals: Effective Strategies for Coaching and Mentoring.* Surrey: Gower.

Gable, S.L., Reis, H.T., Impett, E.A. and Asher, E.R. (2004) 'What do you do when things go right? The intrapersonal and interpersonal benefits of sharing positive events', *Journal of Personality and Social Psychology, 87*: 228–45.

Golwitzer, P.M. (1999) 'Implementation intentions: simple effects of simple plans', *American Psychologist, 54* (7): 493–503.

Grant, A.M. (2005) 'What is evidence-based executive, workplace and life coaching?' In M. Cavanagh, A.M. Grant and T. Kemp (eds), *Evidence-based Coaching: Contributions from the Behavioral Sciences* (Vol. 1). Bowen Hills, QLD: Australian Academic Press. pp. 1–13.

Grant, A.M. (2006) 'An integrated goal focused approach to executive coaching'. In D.R. Stober and A.M. Grant (eds), *Evidence-based Coaching Handbook: Putting Best Practice to Work for Your Clients.* Hoboken, NJ: Wiley.

Jackson, P. and McKergow, M. (2007) *The Solutions Focus: Making Change SIMPLE*, 2nd edn. London: Nicholas Brealey.

Locke, E.A. (1996) 'Motivating through conscious goal setting', *Applied and Preventative Psychology, 5*: 117–24.

O'Bree, M. (2002) *The Leadership Coaching Guide: Growing You and Your Organisation.* Sydney: Australian Growth Coaching.

Rand, K. and Cheavens, J. (2009) 'Hope theory'. In S.J. Lopez and C.R. Snyder (eds), *Oxford Handbook of Positive Psychology.* Oxford: Oxford University Press.

Shennan, G. (2014) *Solution Focused Practice: Effective Communication to Facilitate Change.* Basingstoke: Palgrave Macmillan.

van Nieuwerburgh, C. (2014) *An Introduction to Coaching Skills: A Practical Guide.* London: Sage.

Whitmore, J. (2009) *Coaching for Performance: GROWing People, Performance and Purpose,* 4th edn. London: Nicholas Brealey.

John Campbell is the Executive Director of Growth International where he leads a team of coaches and facilitators that provides coaching and coach training services to educators across Australia, the Asia Pacific region and the UK. He is an experienced and inspirational executive coach and facilitator. In addition to his teaching qualifications he holds Master's degrees in Organisational Communication (University of Technology, Sydney) and in the Psychology of Coaching (University of Sydney).

FRAMEWORK FOR PRACTITIONERS 3: SUPPORTING THE DEVELOPMENT OF COACHING CULTURES

TIM HAWKES

Tim Hawkes, Managing Director, Unlimited Potential

In our experience, organisations come to the decision to work towards coaching cultures in three different ways:

1. *Organisation led* – The senior team within the organisation understands and sees the benefits of coaching within their organisation and requests the Learning and Development function to put together a strategy.
2. *Director led* – One or two directors see the importance of coaching and begin an initiative to put together a coaching strategy.
3. *HR department led* – Individuals within the Learning and Development team see the importance of a coaching culture and begin a programme to develop its strategy from within, managing upwards.

Whichever of these is the initiator of the organisational coaching culture the responsibility of implementation usually falls to the Human Resources, Organisational Development or Learning and Development teams. There is growing research on coaching cultures (discussed in Chapter 16) but limited practical guidance.

Two of the biggest mistakes made by organisations implementing a coaching culture

- *Unstructured external coach programme* – Non-vetted external coaches delivering independent programmes which are not aligned to the organisation's cultural strategy.
- *Death by coach training* – Providing more and more coach training as a way of shoe-horning in a coaching culture.

We believe that it is important for practitioners to be aware of the constituent parts of a coaching culture. We propose that there are nine dimensions.

NINE DIMENSIONS OF A COACHING CULTURE

These dimensions are key elements for ensuring that a coaching culture is embedded within an organisation. We believe that all nine dimensions are necessary for a coaching culture to flourish:

1. *Develop Coaching Resources* – Provide a place of reference for coaching.
2. *Improve Workforce 'Coachability'* – Prepare the workforce for coaching.
3. *Go from Coachee to Coach* – Develop potential within all individuals to become coaches.
4. *Build Coaching Skills* – Develop a formal programme of coaching training.
5. *Create Internal Coaching Groups* – Embed the coaching for lifelong development.
6. *Deliver an Internal Coach System* – Formally agree future initiatives that coaches support.
7. *Use External Coaches* – Bring in outside qualified expertise to accelerate learning/understanding.
8. *Promote Advocates for Coaching* – Create role models to set the desired standard.
9. *Enjoy a Self-sustaining Coaching Culture* – Create a business where knowledge and wisdom are shared openly.

These nine dimensions fit into the Embark Coaching Culture Model (the Embark Coaching Culture Framework created by Tim Hawkes and Stuart Haden) which helps us understand where in the organisation these dimensions fit and at what point in the journey the organisation is.

THE EMBARK COACHING CULTURE MODEL

This model provides a helpful framework which can support practitioners to identify what is required to develop a successful coaching culture regardless of the starting point.

The model breaks the coaching culture down into two axes which help identify where an organisation is on the 'coaching map'.

Axis 1 – Your Organisation

For a successful coaching culture to exist, coaching skills must be exhibited at all levels. It should not be reserved for senior management, it is for everybody. With this in mind the model targets the organisation at three levels as follows.

- *Developing the workforce* – Focus on your non-management population. This can be considered as the majority of your employees.

- *Developing your middle/junior managers* – This level focuses on new and aspiring managers, technical experts and managers that hold middle-ranking responsible jobs.
- *Developing the senior managers* – This level focuses on your strategic thinking management population and is restricted to the few high-level managers in your organisation.

Axis 2 – Coaching Maturity

The Embark Model uses three levels of coaching maturity to demonstrate progress. It adopts the well-known approach of Knowing, the lowest level, through to Being, the highest level.

- *Knowing Coaching* – The belief and knowledge that coaching exists with an understanding of what it is, maybe some training taking place, and reading coaching books and materials.
- *Doing Coaching* – Actively using coaching techniques within the workplace, and being aware of when individuals, teams, organisations are using coaching techniques.
- *Being Coaching* – Coaching is a way of life, fully understood and delivered in a meaningful way with knowledge of key tools and techniques effective in developing individuals. The coaching is self-sustaining when individuals are 'being' coaching.

To put these together we created a nine-box matrix or map

Table F3.1   Mapping the future of culture change

	Knowing	Doing	Being
Workforce	1. Develop resources	2. Improve workforce coachability	3. Go from coachee to coach
Junior and middle managers	4. Build coaching skills	5. Create internal coaching groups	6. Deliver internal coach system
Senior managers	7. Use external coaches	8. Promote advocates for coaching	9. Enjoy a self-sustaining coaching culture

By ranking each of the dimensions through an organisational survey the organisation can clearly understand where its weaknesses are in terms of a coaching culture, avoiding some of the common pitfalls.

WHAT CAN WE LEARN FROM EMBARK?

Over 800 people have completed the Unlimited Potential Embark coaching culture diagnostic from organisations such as British Gas and the University of Law. The combined results of all these companies give us a picture where organisations think their coaching culture currently stands.

The most startling outcome of these surveys is that in almost every organisation (there are a few exceptions) Dimension 2, 'Improve Workforce Coachability', vies with Dimension 4, 'Build Coaching Skills', for the top spot. Whilst we know that organisations are spending a significant amount of money on internal coach training programmes (Dimension 4), it is less clear what money they are spending on 'Improving Workforce Coachability'.

Since the work that we have done with organisations indicates that little development has gone into workforce coachability, we would question whether some organisations make the assumption that their workforces are inherently coachable. The lowest scoring dimensions in the survey tend to be 9 and 6, 'enjoy a self-sustaining coaching culture' and 'deliver internal coach system'. The self-sustaining culture is no surprise as this is a result of all the other dimensions working together. As for delivering internal coach systems, the evidence is that organisations are training internal coaches, putting them to work in the organisation, but the internal coaching mechanism is not fully supported.

CONCLUSION

The conclusion that we have drawn from analysing client results and looking at organisational coaching cultures across the world is that true success comes at the moment of interaction, i.e. the moment when one person asks the critical question that needs to be asked and then listens to the answer.

Success in a coaching culture relies on every individual having the knowledge, confidence and support to ask the high quality well-timed coaching question and be prepared to listen, *really* listen, to the answer.

Tim is a Managing Director of Unlimited Potential, co-founder of the Embark™ coaching culture diagnostic tool and also a Chartered Mechanical Engineer. Working globally over the last ten years Tim has delivered programmes ranging from one-to-one coaching through to organisational coaching culture development programmes, relying on high quality coaching as the basis of all of his work. He specialises in assessing organisational coaching culture through his unique Embark™ coaching culture diagnostic. He has worked for the University of Warnick MBA on diversity and also delivered coaching change programmes for organisations such as the Royal Mint, National Archives, Cognizant and Radisson Edwardian.

PERSPECTIVE FROM PRACTICE 1: WHAT WE KNOW FROM ELITE SPORTS

PAT McCARRY

Competitive environments at the highest level can be considered rigorous laboratories for effective coaching practice and as such offer a great deal that can be transferred to many other fields, including business, health and education.

Coaching in team sport is a unique and sometimes complex role, clearly distinct in nature from coaching in other contexts. This is because the sports coach is a key central figure in influencing the achievement of desired outcomes for sports organisations and teams, and as such is held accountable and placed under constant scrutiny. There is no peripheral role for the coach as competitive games take place regularly where the performance levels of the team are tested and exposed under microscopic analysis for all to see. This high pressure environment, whilst exciting, can also be highly stressful. For example, in football three consecutive defeats can result in the termination of a contract. It is important to remember that the team coach works within a network of relationships that can include stakeholders with conflicting interests, such as owners, directors, sponsors and fans who all make increasing demands on the coach and players.

Feedback in this profession for both players and coach is constant, conflicting, and at times unforgiving. In terms of performance on the field or court, however, the coach is in constant receipt of qualitative and quantitative data on an unprecedented scale which sometimes makes it necessary to employ a comprehensive backroom staff. The coach's observations during the game coupled with extensively detailed computerised match analysis will immediately provide the coach and staff team with a wealth of information regarding individual players' performances in addition to the team as a whole. It is this analysis and detailed assessment of the forthcoming opponents that inform immediate planning for the coaching sessions. From this you the reader can see the perfect feedback loop inherent in team sport that is possibly more ambiguous in most other professional contexts. In sport, the coach is never without clear performance goals and their skill lies in converting these demanding goals into high quality, structured coaching sessions in an effective and highly interactive learning environment. The coach has limited time to make an impact before the next game and must therefore take every possible opportunity to maximise improvement in what has become a ruthlessly competitive arena.

TRANSFERRABLE LEARNING

Create and maintain a purpose-driven and values-based culture

What does your organisation stand for? Is there a clearly understood and easily expressed purpose? Do your employees feel part of something that they care about and that has personal meaning for them? In sports terms, what are they playing for?

Have a clear vision and strategy for recruitment

How rigorous is your recruitment policy? Is there clarity around what skills and characteristics are needed to fit into particular roles in your team? Who is on the recruitment team and why? The most successful sports team in history, the New Zealand All Blacks rugby team, recruit mainly based on character because they believe the requisite talent can be developed given a baseline of skill.

Model and expect high standards of behaviour and performance

The management team need to model the very highest standards in terms of behaviour and performance. If they do not, then they cannot expect the rest of the team or staff to do so. A good question for leaders to ask is 'How do I affect my staff or team when I interact with them?' An even better practice would be to check this out with peers and staff directly.

Value and grow the staff through a conscious and challenging development process

The staff or team are the greatest asset and need to be valued as such. The way that leaders genuinely care about them and grow them will be reflected in their morale, performance and behaviour. This includes the provision of regular feedback and access to coaching. The aim in sport is to improve the team's motivation, morale and performance constantly because the team is only ever a short period of time away from the next test. The team's managers cannot wait until the next formal appraisal date because the improvement needs to happen immediately. The approach is rigorous, rewarding, and demands total commitment. To ensure progress and minimise burnout, it is key that players see practice as an enjoyable, stimulating learning experience where they can grow, be motivated, and have opportunities to express themselves.

Encourage and model honesty and transparency

So often in the past a 'them and us' attitude has prevailed between management and staff. The outcome of this has been that management will hold the power even more tightly. If this is the case then there can never be trust and loyalty cannot be taken for granted. In sport, it is accepted that the performance and behaviour of the team are directly influenced by the coach and management team. This healthy approach to accountability enables both individuals and the team to continually improve.

Create challenges and goals that excite and stimulate

Sports teams and individuals thrive on exciting challenges that stretch and motivate them. There will be team goals and also individual goals regarding development and performance. If the players are involved in holding each other accountable and supporting each other when times are difficult, then the hard work is made more manageable and enjoyable. There is something wonderful about being part of something greater than oneself and having an opportunity to test this growth and performance level regularly through competitive fixtures. In addition, the majority of individuals involved in competitive sports enjoy what they do. This can be stressful and exhausting but it is enjoyable and has a constant and clear focus. It is worth considering how this can be replicated in other work environments. How can the environment be a more enjoyable and stimulating place to work in? People often spend a good deal of their day in a working environment, so it is prudent and humane to consider how this time can be as enjoyable, productive and rewarding as possible.

Pat McCarry is an executive coach who also runs courses for the professional development of football coaches. He has a BSc in Sports Science and Management and a PGCE in secondary education from Loughborough University. He worked in education as a teacher, governor and committed member of senior management for ten years. In 1999 he became Director of

Coaching and Professional Development for UK Elite Soccer, the second-largest coaching provider in the US where he developed coaches across 30 states. He is currently completing an MA in coaching at Warwick University and has a passion for innovative leadership programmes.

17

TOWARDS A PHILOSOPHY OF COACHING?

CHRISTIAN VAN NIEUWERBURGH

Coaching has blossomed as a practice and is continuing to flourish as an industry in the early twenty-first century. It is now a well-established profession with numerous professional associations that have members across the world. As we have seen in this book, coaching is in use across a broad range of organisational settings and is widely accepted as a beneficial intervention to support individuals, enhance performance and improve leadership. Coaching is being used systematically within educational systems, the health sector, in local government, and in commercial organisations. A survey of the use of coaching across these environments is encouraging and seems to bode well for the future of the profession. Let us also hope that it bodes well for individuals, our schools, our workplaces and our societies.

While the practical application of coaching seems to be delivering positive results to clients and organisations, there have been significant steps towards the establishment of coaching as an academic discipline. Higher education institutions such as the University of Sydney, City University and the University of East London launched ground-breaking 'coaching psychology' programmes in the first decade of the new millenium. Postgraduate coaching programmes are now available in many universities all over the world. The emergence of these programmes has led to a concurrent increase in the number of academic journals focused on the discipline of coaching. These journals continue to grow in esteem and regularly publish high-quality academic papers. Within the field of psychology, there have been determined moves towards recognising 'coaching psychology' as an entity in its own right. The British Psychological Society and the Australian Psychological Society both have special interest groups dedicated to coaching psychology. More recently, the International Society for Coaching Psychology has been formed. So it clear that the influence of coaching has seen rapid growth that has been supported professionally, academically and by the field of psychology. In comparison, there has been less exploration about the philosophical underpinnings of the field.

WHY DO WE NEED A PHILOSOPHY OF COACHING?

As we move from the relatively straightforward application of coaching with individuals (one-to-one coaching) to theorising about the potential impact of coaching across organisational settings and to a wider range of stakeholders, it becomes necessary to spend time revisiting some of the *fundamental principles* of coaching. Not doing so may put the future of coaching in jeopardy. There is a risk that coaching will simply come to be seen as the application of conversational frameworks. Even more worryingly, organisational demands for 'efficiency' and 'results' can lead to adaptations to the coaching process that will undermine some of its core principles. For example, potential organisational clients may demand a 'directive' coaching approach for its senior leaders or could minimise the time available for the training or supervision of internal coaches. Another ongoing concern is that the commercial pressures on executive coaches can drive some within the profession to make unsubstantiated and exaggerated claims about the benefits of coaching. A very topical issue at present arises from a positive phenomenon: the implementation of coaching interventions on a large scale, sometimes across multiple locations (e.g. multinational organisations). The complexities of such an endeavour can sometimes necessitate an undue focus on process and administrative factors (that may impact negatively on individual experiences of coaching). The final risk, which we have tried to avoid in this book, is the desire to portray coaching as the answer to all challenges across virtually any organisational setting.

COACHING: AN ART OR A SCIENCE?

Following on from the final risk mentioned above, coaching has been described as both an art and a science (Downey, 2003). This description can be used to present coaching as all things to all people. Many organisational clients seem to be more open to coaching if led to believe that coaching can be *proven* to deliver results through scientific experimentation. On the other hand, a significant number of people attracted to coaching as a profession may be drawn to the 'artistic' aspect of coaching.

It has been argued that effective coaching consists of three elements: the coaching process, the skills of coaching and a 'way of being' (van Nieuwerburgh, 2014). Pressure to understand coaching as a 'science' (driven by the academic community, the field of psychology and many organisational clients) places excessive weight on the process and skills of coaching. This is because scientific research can be undertaken only on these tangible elements. When designing scientific experiments relating to the impact of coaching, it is relatively more straightforward to ensure, for example, that all participating coaches use a particular process and have similar levels of skill. Indeed, most scientifically rigorous quantitative research over the last decade has focused on these two elements (see Chapter 13: The Current State of Research). The third element ('way of being') is the least tangible. It is less clearly defined than the other two elements and therefore less amenable to scientific study. However, some would argue that the coach's 'way of being' may have the most significant impact on the client's experience.

It is proposed here that coaching is indeed both an art and an applied science. This assertion is not driven by a desire to appeal to both sets of stakeholders but as a way of recognising the richness of the intervention and the complexity of the field. While further quantitative research is needed on the 'scientific' elements of coaching (i.e. the coaching process and coaching-related skills), further qualitative research is needed to deepen our understanding of the 'way of being' of coaches. Enhanced understanding of both the 'scientific' and 'artistic' aspects of coaching will support the further development of coaching in its various settings. Most importantly, it will allow us to support our clients (both individual and organisational) better.

INITIAL THOUGHTS TOWARDS A PHILOSOPHY OF COACHING

So it can be argued that there is a need for a philosophy of coaching. But from where can such a philosophy emerge? If we are claiming that coaching is an applied psychology, or an applied science or an art (or all of these), then the philosophical context for it could emerge from praxis. In other words, the 'doing' of coaching can inform the 'thinking' about its successful application. Coaching is a non-directive approach to collaborative discussion, intention-setting and idea generation. The practice of coaching is underpinned by a number of theoretical principles.

Firstly, coaching is a *non-judgemental* way of talking to others. This means that a coach must embrace the notion that their role does not allow for 'making judgments' or otherwise evaluating the performance of a client. Accepting that most of our everyday conversational partners will make judgments throughout our interactions, coaching should be notable for creating environments in which coachees do *not* feel judged. One of the most important conditions for the type of honest conversations we seek is the freedom to speak without fearing criticism or disapproval.

There is a significant challenge associated with the need for a coach to remain non-judgmental throughout their interaction with a client. Philosophically speaking, this means that a coach should only apply ethical codes of practice and morally assess their *own* behaviour and thoughts. Any attempt to impose their moral world-view is firstly judgmental and secondly implies a belief in their own moral superiority. As a matter of principle, the client should not feel judged by the coach, regardless of what they say or do during the coaching conversation. This is one of the factors that can create an environment in which a client can honestly explore their fears, relationships, weaknesses, strengths and aspirations.

Secondly, a coaching relationship should be characterised by *mutual respect*. This respectful approach covers the interactions between coach and client but also extends to the coach's acceptance of the client's right to self-determination. In other words, the coach must accept, from a philosophical stance, the client's right to make choices relating to their life and future direction. To take this idea one step further, any attempt by the coach to determine or influence the choices of their client is to actively undermine that client's autonomy. The coach should demonstrate respect of their client as an autonomous human being capable of finding their own solutions.

Thirdly, along with autonomy and the right to self-determination, clients should be expected to take *personal responsibility* for the situations they find themselves in. Coaches should avoid actions or comments that divert responsibility away from their clients. This can happen inadvertently when a coach may allow a client to continually blame others for their current situation (therefore presenting as 'helpless'). A coach can also undermine a client's sense of personal responsibility by *taking responsibility* for helping that client to move forward. Once a coach has supported a client to create a safe reflective space, it becomes the client's responsibility to make full use of this space in order to make courageous choices that will help them achieve more of their potential.

Social constructionism

The practice of coaching is predicated on acceptance of a *social constructionist view* of the world. Coaching is, after all, a conversational intervention. What would be the point of spending hours discussing strategies for achieving goals if the future was already pre-determined? Coaching relies on the belief that a client assumes that through conversation they will be able to imagine and influence their own future.

Principled non-directivity

The process of coaching is valued because it is presented as one that generates self-directed learning and personal insights. For the process to work most effectively, the coach should therefore adopt the position of principled non-directivity (Rogers, 1961). In other words, the coach must be clear that their role is not to direct a client towards a solution or desired outcome. In fact, the coach should take an impartial view, ensuring that they do not have an agenda (hidden or otherwise). The coach should remain, at all times, a collaborator or 'thinking partner' (Kline, 1999), rather than a teacher, advisor, consultant or sage. The purpose of coaching is to facilitate *self-directed* learning and development. While the coach should, as a matter of principle, avoid *telling* or *advising* the client about how they should move forward, the coach may manage the conversational process. In fact, this is the coach's primary role.

TENTATIVE FIRST STEPS TOWARDS A PHILOSOPHY OF COACHING

If the idea of creating a 'philosophy of coaching' is considered helpful, it will be necessary for practitioners (i.e. coaches), the providers of coach training (whether internal or external), purchasers of coaching-related services, professional coaching bodies and academics to consider whether the effective practice of coaching and its continued development might require further philosophical exploration.

Maturity of the coaching profession

Perhaps this philosophy can play a role in supporting the ethical maturity of the profession? Without an underpinning philosophy, coaches may inadvertently leave themselves open to moral judgment and criticism. The lack of a 'moral compass' for coaches may also undermine the profession through an absence of consistency in approach. In line with the philosophy proposed here, it will be clear that coaches cannot be judged on the actions (moral or immoral) of their clients. However, it becomes incumbent on coaches to support their clients to assess their actions based on those clients' ethical values and moral principles.

There is a hard truth that many coaches will have to face. Their role is not to make the world a better place, nor is it their role to change the organisations in which they work. It is too easy for an external coach to make judgments about a client's organisation. There are many professional roles (other than coach) that a person might wish to adopt if they are interested in influencing the way organisations are managed. A coach *must* remain focused on their primary roles of creating a safe environment for learning and providing personalised, focused support for coachees as they strive to achieve more of their potential.

What has emerged

As mentioned in the introduction, one of the key drivers behind this writing project was to understand what is *unique* about working within certain professional contexts. As a reader, you will have noticed some key differences about coaching within the various organisational settings:

- Organisations and contexts have different hierarchical structures.
- Some key concerns seem to be more prevalent in some contexts than others.
- The extent to which Return on Investment (ROI) is measured varies.

- The way in which ROI is measured can be different.
- Career paths can be more complex in some organisations than others.
- The relative priority given to the wellbeing of staff can be variable.
- Some contexts give more importance to coaching supervision.
- The extent to which coaching is used to support performance management varies between contexts.
- In some professional contexts, there seems to be pressure to adopt more directive approaches to coaching.

At the same time, some themes emerge as relatively consistent across contexts:

- Broadly speaking, senior leaders seem to prefer being coached by external executive coaches.
- Generally, middle leaders and other staff tend to be coached by internal coaches.
- External coaches can have a role in supporting internal coaches.
- Despite the argument that coaches need not be experts in the topic of coaching conversations, professionals, on the whole, see coaches with relevant industry backgrounds as more credible.
- A strong theme to emerge is recognition of the importance of evaluation and assessment of the efficacy of coaching interventions.
- There seems to be broad agreement on the need for high-level, quality-assured training of coaches.
- It emerges that many people recognise that there is no 'one-size-fits all' solution when it comes to coaching.
- It is agreed that coaching is about the *conversation*, and not only that, it is about the quality of the conversation.
- There seems to be consistent interest in 'coaching cultures', with the view that coaching interventions can lead to such cultures.

It is a combination of some of these factors that may contribute to a 'philosophy of coaching' that goes beyond the practical application of coaching interventions and affects professionals more deeply and more profoundly. It seems therefore appropriate that those of us involved in coaching initiatives ensure that a *philosophy of coaching* underpins the work that we do. It is this philosophy that should permeate a coaching culture. It seems therefore that the term 'coaching culture' (see Chapter 16: Towards a Coaching Culture) is itself now open to challenge. Maybe we are simply talking about an excellent organisational culture. Of course, we believe that coaching conversations and approaches will be an integral part of such a culture. But the defining characteristic of such a culture is not the fact that coaching is taking place. One could argue, for example, that there may be organisations that have fully adopted coaching initiatives but have not seen a dramatic improvement in the organisational culture. It seems that the defining characteristics of the cultures that we aspire to must relate to the experience of the people within those organisations. Maybe when we talk about 'coaching cultures' we are thinking about productive and healthy workplaces where human beings flourish. Maybe 'coaching cultures' exist in organisations that focus on the subjective wellbeing of individual professionals who have a shared goal, are mutually respectful, and operate in trusting and supportive environments.

This raises an uncomfortable question for us. Is it the coaching interventions that need to improve, or is it the professional contexts that need to change? This is not a question that must be answered straightaway, but one that should be asked nonetheless. For the time being, we should remember that the primary role of a coach is to support *individuals* to achieve more of their potential. Organisational cultures *may* change as a result of coaching interventions. But this will happen one conversation at a time, one person at a time.

REFERENCES

Downey, M. (2003) *Effective Coaching: Lessons from the Coach's Coach*, 2nd ed. London: Texere.

Kline, N. (1999) *Time to Think: Listening to Ignite the Human Mind*. London: Cassell.

Rogers, C.R. (1961) *On Becoming a Person*. Boston, MA: Houghton-Mifflin.

van Nieuwerburgh, C. (2014) *An Introduction to Coaching Skills: A Practical Guide*. London: Sage.

Figure 17.1   Philosophy of coaching

INDEX

10:9 rule, 59

absenteeism, 199
Acceptance and Commitment Therapy, 16, 188, 205
accountancy firms, 75, 76, 85
accreditation, 221–2
action learning, 86, 97
active intentional learning, 18
active listening, 87, 132, 139, 151, 152
administrative staff, higher education, 148
adolescents, 170–1
  see also schools
affinity, 93
age, 60
Agency Thinking, 237
Alban-Metcalfe, B., 65
alcoholism, 119
Alilovic, K., 220
Alimo-Metcalfe, J., 65
All Blacks rugby team, 246
American Management Association, 38, 58, 61
Anthony, W., 17
Appreciative Inquiry 4D model, 176, 231
Aristotle, 200
arousal, 18
Asia, executive coaching in, 67–8
Association for Coaching, 65, 139, 221
attentional restoration, 22–3, 24
Attentional Restoration Theory, 23
Australia, 23, 131, 137, 148, 170–1, 173, 174, 179, 236
Australian Growth Coaching, 236
Australian Psychological Society, 249
Authentic Happiness, 137
authenticity, 205

autonomous motivation, 201
autonomy, 14, 50, 201, 203–4, 252

Bachkirova, T., 82–3
Ballarat Grammar, 179
banking, 55–6, 58, 60–1, 62, 63–4, 65, 68, 69–70
Barclay, S.R., 45, 47–9
Barclays, 63, 64
Barta, T., 60
basic skills, 15
Bates, P., 115–16
Bennet, H., 117, 121–2
Bentham, Jeremy, 200
Blau, G., 48
Bolier, L., 171
Branham, L., 60
British Psychological Society, 221, 249
Britton, Jan, 99
broaden-and-build theory, 201, 203
Brockmann, E., 17
Brown, C.H., 15, 16, 18, 19
bullying, 206
business schools, 151

Cameron, K., 204
Canada, 148
Capital Health and Wellbeing, 92–3
Capital One, 57
career coaching
  career paths, 44, 45
  career stories, 46–7
  career success, 49–51
  career transitions, 47–9
  consultancies, 43

career coaching *cont.*
  definition, 38
  education, 44
  healthcare, 104–7, 112
  in-house, 44
  human resource management (HR), 44
  Life Design, 44, 46
  narrative coaching, 46–7
  private client work, 43–4
  range of, 42–3
career paths, 44, 45
career stories, 46–7
career success, 49–51
career transitions, 47–9
Carney, Mark, 64
Carter, A., 229
Cavanagh, M., 20
chairing meetings, 108
change management, 80
character strengths, 200
China, 59
CIGAR, 235
City University, 249
client relationship skills, 79
Clinical Commissioning Groups (CCGs), 101, 103,
  109–10
Clutterbuck, D., 228, 230
Coaches Network (Open University), 153
coaching
  approach, 138–9
  art or science, 250–1
  coaching-point-of-contact, 36
  with compassion, 65
  conversations, 180
  cultures *see* coaching cultures
  definitions, 2–4, 117, 132, 145–6, 187, 189
  employing coaches, 223–4
  etymological origin of term, 145
  measuring success, 66–7, 81, 254 *see also* return on
    investment (ROI)
  panels, 66
  philosophy, 249–55
  professional associations, 65, 93, 94, 139, 151, 187,
    221–2, 249
  psychology, 187, 249
  research *see* research
  supervision *see* supervision
  training, 65, 140, 249
coaching cultures
  assessing the existence of, 230
  benefits of, 229
  definition, 228, 230

coaching cultures *cont.*
  developing, 86–7, 97–8, 230–3, 241–4
  Embark Coaching Culture Model, 241–4
  key elements, 228–9
  for learning, 133, 166, 171, 177
  philosophy of, 254–5
  professional services firms, 86
  in schools, 132, 140
  wellbeing at work, 208
Coaching for Performance, 3, 235
Coaching Framework for Local Authorities in Wales, 97–8
Coaching in Education: Getting Better Results for Students,
  Educators and Parents, 173–4
coaching-point-of-contact, 36
cognitive fusion, 21–2
cognitive-behavioural coaching, 65, 124, 179, 188, 219
Collins, Jim, 30
communication skills, 107
compassion, coaching with, 65
competency, 201, 203–4
The Complex Problem Solver, 67–8
Conference of Inclusive Capitalism, 64
confidence, 110–11
confidentiality, 31–2, 81, 86, 95, 112
conflict, 107, 206
Connecting Communities programme, 123
consultancies, career coaching, 43
consultations, 110
continuous professional development (CPD), 153
conversations, 131–2, 140, 180
co-production, 115, 117–19, 123, 207
corporate and investment banking, 58
counselling, 139, 188, 202, 207–8, 220
  see also psychotherapy
Cox, E., 125
CPD (continuous professional development), 153
Creating a Coaching Culture, 97
crisis, financial, 55, 57, 59, 62, 63, 64, 69, 91
critical enquiry, 151–2, 153
cross-selling, 79
Csikszentmihalyi, M., 16, 17–18, 204–5
culture change, 63–4, 65
culture fit, 93
customer orientation, financial services, 58

D'Abate, C.P., 188
Dane, E., 21
Deci, E.L., 11, 12
decision matrix, 106
Defence, Ministry of (MoD), 44
defusion, 21
Deloitte, 56, 76

Dembkowski, S., 97
democratic voluntary involvement, 233
depression, 48, 171, 179
derailment, 59–60
Deutsche Bank, 59
Dev, Gautam, 67–8
Dewey, J., 151
disability, 60
dissertations, 159–66
diversity, 60–1
doctors, 105, 106, 107
Drucker, Peter, 35
DuToit, A., 69

Eastspring Investments, 67–8
education
    career coaching, 44
    definition of coaching in, 132
    see also higher education; schools
The Effective Executive, 35
Eldridge, F., 97
elite sports, 245–7
Ellam-Dyson, V., 33
Ellinger, A.D., 193
Embark Coaching Culture Model, 241–4
emergencies, 31, 32
emotional intelligence (EQ), 65, 169, 229
emotions, positive, 203, 204, 206
Emotions and Behaviour at Work questionnaire, 111
Employee Outlook surveys, 63, 64
employer engagement, 59, 69
employment, benefits of, 38
Empson, L., 76
enabler, coach as, 118
energy, 206
Energy Audit, 24
energy management, 24
environmental mastery, 14
EQ (emotional intelligence), 65, 169, 229
equality, 135
Equity and Excellence: Liberating the NHS, 110
Ereaut, G., 115, 117
ethical practice, financial services, 64
ethnicity, 60
eudaimonic wellbeing, 13–14, 200, 202–3, 205
European Mentoring and Coaching Council, 65, 93, 94,
    139, 221
exceptions questions, 17
executive coaching, 3–4, 44, 61, 62, 67–8, 69–70, 94, 95,
    205, 250, 254
    see also Ridley Report 2013: Trends in the Use of
        Executive Coaching

executive committee meetings, 62
expertise, 65, 77
explicit knowledge, 15, 17

facilitated executive committee meetings, 62
facilitation skills training, 108
The Facilitator of Promotions, 67
fatigue, 23
female professionals, 85
field and forum, 58
Fifth Third Bank Corp, 65
financial crisis (2008), 55, 57, 59, 62, 63, 64, 69, 91
financial services
    challenges facing, 55–6
    coaching panels, 66
    coaching to change culture, 63–4
    ethical practice, 64
    facilitated executive committee meetings, 62
    leadership development, 61
    marketing coaching to, 65–6
    maternity and paternity coaching, 59
    measuring success of coaching, 66–8
    onboarding, 60
    opportunities for coaching in, 68–9
    performance and sales coaching, 58
    promoting diversity, 60–1
    retention, 59–60
    selecting appropriate coaching solutions, 64–5
    staff coaching, 56–8
    succession planning, 62
    talent management, 61
    wellness, 63
First Australian Positive Education Conference, 174
Fischer, M., 115, 117
Flaherty, Paul, 96
flourishing, 200
flow theory, 16, 17–18, 204–5
football, 245
Foundational Certificate for Coaching in Education, 140
Fredrickson, B., 203
Funding Outlook for Councils from 2010/11 to 2019/20, 91
fusion, cognitive, 21–2

Gable, S.L., 238
Gale, N.K., 220
Gander, M., 148
Gardner, F.L., 15, 16, 21
Garvey, B., 117
Geelong Grammar School, 174
gender equality, 60–1, 85
General Practitioners *see* GPs
Gladwell, M., 18

Global Framework for Coaching in Education, 132, 133–7
Goal-Attainment Scaling (GAS), 192–3
Godskesen, Professor Mirjam, 150
Goldsmith, Marshall, 78–9
Goldsmith method, 67
Golwitzer, P.M., 238
González-Doupé, P., 220
Gordon, S., 22
Gormley, H., 228–9
GPs, 101, 103, 104, 109–10, 112, 122
    see also primary care
Grant, A.M., 178–9, 188, 202, 205
gratitude exercises, 203
Great Place to Work Institute, 68
Green, L.S., 174, 175
Green, S., 178–9
Green, Stephen, 62
grief, 48
GROW model, 3, 164, 175, 180, 217, 235–6
Growth Coaching International, 236
Growth Coaching Online, 140, 164
GROWTH model, 160, 163–6, 235–8
Gucciardi, D., 22
Gulliver, Chris, 93–4
The Guru Syndrome, 67
Gyllensen, K., 31–2

Haden, Stuart, 242
Hanin, Y.L., 16, 18
Harford Financial Services Group, 65
Harrington, Nicola, 96
Harter, J., 38
Harvard Business Review, 4
Hawkes, Tim, 242
Hawkins, Peter, 228, 230–1
Hays, K.F., 15, 16, 19
headteacher-based coaching, 134–5
Health, Safety and Well-being Partnership Group, 103
Health and Social Care Act (2012), 101, 110
health and wellness coaching, 119, 125
health coaching, 117, 119, 121–2, 126, 200, 202
healthcare
    career coaching, 104–7, 112
    clinician-patient relationship, 115–16, 117–18
    commissioning of coaching, 104
    dealing with patients, 102
    financial constraints, 103
    GPs, 101, 103, 104, 109–10, 112, 122
    Health and Social Care Act (2012), 101, 110
    in-house coaching, 112
    impact of change, 103–4, 108
    leadership coaching, 108–11, 112

healthcare cont.
    long term health conditions, 122
    multi-professional settings, 102–3
    primary care, 120–1
    private sector, 101
    skills coaching, 107–8
    see also patients
hedonic wellbeing, 200, 202–3
Henley Business School, 228
higher education
    administrative staff, 148
    challenges facing, 145–6, 148
    coaching for PhD students, 147, 149–50, 153, 154
    coaching for research supervision, 159–66
    coaching for staff development, 146–7, 148–9, 153
    coaching for undergraduate students, 147–8, 150–2, 153, 159–66
    Leadership Foundation for Higher Education, 146–7
    mentoring, 147, 159–60, 161, 165, 166
    Positive Education see Positive Education
Hogan Assessments, 111
Holland, J., 106
Holt, Natalie, 92–3
Hope Theory, 237
Horta-Orsorio, Antonio, 63
House of Care Model, 121–2, 126
Houses of Parliament, 44
Howard, George, 217
HR Magazine, 59, 93–4
HSBC, 62
human resource management (HR)
    career coaching, 44
    developing coaching cultures, 241
    manager as coach, 36
    perspective on performance, 13
humanistic coaching, 48

ICF (International Coach Federation), 65, 139, 187, 221
Ideal Performance State, 16
Imperial College, 148, 153
implicit knowledge, 15, 17
India, 229
Individual Zones of Optimal Functioning (IZOF), 16, 18
informal coaching, 120, 126, 127
Ingleton, Coral, 95–6
Institute of Business Consulting, 93
Institute of Coaching, 151
Institute of Employment Studies, 104
Institute of Leadership and Management, 227–8
instructional coaching, 135
insurance companies, 55, 63
International Coach Federation (ICF), 65, 139, 187, 221

International Society for Coaching Psychology, 249
International Symposium for Coaching and Positive
    Psychology in Education (ISCAPPED), 174
interpersonal skills, 107
intrapersonal attunement, 20
intuitions, 21
Inverted U hypothesis, 18
investment banking, 58
IQ (intelligence quotient), 65
Isaacs, W., 20
issue-led coaching, 84

Janssens, M., 13
Jarvis, P., 214, 215, 220
Jastrzebska, K., 230–1
Jenkins, Anthony, 64
job
    for life, 45
    post job-loss career growth, 48
    satisfaction, 50

Kabat, Kevin, 65
Kelly, George, 220
Kent Coaching and Mentoring Network, 95–6
Kent County Council, 95, 96
Kent Fire and Rescue Services, 95, 96
Kim, S., 192–3
Kitwood, Tom, 102
Kline, Nancy, 83
Knight, Dr Jim, 135, 166
Knox Grammar School, 174, 179
kocsi, 145
Kubler-Ross, E., 48

Lambon, Professor Matthew, 147
leader as coach, 30, 134, 137
leadership
    coaching, 37, 57, 61, 92–3, 101, 108–11, 112, 133–4,
        179, 194, 236 *see also* executive coaching
    development, 61
    positive, 204
The Leadership Coaching Guide: Growing you and your
    Organisation, 236
Leadership Foundation for Higher Education, 146–7
Lee, A., 149
Lesson Study, 135
LGA (Local Government Association), 91
life coaching, 3–4
Life Design, 44, 46
life-line exercises, 106
lifelong learning, 46
Linley, P.A., 204

literacy, 135
Lloyds, 63
local authorities *see* local government
local government
    coach characteristics, 95
    Coaching Framework for Local Authorities in Wales,
        97–8
    coaching leaders, 92–3
    collaborative approaches, 94, 95–6, 98
    cross-sector coaching, 96
    effectiveness of coaching, 98–9
    executive coaching, 94, 95
    financial constraints, 91, 98
    internal coaches, 92, 94, 95
    leadership dynamics, 91, 92
    strategies for introducing coaching, 97–8, 99
    team coaching, 96–7
Local Government Association (LGA), 91
Loehr, J., 16, 24
London Employment Survey, 55
Lorreto Kirribilli, 174, 179
Lyubomirsky, S., 171, 205

Magyar-Moe, J.L., 205
management of change, 80
managerial coaching
    approaches, 34–5
    benefits of, 229
    definition, 30–1
    external coaching, 29
    implementing, 37–8
    research findings, 192–3
    training considerations, 35–6, 37
    uniqueness of role, 31–3
marketing, 65–6
maternity coaching, 59, 85
Mathieu, A., 58
Mayer, John, 220, 221–2
McKee, A., 229
McKinsey, 58, 60
McLeod, P.J., 149
meaning, 205
meditation, 19
    see also mindfulness
meetings
    chairing of, 108
    executive committee, 62
Megginson, Professor David, 94, 97, 228, 230
Melbourne Declaration on Educational Goals for Young
    Australians, 173
Mellon Learning Curve Research Study, 60
mental illness, 63, 169, 170–1, 176

mental toughness, 21–2, 23, 172, 175
Mental Toughness Questionnaire, 111
mentoring, 3, 93, 117, 132, 138, 147, 150, 159–60, 161, 165, 166
Mewburn, I., 149
Middelfart Sparekasse Bank, 68
mindfulness, 15, 16, 19, 20–2, 63, 175, 203, 205
Mindfulness-Acceptance-Commitment (MAC), 21–2
MINDSPACE, 121
Ministry of Defence (MoD), 44
Mintzberg, H., 124
Moore, Z.E., 15, 16, 21
mortality, 38
motivation, 201
motivational interviewing, 48, 124, 188
Mroz, D., 177
Mukherjee, S., 37, 229
Munich Re, 61
MWM Consulting, 62
My Health, My Way Dorset, 122
Myers Briggs Type Indicator, 111

narrative coaching, 44, 46–7, 49, 188, 194
National Health Service (NHS), 101, 111, 112, 115, 117, 121–2
  see also healthcare; primary care
nature, 23, 24
near-shoring, 56
negative emotions, 203
Neuro Linguistic Programming (NLP), 188
NHS (National Health Service), 101, 110, 111, 112, 115, 117, 121–2
  see also healthcare; primary care
NHS East Midlands, 108
NHS England, 109
NHS National Leadership, 104
NHS Trusts, 101, 103
Nicholson, N., 48
NLP (Neuro Linguistic Programming), 188
non-learning, 215
North West Employers, 96–7
Nuffield Trust, 101
numeracy, 135
nurses, 101, 103, 104, 107, 187

Oades, L.G., 202
objective success, 50
O'Bree, Mandy, 236
O'Connor, M., 172
offshoring, 56
Olivero, G., 194
on demand coaching, 93

onboarding, 60
Online Etymology Dictionary, 145
Open University, 153
Open Warwick, 148
optimal functioning, 11–28
optimism, 205
oscillations, 24

Palmer, S., 31–2, 33
panels, coaching, 66
parent coaching, 137
Parliament, 44
partners, 75, 76, 82–3, 85
Partnership Principles, 135
Passmore, J., 202, 230–1
paternity coaching, 59
Pathways Thinking, 237
patients
  coaching competencies, 124
  coaching definitions, 117
  coaching in the UK, 119–20
  co-production, 116, 117–19
  dealing with, 102
  definition of, 116
  developing patient leaders, 123
  formal and informal coaching, 120
  health coaching *see* health coaching
  impact of coaching, 125–6
  long term health conditions, 122, 125
  promoting patient involvement, 123–4
  promoting social inclusion, 122–3
  self-management coaching, 122
  strategies for introducing coaching, 126
  see also healthcare
peak performance
  definition, 12
  eudaimonic perspective, 13–14
  nature of, 11–12
  subjective accompaniments, 11
  theoretical models, 15, 16
peer support, 36, 37, 38
peer-based coaching
  business schools, 151
  schools, 135–6, 147
  universities, 148–9
  wellbeing at work, 208
The Peninsula School, 179
performance
  coaching, 58
  definition, 4
  management, 32
  strengths, 200

PERMA model, 170, 171, 173, 174–5, 177–8, 201
personal agency, 217
personal construct coaching, 219
personal growth, 14
personal intelligence, 221–2
personal learning, 214–19
personality coherence, 15
personnel management *see* human resource management (HR)
Peterson, D.B., 190, 200
PhD students
    coaching for, 147, 149–50, 153, 154
    mentoring by, 150
    supervisors, 149–50
philosophy, 249–55
positive deviance, 177
Positive Education, 136, 137, 140, 169–70, 171–2, 173–4, 176–81
Positive Education Schools Association (PESA), 173, 180
Positive Education Summit (2013), 173
positive emotions, 203, 204, 206
positive leadership, 204
Positive Organizational Scholarship, 176–7
positive psychology, 136, 137, 140, 169–72, 178, 188
    see also Positive Education
positive psychology coaching (PPC), 174, 202
positive relationships, 14, 204
Positive Youth Development, 172
post job-loss career growth, 48
Pousa, C., 58
practice, 15, 18
preparation, 15, 18
presenteeism, 199, 206
primary care, 120–1
    see also GPs
principled non-directivity, 252
Privette, G., 12
Prochaska, J.O., 47
procrastination, 206
Proctor, C., 200
professional associations, 65, 139, 221–2, 249
professional development
    for coaches *see* continuous professional development (CPD)
    coaching for *see* career coaching
professional services firms
    characteristics of, 75–80
    coaching below partner level, 83–4
    coaching female professionals, 85
    coaching partners, 82–3
    coaching roles, 80–1
    coaching support for teams, 85–6

professional services firms *cont.*
    developing coaching cultures, 86
    embedding coaching skills, 86–7
    issue-led coaching, 84
    measuring coaching effectiveness, 81
    progression and leverage, 78–9
    remedial coaching, 84
    strategies for coaches, 88
    talent development, 85
    team coaching, 85–6
pros and cons list, 106
psychoeducation, 15, 17–18
psychological skills training (PST), 18
psychological wellbeing, 200
    see also wellbeing; wellbeing at work
psychology, 187, 249
psychotherapy, 139, 188, 189
    see also counselling
The Public Accounting Report 2010, 85
public sector, coaching in, 92–4
purpose, 14, 205
PwC, 59, 76

qualifications, 65
Quinn, S., 177

Rath, T., 38
Realise2 strengths assessment, 179, 204
Rear, Andy, 61
redundancy, 42, 43, 45, 47, 48, 56
reflection, 151–2, 153
reflective practice, 216
REGROW, 235
Reid, J., 105, 106
relatedness, 201, 203–4
relief cover, 138
remedial coaching, 84
research
    into coaching effectiveness, 188–90, 191–3
    into coaching in higher education, 147
    into coaching in human resource development, 193–4
    into coaching in schools, 139
    coaching literature, 187–8
    evaluative versus formative research, 190–1
    on managers as coaches, 192–3
    methodological limitations of current research, 189–90
    need for, 4
    supervision of undergraduate dissertations, 159–66
resilience, 57, 63, 92–3, 110, 111, 169, 170, 175, 203, 205
retention, 59–60
return on investment (ROI), 66–7, 93, 192–3, 208, 253–4

Ridley Report 2013: Trends in the Use of Executive Coaching, 76, 82, 86, 87, 94–5, 97
Rogers, J., 37
ROI (return on investment), 66–7, 93, 192–3, 208, 253–4
Ryff, C.D., 14
Rynsaardt, J., 178–9

Salanova, M., 205
salary bubbles, 56
sales coaching, 58
Sants, Hector, 63
Savickas, M., 44, 45, 46
schools
    coach training programmes, 140
    coaching cultures, 132, 140
    coaching to enhance professional practice, 134–6
    conversations, 131–2
    counselling and psychotherapy, 139
    ethical challenges, 138–9
    evidence-based coaching, 171–2, 173–81
    Global Framework for Coaching in Education, 132, 133
    headteacher-based coaching, 134–5
    instructional coaching, 135
    leadership coaching, 133–4, 179
    mentoring, 138
    open classrooms, 137–8
    parent coaching, 137
    peer-based coaching, 135–6, 147
    Positive Education *see* Positive Education
    relief cover, 138
    research, 139
    role of positive psychology in, 169–73
    student coaching, 136
    teacher coaching, 135, 172, 178–9, 187
    see also higher education
Schwartz, T., 16, 24
Scotch College, 179
sedentary work, 206
self-acceptance, 14, 33
self-care, 15, 22–4
self-determination theory, 201
self-directed learning, 252
self-knowledge, 15, 20
self-management, 15
self-management coaching, 122
self-promotion, 44
self-regulation, 21, 205, 206
Seligman, Martin, 137, 170, 200, 201
Sim, S., 69
Sin, N.L., 171
Sinclair, A., 104
sitting, 206

skill shortages, 56
sleep, 23, 24, 206
social constructionism, 252
social inclusion, 122–3
solicitors, 85
solution-focused coaching, 17, 65, 179, 188, 194, 237, 238
Spence, G.B., 11, 12, 20, 202
sports coaching, 57, 245–7
Standard Bank, 56
Standard Chartered, 57
Steinert, Y., 149
stewardship, 64
Steyaert, C., 13
Strategy Safari, 124
strengths coaching, 57, 200, 204
stress
    education, 148
    financial services, 63, 65
    healthcare, 103
student coaching, 136
Stutley, Hazel, 123
success
    measuring, 66–8
    subjective and objective, 50
    see also return on investment (ROI)
succession planning, 62
Suffolk Coaching and Mentoring Partnership, 96
Suffolk County Council, 96
suicide, 38
supervision
    for coaches working in organisations, 153, 219–21
    for managerial coaching, 37
    personal learning, 214–19
    professional associations, 221–2
    strategies for setting up, 223–4
    of undergraduate's dissertations, 159–66
Sydney Business School, 174
Sydney Girls High School, 178–9

tacit knowledge, 17
talent development, 85
talent management coaching, 61, 69
task variety, 50
teachers, coaching of, 135, 172, 178–9, 187
team coaching
    local government, 96–7
    professional services firms, 85–6
team management skills, 79–80
team sports, 245–7
therapy, 139, 188, 189
    see also counselling
thinking partner, 252

time management, 108, 206
time pressure, 33, 36, 38
Time to Think coaching, 83
tiredness, 23
Towler, J., 219–20
training, 65, 140, 194, 249
transformational leadership, 65
transtheoretical model of change, 47
Tripartite Model for Research Supervision, 160–3,
      165–6

UK City Mental Health Alliance (CMHA), 63
unconscious conflict, 65
undergraduate students, 147–8, 150–2, 153, 159–66
Understanding Human Nature, 217
United Arab Emirates, 59–60
United States of America (USA), 56, 119, 131, 135,
      148, 170
universities *see* higher education
University of Adelaide, 149
University of Amsterdam, 187
University of East London, 174, 187, 249
University of Sydney, 174, 187, 249
University of Warwick, 148
Unlimited Potential, 241, 243
USA (United States of America), 56, 119, 131, 135,
      148, 170

Valk, Penny, 227
values, 205
Values in Action, 200
van Nieuwerburgh, C., 132, 166, 173–4, 175, 228–9, 231
VIA Character Strengths Survey, 179
Viney, R., 105
visioning, 65
visualisation, 18, 106, 107
von Nordenflycht, A., 76

Wales, 97–8
war for talent, 85
Water, L., 171
Watts, M.H., 214, 217

Way of Being, 166
wellbeing
    coaching, 117
    eudaimonic, 200, 202–3, 205
    hedonic, 200, 202–3
    keys factors underpinning, 170
    Ryff's model of, 14
    theory, 201
    at work *see* wellbeing at work
Wellbeing and Engagement Framework (WBEF), 177–8, 179
wellbeing at work
    broaden-and-build theory, 201, 203
    coaching for, 199–200, 202–8
    common challenges to, 206
    eudaimonic wellbeing, 200, 202–3, 205
    financial services, 63, 69
    hedonic wellbeing, 200, 202–3
    self-determination theory, 201
    strengths theory, 200
    wellbeing theory, 201
wellness *see* wellbeing; wellbeing at work
Welsh Local Government Association, 97
West, M.A., 48
West Midlands Coaching Pool, 65, 99
Whitmore, Sir John, 3, 132, 235
WHO (World Health Organization), 171
willpower, 205, 206
Wolever, R., 125
women *see* female professionals; gender equality
work
    environment, 50
    identity, 51
workaholism, 12
work-life interference, 206
World Association of Business Coaches, 221
World Health Organization (WHO), 171

Yates, J., 38
Yerkes Dodson law, 18
young people, 170–1
    see also higher education; schools
youth development, positive, 172